MARY LYNN KITTELSON

SOUNDING THE SOUL

*To Deb, Ah, how I have appreciated your sounds -- and resonances. Your work is lovely! Hope to hear you some more, Mary Lynn (Kittelson)*

# Sounding the Soul

## *Listening to the Psyche*

Mary Lynn Kittelson

**DAIMON**

Parts of this book originally appeared as "The Acoustic Vessel" in *The Interactive Field in Analysis,* Volume One, ed. by Murray Stein. © Chiron Publications 1995. Reprinted by permission of the publisher.

Cover illustration: "Orpheus." Pastel on paper, ca. 1903–1910, 68.8 x 56.8 cm. Odilon Redon, French, 1840–1916. © The Cleveland Museum of Art, 1995, Gift from J.H. Wade, 26.25.

Photo of the author by Steve Roach.

Illustration: "The Annunciation," Master of the Retable of the Reyes Catolicos (15th century, Spanish), courtesy of the Fine Arts Museum of San Francisco, M.H. de Young Memorial Museum, Gift of the Samuel H. Kress Foundation.

Shell illustrations taken from *Iconographic Encyclopaedia of Science, Literature and Art,* ed. by J.G. Heck. New York, 1851, Rudolph Garrigue, Publisher (Plates 75 + 76).

Thanks to Alan Halm for the drawing of the ear.
Thanks to Sonjie Johnson for proofreading.

Printed in Canada

ISBN 3-85630-554-8

© 1996 Daimon, Einsiedeln, Switzerland

*And it was almost a girl who, stepping from*
*this single harmony of song and lyre,*
*appeared to me through her diaphanous form*
*and made herself a bed inside my ear.*

*And slept in me. Her sleep was everything ...*
*all wonders that had ever seized my heart*

Rainer Maria Rilke
Excerpt from *The Sonnets to Orpheus*
I,2

# Contents

# Foreword

From the sound of it, Kittelson knows what she is talking about in this delightful, phenomenological account of how hearing matters to us. Acoustic imagination is given free rein to run circles around visual insight in her ear-based study of human communication that uses dream-telling, telephone conversations, poetry, inner monologues, silent exchange and music to explore the territory of sound. It resonates with meaning and is full of surprises. My first experience of this book reminded me of crawling into a dream closet to find a hidden door that opens into a vast and unknown chamber. It is astonishing to suddenly have so huge a resource at our disposal.

Kittelson's ear awareness finds side-doors into the topic. She lets us in on a secret as intriguing as Freud's footnote about the gradually diminishing sense of smell in human beings: we have a lapsed instinct for interiority. For turning inward, for spiralling deep into the dark, for following evocative reverberations to their source. Ever since the invention of the light bulb our eyes have worked overtime while our ears go slowly numb. Being assailed by sound (TV, air traffic, boom boxes, etc.) is a far cry from the old time community occupation of listening to one another after the sun went down. Airwaves carrying sounds intended for hearing have a way of weaving unraveled beings back together – a point noted in the section on the healing flow of sound.

But the book is no end-of-the-era death knell. She does not write in mourning, but in lively pursuit of the language of hearing, an ode to the persistent primacy of the ear. We haven't really lost it. It's right here, she says, right around the corner from our noses.

It has been a pleasure to actually work around the corner, in the same office as the author, while this book was being written. Her curiosity about sound pervaded the atmosphere making me acutely aware of echoing footsteps, voice patterns, sounds in dreams, involuntary noises, the quality of my own listening, and sound carrying between rooms. I felt as if she lent me her ear, adding another dimension to my own therapeutic listening position. Her work is not for professional listeners only – we are all ears! Anyone eager to sit in the ear's theatre will find this a program for following its labyrinthine drama. Even though the therapy room provided Kittelson's laboratory, the scenes that take place there are not confined. Like the invisible waves of her subject, the soul of sound work moves unimpeded from context to context. Sometimes as the scientist, sometimes the depth psychologist, often the poet, she cultivates the animated art of listening to ourselves talking. I find her effort on behalf of the ear a welcome response to James Joyce's prayer ("Loud, save us!") that "sound sense be made kin again."

Nor Hall, Ph.D.

# Introduction: Essential Sound

*The universe is more like music than like matter.*

Donald Hatch Andrews
(modern physicist)

Sound resonates at the very core of our being. From the first miracle of a newborn's squall, to the last rattle of breath leaving a dying person, sound means energy and life. The auditory world sounds and re-sounds, all around. Within its vibrant reality, we are sounding. And things are sounding us. Day and night, it informs us, and helps us form our worlds, within and without.

Ears cupped, bodies humming, we live within sound. We vocalize from our own bodies, expressing our energy through vibration and resonance. In society, in nature, the acoustic array is rich and various. The whispers of breaths and the pad of footfalls play out their rhythms. Technology pulses and thrums, beeps and clicks. Insects buzz, dogs bark, children shout, water gushes, cars and jets roar and recede. From the vibrating air and ground, from reverberating objects, and from all the beings we encounter, sound surrounds us, and enters our being.

However, we rarely notice sound or its companion, silence, except subliminally. For most of us, auditory signals are mere muffled background, vague atmosphere, or irritating noise. Auditorily speaking, our ears are dulled and overloaded. We rarely note, at least consciously, the effect of a person's voice or ponder a quality of resonance or silence. We almost never notice the reality, much less the details, of how auditory energy carries meaning. Primary elements like rhythm, echo and timbre go in one ear and right out the other. It is just like during a film, when we "viewers" hardly notice the sound track at all. Yet the sound is moving things along, enriching and interpreting the film steadily, invisibly – and powerfully.

Oddly enough, one reason for our unconsciousness involves the very fact that auditory energy is so basic. The auditory channel is set to go, from very early on in life. Even before birth, fetuses in the womb react to sound, startling at loud sounds from outside of the womb. The middle ear bones are the only bones in the body that are fully mature in size at birth. Immediately after birth, human infants are able to hear with considerable differentiation. Visual differentiation develops over the months, but the auditory channel is ready from the start.

We are also vocal creatures, from the first breath. Our voices sound, in original moments and replayed ones. A myriad of vibrations and rhythms, resonances and silences hold us, vibrate us, move us, all through the life process. Sound is always moving us. Indeed, this fact is a literal, as well as metaphorical, reality. We are in constant reverberation with the world, with ourselves. Ancient tradition has given voice to this fact. "The ear is the way," it says in the Upanishads. "Hear, and your soul shall live," declares Isaiah in the Old Testament.

However, we are in an aurally dulled state. The eyes are frontal, in terms of their physical placement as well as our self-conception. The position of the ears is resoundingly to the side. The eyes appear to us to be the most vital of the five senses. We conceive of ourselves as an eye-minded culture, a vision-based species. People think in terms of what they *see* and how things *look*. Indeed, the "eyes" have it. In personal relationships and in soul work, it is the eyes that we long to gaze into – a lover's, a friend's or our own in the mirror. They are "windows to the soul." We long to catch somebody's gaze, to be "seen." "Beautiful, beautiful brown eyes," we sing, "Smoke gets in your eyes," and "You can't hide your lyin' eyes." Pain, knowledge, and love reside in a glance, a gaze; truth is revealed in a long, careful "look" at things. The eyes, we assume, are the real center of knowing. Even the very sounds of these eye-words assert their dominance! Whether we speak of "eyes" or "ayes" or "I's," it is the visual world which seems to affirm our being.

The ears, to the side, are more problematic. There is something questionable about them. Even their shape suggests a question mark. Auditory perception resists the direct pathway. Its ways are labyrinthine, echoic. Its essence is vibration, resonance. Next to the upfront, brazen eyes, the ears are easily embarrassed, and embarrassing. If directly peered at, in the spotlight or during an exposed moment, they turn red. Sometimes, the ears have a sideways sexual quality. They flame up, get red-hot. They also suggest waxy, earthy, shadowy ties. The ears are eloquent, in their burning, in their mysterious fluids and curves and chambers. It is such associations which tie the ears to the deepest roots of our being.

In seeking for the depths, vision is not necessarily the sensory channel of choice. In the deep, in the underworld, in dreams, the search is for resonance. It is for meaning *beyond* appearance. The process of seeing has its biases, as all the senses do. The process of seeing, for example, makes perception of the subjective seer very difficult. As Berendt points out, in looking at something, we do not see our own "I" or face. With all of the other sensory channels, perception of self is possible. We can directly hear, smell, taste, and touch ourselves.[1]

It is in the very nature of seeing to create what is, in some ways, an artificially separate relationship. In seeing things, we necessarily experience them at a distance from us. There must be space between a seer and a visually perceived object. If the object is too close, it blurs. It darkens. A visual object must be far enough away so that we can see it, as separated and distant. Furthermore, in looking at an object, we usually focus, homing in on a clear view. In visual mode, we sharpen the perceived boundaries between objects and their surroundings and between objects and ourselves. We adjust vision until we perceive a hard line to things. Berendt makes the claim that perception through the eyes encourages more distance, while perception through the ears is more experiential. The closer we edge up on something, he says, the more judging changes imperceptibly into experiencing.[2] Indeed, our assumptions, both phenomenological and philosophical, have been shaped by the process of visual perception, by the nature of seeing.

Light is necessary for seeing. It is not necessary to any of the other senses. In eye-minded mode, light is associated with seeking consciousness, with seeking a separate stance. In an up-front, separating-out style, seeing and light create "consciousness." In eye-minded illumination, we are like Prometheus; we have to have the light. So eye-centered are we that, in the metaphors of our language, we actually equate *seeing* something with *understanding* it. "*Look* here!" we say, or "I *see* what you mean." "It *appears* to me," we comment, or "He *observed* this or that," or simply, "Open

[1] Joachim-Ernst Berendt, *The Third Ear: On Listening to the World*, New York (Henry Holt and Company, 1988), p. 28
[2] Ibid., p. 178.

your *eyes!*" In fact, we go so far as to say: "*Seeing* is believing." We really do talk as if we were exclusive creatures of light. As the dim and dark descend, every evening, on our well-lit days, how quick we are to turn on the lights!

We need to notice this domination of the visual mode. We need to awaken to the fact that perception occurs along different pathways, and comes in many styles. Each of the human sensory processes have propensities toward distinctive, let us say, angles of understanding. All the senses are capable of making fine differentiations. The imaginative world of dreams, fantasies and myths expresses itself in auditory images, as well as visual ones. In hearing things when awake, and in our dreams and fantasies while unconscious, we are experiencing *images,* just as we do when seeing things. In Jungian thought, *images are the language of the psyche.* When discussing how people can work with images, Jung specifically mentions "acoustic images" and "audio-verbal types,"[3] among other types. Working with images, be they visual, auditory, kinesthetic or in another mode, is central to understanding the psyche, and especially the unconscious.

In breaking away from the tyranny of "seeing," conceiving of images as *only* visual, we discover the acoustic world, replete with evocative vibration and sound. It is full of meaning, defining our impressions, enlivening our days and nights. Indeed, in Western culture especially, we might well ask ourselves what this preponderance of eye consciousness means. What might we be missing?

In *The Listening Self,* M. Levin speaks of the domination of "oculocentrism." The nature of the Gaze, says Levin, is practical and aggressively active. The physics of vision tends

[3] C.G. Jung, *The Collected Works of C.G. Jung,* H. Read, M. Fordham, G. Adler and W. McGuire, Eds., (Bollingen Series XX, 2nd Ed.), R.F.C. Hull, Trans., Princeton, NJ (Princeton University Press), Vol. 8, para. 608 and 170.

to overvalue constancy, uniformity, permanence; it stresses
unity, totality, clarity, and distinctness. In modern times, our
capacity to listen fully and well is limited, and is linked to a
"loss of Being" or a "loss of meaning"; historically, it is
linked to an experience of nihilism.[4] A sense of wholeness
and fullness, and the awareness of the world as resonance
are lacking.

Auditory images evoke an archetypally feminine mode.
Hearing is vibratory, surrounding, surrounded by. Participatory, flowing, receptive, audition is replete with images of
cupping, dark and fleshy passages, moist and hairy sensitivity, and watery labyrinths. Acoustic energy is received into
openings. It pulses and curves inward along dark canals. It
coils in moisture and fluid. And finally, it sparks along
neural passages that create new response, new life. The
process of hearing is linked with creation, insemination,
pregnancy and birth.

The images of the hearing process suggest a gestation of
meaning. The spherical waves in the "bath of sound" create
a sense of rounded vessel. Hearing sound means mutual
vibration. Held, contained within a field of energy, energy
participates, resonates. Its essence suggests a taking-in, in
contrast to an outgoing thrust of rays. Listening is erotic,
lush with curves and fluidity. It resonates a back-and-forth
rhythm of reception, as it rocks us, bone to bone, fluid to
fluid.

Other writers have also commented on this essential
feminine eros of listening. H.-J. Berendt commented on the
eye-dominance in our culture, which developed alongside
of patriarchy. The eyes, he said, are associated with yang
energy, with the sun and masculinity. The ear, however,
partakes in yin energies, of the moon and femininity.[5] James

---

[4] David M. Levin, *The Listening Self: Personal Growth, Social Change and the Closure of Metaphysics*, London and NY (Routledge), 1989, p. 6 and 31.
[5] Berendt, p. 27.

Hillman also connected listening with an archetypally feminine receptivity. In describing the dominance of seeing, he commented on the tendency of the ego to identify with seeing in seeking "the light of consciousness." A more passive awareness, a "receptive consciousness," is involved in listening. "We receive the other as if he were music," said Hillman, "listening to the rhythm and cadence of his tale, its thematic repetitions, and the disharmonies." Conceiving and gestating a new solution to a problem, he says, "occurs only after we have been fully penetrated by it, felt its impact, and let it settle in silence."[6]

This archetypally feminine attitude is a necessary mate to hardline focus, to sharply penetrating and separating consciousness. It is in a patriarchal setting, when the goal is a keen and bright consciousness, that people identify more with seeking light. It is still resoundingly the case that the more distanced and hardline mode of perception is generally more highly valued in our culture. Mainstream society, almost reflexively, calls on the concepts of "objectivity" and "observable differences" to support validity or truth. And what profusion and contradictoriness, what utter cacophony its jungle of data has engendered!

Even the so-called experts in "sanity," clinical psychologists, generally overvalue rationality, "objective" thinking. In modern psychotherapy, active, thrusting styles are predominant, promoting control, rationality and directedness. "Proactivity," not "reactivity," is the vogue. The fuzzier, more ambivalent and associative tendencies of the psyche fall into the shadows, where we lose relationship with them. Depth psychology suffers mightily when goaded into this mental Sousa march, straight down the street. As so much of myth suggests, it is the fate of the psyche to wander in the

---

[6] James Hillman, *Insearch: Psychology and Religion*, Irving, TX (Spring Publications), 1979, p. 22.

labyrinth. It is just this irrational, associative, layered world of symbol and image that is the very nature – the very language – of the psyche. In visual mode, we more easily remain deaf to this kind of multiplicity, to the necessary *unclarity* of the psyche.

Ear reception selects out different information, different aspects of perception. Ear-mindedness also affects how we feel about and interpret those perceptions. When the world, both inside and outside, is heard to resonate and echo, that is, when it reaches us through sound, consciousness becomes participatory. This idea of participatory consciousness is a radical departure from our old sense of what knowledge and science consist of. However, it is in keeping with the theories of modern physics, with the Principle of Uncertainty, and with Field Theory.

The Western world is in the middle of a revolution regarding the nature of the universe. This revolution has affected not only what we conceive of as the "facts" about the universe, but also how we go about functioning in and understanding this universe. Modern physicists say that we are in a state of constant, reciprocal vibration with matter and energy. Matter and energy now appear inseparable. Matter is looking more and more like force or energy, and less and less like something solid or set. The more atomic and subatomic our outlook, the less solid that matter appears.

Matter has become inseparable from its field. It is the *vibration* of matter which is now studied, and with it, the accompanying "vibration" of the scientific observer. A person's vibratory effect on an experiment or situation is now taken into account. This is to say that pure objectivity, made up of distance, clarity and sharp difference, is no longer conceived of as a *scientifically accurate* basis from which to discover "reality."

The findings of modern physics, even decades ago, influenced C.G. Jung, and reinforced his ideas in regards to psychology. Jung, a firm believer in scientific method, described himself as an empiricist, studying the phenomena of the psyche. The subjectivity of the observer or analyst must be noticed and taken into account. In discovering the "truth" of a situation, an accurate observer, said Jung, must take his or her own vibratory field of energy into account.

Both the Freudian and Jungian schools among others, have continued to develop these ideas. In modern times, psychoanalyst Evelyne Schwaber has particularly stressed the participatory aspect of the interchange. Theory-based interpretations or assumptions are based on the analyst's inference, she says, and imply that the patient's experience in the transference, for example, is devoid of his or her perception of the analyst's responses to him or her. However, the field is interactive; psychic experience, she says, is not separable from its context.[7] Thus it is vital that analysts be aware of their chosen perspective.

It is precisely in learning to take the participatory aspects into account where the pathway of audition, with its vibratory mix of inner-and-outer, is so valuable. Ear-mindedness is well-suited for work from within a field of energy. It recognizes more fully the participatory base from which we are operating. In hearing, sound surrounds us. We experience its vibrations as coming toward us. Hearing persons perceive themselves as surrounded, animated within a force-field of sound waves. In fact, hearers are even "surrounded" and animated inside our bodies, for sound waves literally enter the body. In contrast to seeing, hearing is a more flowing experience between inner and outer. Acoustic energy naturally evokes both breadth and depth. Sound

[7] Richard Chessick, M.D., Ph.D., *The Technique and Practice of Listening in Intensive Psychotherapy*, Northvale, NJ (Jason Aronson Inc.), 1989, pp. 16-19.

enters and then resounds onward, inward, and outward. Sound, resonance and silence involve reverberating space, which naturally encourages and deepens reflection or retro-hearing and re-experience. Sound is alive with flow, rhythm, layers of vibration. And so is silence. Through careful and imaginative listening, the perceptual richness of the acoustic realm, and the myriad of ways it manifests, can become a more conscious experience, moving us along the way.

Sound and reverberation call especially to those layers of experience that hover near consciousness. They take their meaning from the laws of vibration and associativeness. Indirectness, likenesses, hold sway in the night world. Unconsciously, we receive a great deal from the side, from our ears. This world of acoustic perception is one that we are subliminally in tune with. Indeed, we are deeply dependent upon it.

In exploring the depths, vision is the last perceptual mode to center in. Sight leaves us in the dark. Depth work intrinsically entails working in the dark and with the dark. In darkness, we are by no means bereft of our ears, nor for that matter, our other senses. Indeed, they may seem intensified. Working with a more unconscious mode of perception like audition, in its very essence, invites depth work. It is a "natural."

*         *
*

So, an ear-based style, an auditory mode, invites depth perception. My interest in this topic was born of my frustration at what I heard as an overemphasis on visual attitudes and visual image work in the field of Jungian psychology. While discussing images and cases, I realized again and again that I was most engaged with aspects of sound, voice, resonance, and vibration. In this book, I explore the importance of audition and the soul, and discuss some ways to work with audition as a means of communicating deeply, especially in the area of psychotherapy.

The first part contains some basic facts and images concerning sound and audition. The second describes some of the specific ways that auditory images provide shape and revelation in depth psychological work. Included are examples of work within an "acoustic vessel," that is, certain auditory-based moments in the psychoanalytic process. They aim to enliven the sense of auditory image and open the ear to imagination to help readers understand those moments, as well as begin to notice new ones in their own lives. Some pieces of auditory dream-work are found throughout the book.

While most examples of auditory work involve scenarios in a therapy setting, I am talking about more than therapy. I am interested in depth communication between people, and between people and their images. Auditory energy is image; it is meaning. I mean to evoke ear-minded ways of noticing and interacting with auditory images, of relating and learning from the auditory experience within ourselves, in our surroundings and in relationship with others. This book is an ode to listening. We need to open our ears. And we need to open our imaginations to what we hear and how we are sounded.

So, what if we conceived of ourselves as auditory beings instead of visual ones? Our style would shift, and so would our availability to the world, inside and out. Centering in sound entails receptive interaction with the unconscious. It brings in a participatory style of consciousness. Rather than "bringing light" to unconscious energies, it means, first of all, being alive, resonant, to it, such as it is.

# I. Sound: Facts and Images

# 1. Sound in Modern Society

Talk-talk-talk. Bleah-bleah-bleah! In our culture, we talk so much, and often so senselessly, that it can be difficult to take the experience seriously. More and more, in our modern environment, the words and sounds we hear are noise, and not meaningful sound. In city streets, stores, in homes and in the media, sensory competitiveness prevails. No wonder that we do not stop to listen, much less listen well. If we did, we would probably want to cover our ears.

The sounds of our society are just too much. Commonly, they are loud, repetitious, mindlessly trivial or shrill. Speech and music are the auditory experiences that we are most conscious of, and the ones we could think carry the most meaning. Yet often they are raucous, empty, boring, even smaller than smalltalk. Hyped-up headline-talk insults our understanding. Words in public places, in the media, on the telephone sound like a blurred, incessant jumble. We close our ears to the sounds of our society, its cajoling, seducing, urging and thrill-seeking.

Auditorily, even on the news, we are tortured by the whanging of pesky sound bytes. Only rarely do we get the chance to chew on anything substantial, much less digest it. The American media is beset by conflictual style news reporting, falsely dramatic features, and waves of societal and political hysteria. Data, the so-called facts, often contradict, and are used in manipulative ways. Such are the auditory manifestations of the Information BOOM. Increasingly, the vocal sounds of our own species sound piercing, taut, out of control. Indeed, dogs are not the only species who bark and howl in this auditory environment. The neediness, the frustration of not being heard, rings out in our voices, in their edginess, their jangling timbres. Human voices are showing the strain. "Yakety-yak-yak-yak!" Indeed, we necessarily avoid careful listening. Why even try?

In the midst of all this overstimulation, it is too much auditory energy, and in particular, noise, which we describe as toxic, as "noise pollution." We do not usually talk about visual, tactile or kinesthetic atmosphere as "polluted." But we do use the phrase "noise pollution." Sound is like the air we breathe, the water we drink and the soil we live on. However, most people do not take noise pollution seriously. Turning a deaf ear, they assume that things they cannot see and touch are not quite real. The importance of the world of sound is somehow not believable.

However, the effects of noise are "real." Noise exerts a powerful effect on our quality of life. As auditorily sensitive people notice, roaring motors, airport thundering, honking horns, blaring sirens and screeching brakes occur in regular – and high intensity – doses. In many places, public and private, there is a cacophony of radio, TV, video and stereo sounds playing at various volume levels. Saccharine background "musak" is a torture to some ears. And ending up "on hold" on the telephone often means a period of auditory torment, with unpalatable music or ads. Also present in many environments are all of the indeterminate hummings and thrummings of household and office appliances and technology, vibrating at different levels of pitch and volume. Some people are highly reactive to such "background" sounds, often unconsciously so.

Although paying relatively little conscious heed to auditory energy, C.G. Jung detested noise. He railed impressively against it in a letter to Karl Oftinger in 1957, and his remarks strike an uncomfortable chord in their application to modern American society. Jung's list of auditory "evils" includes not only noise, but the gramophone, the radio, and the "blight" of television. Children can no longer concentrate because "so much is fed into them from outside that they no longer have to think of something they could do from inside themselves, which requires concentration." Their infantile dependence on the outside, he says, is thereby increased and prolonged into later life, when it becomes fixed in the well-known attitude that every inconvenience should be abolished by order of the State."[8]

His next words are even more striking:

> *The alarming pollution of our water supplies, the steady increase of radioactivity, and the sombre threat of overpopulation with its genocidal tendencies have already led to a widespread though not generally conscious fear which loves noise because it stops the fear from being heard. Noise is welcome because it drowns out the instinctive warning. Fear seeks noisy company and pandemonium to scare away the demons. (The primitive equivalents are yells, bullroarers, drums, firecrackers, bells, etc.). ... Noise protects us from painful reflection, it scatters our anxious dreams, it assures us that we are all in the same boat and creating such a racket that nobody will dare to attack us.[9]*

Modern "civilization," said Jung, is predominantly extraverted and abhors all inwardness. Its noise is an integral component. We secretly want noise, because when a person is empty inside, he or she becomes somebody by creating a lot of noise.

[8] C.G. Jung, *Selected Letters of C. G. Jung*, 1909-1961, Sel.and Ed. by G. Adler, R.F.C. Hull, Trans., (Bolligen Series), Princeton NJ (Princeton University Press), 1984, p. 162.
[9] Ibid., pp. 162-64.

Upon returning home after living in a European culture
for eight years, I was struck most of all by the auditory aspect
of America. Before I became used to it again, the atmosphere of unrelenting, extraverted chattering was disturbing. It seemed that strangers were "disclosing" the most
intimate and shocking things. There seemed to be so much,
and such indiscriminate talk – and so little listening or real
responsiveness. No wonder, I remember thinking, that in
this country, so many people seek the attentive ear of a
therapist. Often, it is only in starting therapy that people
notice how used they are to not being listened to.

In the dictionary, "noise" is defined as "unwanted
sound." It refers to "loud, confused or disturbing sound."
The experience of noise holds us close to its root, the Latin
word for "nausea." The human body and mind are strongly
affected by noise. In cases of loud or sudden noise, these
physical reactions occur: blood vessels constrict, skin pales,
pupils dilate, eyes close; people wince, hold their breath and
tense their muscles. These are signals of significant disturbance. Life at a high decibel level is destructive both physically and psychologically. Noise is rated as "a major contrib-
uting cause" of ulcers, heart disease and attacks, strokes,
high blood pressure, as well as psychoses and neuroses,
states the former Surgeon General of the U.S. Public Health
Service. It has been linked with birth defects and low birth
rates in other studies.

The direct effects of noise are most harmful to the tissues
it first impinges upon, the hearing apparatus. Noise in the
work place, the home, and the recreational environment,
now accounts for more hearing losses than all other causes
combined. It is the auditory system itself which suffers most,
not only sensorily but also in terms of damage to its functional ability. Too much noise not only necessitates tempo-
rarily turning a deaf ear. It literally causes auditory damage
and deafness.

We seek respite. Some people invest a great deal of time and money in high quality sound systems. Newer technologies are constantly in the making, as people seek more and more refinement acoustically. "Walkman" earphones are everywhere, on joggers, bikers, bus-riders, people in waiting rooms. With so little invitation to listen, people are, understandably, retreating into auditory worlds of their own. They are enclosing themselves in auditory spaces of their own choosing and under their own control.

However, we need sound. Technically speaking, it is not so much the "quiet" that we seek. It is rather the right amount of sound. And it is as well the right kind – meaningful sound. The much sought-after "quiet" of the country is not really so quiet. It is replete with softer sounds, with a greater and more subtle ebb and flow of sounds. It has pauses and silence. Actually, some level of sound is a constant in the world, even when things are "quiet." Absolute silence is almost impossible for hearing people to experience. Whether conscious of it or not, we are in fact strongly dependent upon sound, even when its presence is subtle or peripheral. But we would notice its absence immediately upon stepping into a "sound-proof" room. Such a room must be elaborately constructed with special foundations and very thick insulation. Even then, only 99.98% of the sound can be eliminated.

Experiencing soundlessness – or relative soundlessness – is a disturbing experience for most hearing people, producing feelings of emptiness and deadness. They report feeling "unnerved," that their voices "go nowhere," and that they can hear their hearts beat. Helen Keller, who was both deaf and blind, stated that deafness produced a loss worse than blindness. Soundlessness shuts us away from our acoustic background, away from the surrounding vibratory field that hearing people are so used to. We lose contact with the humming, murmuring energy around us.

Sound is a necessary "container," a vibrating and animating energy all around. According to some sources, people who experience deafness are more prone to depression and paranoia. This is probably so for many reasons, unless the person has the cultural experience and support of a deaf community.[10] For hearing impaired people with their primary identity in the hearing world, profound deafness, unlike blindness, makes understanding vocal speech difficult or impossible. It limits the ability to express oneself. With such restrictions, life can become a severely isolating and frustrating experience.

For the hearing, some sound, even if distorted or meaningless, provides a sense of well-being. With the aid of modern medical technology, cochlear or inner ear transplants are possible. However, the auditory information received via such a transplant is distorted. Experts claim that the chief advantage is the psychological value of receiving even distorted information. Apparently, hearing follows a principle similar to the psychological principle, so immediately noticeable in interacting with children: any attention, even if negative, is better than no attention at all. The presence of sound, even if distorted, offers a sense of surroundings, contact, and containment.

So we need sound, we seek some sound, any sound, rather than endure soundlessness. Its effects upon mind and body are vital. Nonetheless, its importance does not mean that we are particularly conscious of sounds as we hear them. The Neurolinguistic Programmers Bandler and Grinder report that of the three sensory channels (auditory, visual and kinesthetic), Americans pay the least attention to

[10] Deaf culture is alive and well. It is claiming recognition for its existence, as well as for its unique advantages. For a (by no means complimentary) description of a deaf person's experience of the hearing world and of the richness of deaf culture, read Joanne Greenberg's book, *In this Sign*, Oliver Sack's *Seeing Voices*, or see the film, "Under a Lesser God."

auditory information. They report that most people do not actually hear the sequence of words and the intonation pattern of what they, or other people, say. They are only aware of the pictures, feelings and internal dialogue that they have in response to what they hear. Few people are able to repeat back, in the same intonation, what you say to them.[11] Clearly, we are not a very ear-minded culture. If something does enter one ear, it tends to go out the other.

One tragic mishandling of sound occurred in Waco, Texas, in April of 1993. A violent confrontation occurred between the Branch Davidians, a militant religious sect, and the FBI and Bureau of Alcohol, Tobacco and Firearms. In the almost two-month stand-off which followed, the inhabitants, holed up in their compound, were surrounded with blaring noise and threats from loudspeakers and sometimes, the sound of shots and tanks. The ordeal ended in profound and, many feel, unnecessary tragedy, with most of the group members apparently immolating themselves by fire.

The auditory atmosphere in particular was destructive. Loud, ugly sounds and music were inflicted on the group, as auditory torture, late into the night. However, sound and music could have been orchestrated as a helpful energy. Music therapist Robert L. Tusler suggested that the compound should have been surrounded with amplifiers, and broadcasting should have been constant, keeping the volume low. At first, hymns familiar to members, especially instrumental ones, should have been played, alternating with quiet, mildly emotional short instrumental compositions. Then gradually such hymns as "Amazing Grace" and "Were You There When They Crucified My Lord" should have been introduced, avoiding martial or aggressive songs.

---

[11] Richard Bandler and John Grinder, *Frogs into Princes: Neurolinguistic Programming,* John O. Stevens, Ed., Moab, UT (Real People Press), 1979, p. 124.

As the weeks went by, the emotional content of the instrumental music should have been lengthened and strengthened, keeping all texts simple and direct, emphasizing the love, mercy and forgiveness expressed in the New Testament.

While this treatment might sound naive and idealistic, Tusler stated that his experience bears out its possibilities. "We know where violence leads," he said at the end of his article, "and we know how music has been used in mobilizing people for war by numbing individual conscience. Can we not experiment with what music can do in place of bullets?"[12]

In considering the place of audition and sound in our own lives, it is vital to take this societal mishandling of sound and silence into account. It is the larger auditory habitat for our individual expression and communication. In the midst of this auditory overload, it is not easy to switch over to a more sensitive kind of hearing and listening, in regard to either words or sound. As the backdrop for our communication at more individual levels, these broader environmental conditions affect our interactions in families and friendships and in therapeutic encounters alike.

We need to hear and be heard. We need to feel ourselves to be acoustically alive, as beings vibrating and being vibrated to! "ECHO!!" at least one spray painter was inscribing on the walls all over the city of Zurich in the late 1980s. We need to hear and be heard within an atmosphere of enough resonance and enough differentiation.

---

[12] Robert L. Tusler, *Fellowship*, Sept/Oct. 1993, p. 31.

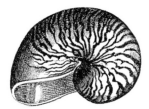

# 2. The Phenomenon of Sound

How is the phenomenon of sound related, in fact and image, to the psyche and depth understanding? What exactly happens when something sounds?

Sound occurs through vibration. An object has perhaps been struck, or set into motion due to corresponding vibrations. As it vibrates, it actually compresses or squeezes the air directly around it. Then, in extremely rapid and minute movements, as the sounding object snaps back, the medium of air again expands, compressing the air in front of it. And so the sound waves travel on, transferring and countertransferring their energies. Sound brings its medium and its surroundings into corresponding vibration, creating what is really a force field of acoustic energy.

Sound travels in an expanding, wavelike motion. Physicists describe waves as being either one-, two- or three-dimensional. Sound is the most familiar force which has a three-dimensional wave. It possesses height, width and depth, symbolically suggesting an inherent sense of depth. The acoustic waves around a sounding object are spherical in shape. Acoustic energy moves out in ever-expanding orbs of energy. It moves through its medium in a layer-by-layer motion, creating in fact, spheres of interactive energy. These concentric circles have a wavelike, back-and-forth movement or vibration around each sound-producer and as well, around each reverberating hearer.

All of this movement is going on so commonly, so naturally, that it seems effortless. But the energy present is considerable. The task of moving sound through air, as already mentioned, is made difficult by the fact that air is relatively inelastic. Neither is air as light in weight as might be assumed. In the open, at half a kilometer's distance, the air weighs more than one million tons. Only bit by bit, in acoustically expanding waves, can auditory energy move at all.

So there is a great deal going on when something sounds, and it all "works." Sound is extremely effective in its movement. It makes tiny, subtle and rounded advances. Sound is a potent force, which moves in a layered way. Sound is in fact so powerful, it actually heats the air. No wonder it is our chosen means for so much communication.

Basically, sound sets into minute movement most of the objects it comes into contact with. A sounding object creates a dynamic space, not only the air, but almost everything within its immediate environment: vases, plants, chairs, the walls themselves. Actually, a sound wave enters and passes through only those objects whose dimensions are bigger than the length of that sound's wavelength, bouncing off equal- or smaller-sized objects. But in actuality, most objects will vibrate with most sounds because of overtones.

By its very nature, sound requires vibratory reaction of everything around it, and human hearers are by no means excluded. Our bones, our skin, our hair, our tiny eardrums and middle ear bones, all vibrate to some small extent when in contact with sound. And this is so, whether we have middle ear or cochlear damage (problems receiving the sound auditorily), or nerve deafness (inability to interpret the sound). *We still vibrate.* This essential effect of sound, its ability literally to move us, gives it a power in our lives. But it also means that sound is inescapable.

Sound is enriched and re-sounded in an enclosed space. In conch shells from the beach, sea sounds actually echo on for years, bouncing back and forth, within the labyrinthine inner chamber. The psychotherapeutic process requires a "vessel" too, an interrelational space for an enclosed and vibrant interchange. This sense of container, full of sounds and rhythms and silences, is present between people in many kinds of "in-depth" exchanges, in couples, families, groups, and even audiences and performers. Things echo between participants. And they echo on after the encounter.

This natural resonance, this natural way that sound gets reinforced in enclosed spaces, also occurs in the microcosm of our bodies. The hollow cavities of the body naturally enrich our vocal sounds. There are resonating spaces behind the nostrils and above the roof of the mouth, the mouth itself, and the throat and larynx and trachea which lead down to the chest. We can vary the size and amount of rigidity in these cavities due to the flexibility of our tissues and muscles. This shifting of rigidity occurs continuously and unconsciously when making sounds, vocally and verbally. Intrinsically, sound entails a resonant space, a space for depth communication.

Acoustics, the formal study of sound, generally classifies any one sound as having four qualities: pitch, timbre, volume and fullness. The first, *pitch*, is a complex phenomenon and one which receives a great deal of differentiated attention in Western music. Its facts and images particularly evoke ideas in depth psychology. Basically, the human hearing range is limited to approximately seven octaves, between 27 and 2,456 vibrations per second. A great many more pitches exist outside of this range, which other animals hear and scientific instruments can measure. In our human range, we hear many of the pitches, but only unconsciously or subliminally, for they occur as overtones.

Overtones are of special interest to people interested in the unconscious. Acoustically speaking, overtones are very much like an unconscious field surrounding each consciously registered tone or pitch. Amazingly enough, the structure of overtones resembles the Jungian concept of archetypes. Archetypes are inherited psychic "predispositions to meaning," which automatically occur; they are set psychic propensities, eliciting, in all times and places, certain conceptions or experiences, like "mother" or "daughter" or "shadow" or "wholeness."

Likewise, overtones occur in set relationships, mathematical ones. The first overtone is one octave higher than the fundamental pitch (or whatever pitch is sounded). It was Pythagoras who first discovered that this subliminally heard overtone, one octave higher, was due to the fact that the vibrating string of a musical instrument also vibrates at one half its length. Further overtones result because this string also naturally vibrates in thirds, fourths, fifths, etc. of its length, in a straight mathematical relationship.[13] These differing lengths of vibration are in fact what produce the overtone series of any pitch. There is a fascinating and long-standing relationship between music and mathematics, beginning with Pythagoras. And there is ongoing speculation on the idea of music as an expression of cosmic order.

In comparing acoustics and psychology, we could say that the fundamental tone, the one heard consciously, sounds forth like a certain conscious psychic content. Its overtones, registered subliminally or unconsciously, are the result of given, inherent mathematical and physical relationships. Like unconscious material and the underlying archetypes, these subliminally perceived overtones give the tone a sense of context. They also suggest potentiality, a sense of what is

---

[13] Arthur S. Freese, *You and Your Hearing*, New York (Charles Scribner's Sons), 1979, p. 50.

prone to happen. Just like the archetypes, which provide hidden structure to psychic meaning, the overtones surrounding a given note provide it with a harmonic context. They place the note within a meaningful structure of related pitches, which is the background for the melodies and harmonies which are likely to result.

Harmonic structure is expressed in the use of scales, in the West, seven- or twelve-toned progression of pitches which defines what "key" the musical piece is in. On an unconscious level, these subliminally heard overtones from the sounded fundamental pitch have been the structuring element in these scales, providing the musical "meaning" or context of a piece. So it is almost as if each tone had its own unconscious reality, its own structure and potentiality, surrounding it and giving it meaning. To the Jungian ear, this sounds like the archetypal field which surrounds a psychic content, say, a dream image or memory or a family photo. The dream image of the man with a wound in his side has layers. They unfold themselves as the personal memory of the run-over dog, of the appendectomy when you were five; the photo of the boy with a gash in his thigh in the article on street violence; and most broadly, the symbolic figure of the wounded Fisher King and Christ, a suggestion of the wounded healer or savior archetype.

However, there is controversy regarding whether these overtones are as "set" as some think. As A. Storr points out, the music which has developed in human cultures over time, have not all been based on the Western tonal system. The claim that exact Western pitch intervals or scales are rooted in the natural order of things is not justified. While the octave is universal, and the major fifth possibly so, the major third (making the major triad of the Western musical tradition) is only approximate (a bit sharp). Overtones above that, which suggest the further intervals, are even more dubious. In the overtone series, they occur at such a high pitch that they cannot be heard as clear pitches, but only as timbre and via scientific instruments. It may be, as Storr states, that scales are arbitrary, and their variety potentially endless in defining musical relations within the octave.[14] However, even if it is limited to the octave as structure, and perhaps the major fifth, a "skeletal" sense of an archetypal layer, an underlying propensity toward meaning, remains, linking musical and archetypal meaning.

This vague expectation is rather like having a sense, based on cultural musical background, of what is likely to occur in this certain key during a certain phase "the work" is in. At the deepest level of predisposition to form, there may resonate, unconsciously, subliminally, fundamental auditory principles, rooted in natural law. And whether in a life lived or a musical piece, their individual yet related energies, their note-by-note intervals and melodic passages, their intricate, interweaving harmonies and disharmonies, make up the drama and tension as it plays out. Both acoustically and psychically, these layers have a dynamic and developing dimension. There is a "working through" of potential – a musical, ear-based one – using the harmonic elements as structure. This is very much like a psychological or analytic "working through" of psychic material.

Dane Rudhyar speculates that acoustic meaning occurs in a spiral shape. Visually, it may look like a straight "ladder" of notes, ascending or descending a musical clef. But musically, says Rudhyar, we perceive a melodic phrase as occurring along a spiral of meaning. When the notes ascend or descend, from the fundamental or "tonic" note through the fifth or sixth step (for example, in the ascending scale of C Major: C-D-E-F-G-A), they are musically understood to be curving away from the tonic tone. However, from there on

---

[14] Anthony Storr, *Music and the Mind*. New York (Random House, Ballantine Books), 1992, pp. 54-57.

(from A or B back to C, an octave higher), the tones are understood as "returning home" resolving back to their beginning sound. To the ear, they are curving back to the tonic or fundamental pitch, only an octave higher or lower.[15] This is an auditory spiral, an ongoing curving, leaving and circling around.

The spiral is a basic shape throughout human life, finding its most basic form in the DNA molecule, the basic shape of life itself. It occurs everywhere, even in leaf and hair growth. In Jungian work, the basic process of development of the individual's psyche, the individuation process, is imaged as a spiral. This turning around or "circumambulation" is variously interpreted as moving down into a depth, where conflicts are held in a meaningful wholeness, or up, into a transcendence of oppositional conflict.

So musical meaning, like psychological meaning, is in fact discovered and guided by means of the "spiral" of pitch. Although pitch is only one aspect, the idea that musical meaning is centered in pitch encompasses a great deal of what Westerners understand as musical experience. Musically, our ears are trained on elements of melody and harmony. This musical assumption is so solid a reality that many listeners do not even hold as valid types of music based on, rhythm, as in African music, or on timbre and harmonic overtones, as in the one-toned musical experiences in Siberia, Mongolia and India. In the history of Western music, there are many scales or "modes" which developed in the centuries following classical Greek times. Now, however, most listeners, with little musical training, have narrowed the field to two. They are conscious, if vaguely, of only the "major" and "minor" keys.

---

[15] Dane Rudhyar, *The Magic of Tone and the Art of Music.* London and Boulder Co. (Shambhala Press), 1982, pp. 90-129.

*Timbre* is the second characteristic of sound. The timbre or "tone color" or "texture" of a tone is something that most listeners readily hear, although their descriptions of that timbre might well be highly subjective. Timbre is an especially rich aspect of sound, imaginatively speaking. Actually, it is a pitch-related aspect of sound, because it is the differing combinations of overtones which create the timbre of a tone. Certain musical instruments enhance certain overtones and deaden others. It is the various combinations of overtones which make the timbre of a flute sound clear and sweet or a vibrating guitar string sound metallic or twangy. An instrument like the oboe, which sounds rather complicated and strange, is carrying very little auditory energy at the frequency level (or pitch) of the consciously heard tone. Its overtones predominate, auditorily registered only at a subliminal level. The rich array of overtones of the oboe accounts for its peculiarly plaintive and soulful sound. Whether from a musical instrument, a motor, an animal or the richest of all, the human voice, timbre creates a practically irresistible invitation into an imaginative realm!

A third characteristic of sound is volume. *Volume* describes the amount of acoustic energy which is sounding – the quantitative power of a sound. This aspect might seem like a relatively simple one, readily perceived. And it is, for our capacity to perceive volume differences is a much-used faculty. Present at birth, perception of volume is extremely sensitive. In fact, our ability to differentiate volume changes is so great that it requires a logarithmic scale. "Zero decibels" (0dB) is the faintest sound audible to the human ear. Ten dB signifies a tenfold increase, 30dB a thousandfold increase, etc. And how loud are everyday sounds? Rustling leaves are recorded at 20 dB, whispering in a quiet room at 30 dB, and a dishwasher a 75 dB. Normal conversation is in the 60-80 dB range. A pneumatic drill is measured at 80 dB and thunder at 120 dBs.

Our great auditory sensitivity to volume means that most listeners can at a conscious level perceive a volume change of 3 dB or more. However, this sensitivity is even more impressive in regard to subliminal hearing. Humans can pick up differences registered in *fractions* of a decibel. Why do we need this level of sensitivity? It is largely because this capacity is the one used to locate things. When we turn our heads one way and then the other to "hear" it, we are actually trying to find the place where the sound has exactly the same volume and the same arrival time in both ears. Even newborns have the capacity for volume differentiation to locate people and movement around them. It is basic to our functioning, throughout our lives.

> *Arthur Freese explains that scientists can make sounds appear to come from anywhere around the head by creating differences in time arrival and intensity at the two ears. A subject can even be made to hear a voice coming from his or her own head. When sound waves are beamed so that just as the crest of one sound wave reaches one ear, the trough of the other sound wave reaches the opposite ear, the brain's "direction finder" becomes totally confused. Unable to ignore the presence of the voice and yet automatically seeking to localize the sound, the brain interprets it to be at a point within the subject's own head.*

Freese, *You and Your Hearing*, p. 53

The fourth and last characteristic of sound, *fullness*, is closely related to volume. In packaging, "volume" refers to quantity, to how much a vessel can hold. In the field of acoustics, fullness refers to how full of itself a sound is, how intense it is. Although fullness has a quantitative sense, like volume, it does not exactly designate amount. Rather, it is more the concentration or density of a sound – more like its "weight." Fullness concerns the quality of energy and atmosphere, the richness or thinness of a sound within the acoustic space. Preachers proclaiming great truths, filling up the large acoustical spaces in great cathedrals, need full voices. But they sound overblown, too full of "themselves" if they use the same voice at a tea party or discussion group. Of the four qualities of sound, fullness is the one which has the most directly to do with intensity, with how closely contained a sound or an experience is.

In comparing these four aspects of sound, volume and fullness have more a sense of the amount and intensity of the auditory energy. It is not so much the distinct characteristics of a tone, but rather, "how much" auditory energy it carries. On the other hand, pitch and timbre are more an experience of the qualities of a sound. They tend to express the distinct "personality" in a tone.

*\*
\* \**

So sound as a phenomenon is powerfully moving. It is a subtle, rich and various force. Its energy is wavelike. Each sounding object, whether organic or inorganic, creates its own spherical, expanding waves. Sound requires an elastic medium in which to move, a flexible responsiveness all around it. It creates a force field which animates the air and material objects around it, whether human or not. Sound is full of energy and life. The characteristics a sound possesses, its pitch, timbre, volume and fullness, evoke a high level of responsiveness and differentiation in us, making us sensitive – and highly dependent – receivers of its distinctively psychic energy.

# 3. Sound and the Psyche

*Music is incomparably closer to the world of the psyche than to the world of bodies. … It is a pure manifestation of the psyche.*

V. Zuckerkandl, *Sound and Symbol,* p. 143

There is something about auditory energy which is especially inviting to the psyche. There is something distinctive in its nature, its essence, which gives it special meaning in our lives. Many authors, including Hegel, have written about music as an analogue of "inner life," conceived of as a continuously flowing stream.

## A. Affinities

Sound is vibration and resonance. As such, it has a close affinity with psychic[16] energy. Both auditory and psychic energy are conceived of as nonmaterial. This idea is a given with the psyche. In fact, something "psychic" is, by definition, something which is nonmaterial, something in the mental, emotional or spiritual world. It is something *not* physical. Dane Rudhyar stated that, of the five senses, sound

[16] Throughout this book, the word "psychic" means "having to do with the psyche or soul or spirit," rather than "knowing beyond processes which are believed to be understood," like a seer or a medium at a seance.

is the closest to force itself, to pure, nonmaterial energy. "We do not actually hear Sound," he pointed out, "but the resonance aroused in material instruments by the impact of inaudible currents of energy..."[17] That is to say that when hearing, we are experiencing sound as a force, as energy per se, vibrating through air, through matter and even through ourselves.

After all, in its very essence, sound is vibration. And we experience it directly as such. Actually, light is vibration too. It vibrates at a rate 40 octaves higher than sound. But we do not usually think of light as vibratory, if we think about it at all. If we do, it is probably when it is particularly bright or dim, or when light is in the form of rays or a sunbeam or in contrast to the shadow it casts. But most people are not interested in light as such, leaving that area to painters and photographers. What we are interested in are the colors and shapes of objects which light is illuminating. If we were engaged with light *per se*, we would hold light shows. Sound itself, however, is a common cultural experience. Our "sound shows" are the many kinds of musical events, long popular in human history.

All of the other four senses, vision, taste, touch and smell, tend to be closely bound up with a material source, with something "concrete." We see and feel a red ball, rubbery in the hand. We smell and taste the pumpkin pie. Smell involves an ephermeral sense of something, a trace, but it is trace of *something*, something perhaps unseen or newly released, like mustard in a jar or the fumes of gasoline. In the case of sound, however, only sometimes is it connected to a source – a motor humming, a guitar string twanging. Sound may carry meaning, even though external associations are absent. Sound is perceived as meaningful in itself.

---

[17] Dane Rudhyar, *The Magic of Tone and the Art of Music.* London and Boulder Co. (Shambhala Press), 1982, p. 75.

It carries its own message, its own energy, humming through the air.

It is possible that, in the process of evolution, dependence on the auditory process, instead of vision, was intrinsic to the development of imagination. In his fascinating book called *Thinking Animals*, Paul Shepard speculated that when the first mammals shifted to functioning mainly in the nighttime, not the daytime, dependence on vision shifted to dependence on hearing and smell. Hearing, since it involves distance, movement and direction, develops a sense of stimuli being successive, needing pattern, ordering in time. Information, he said, became integrated cortically, not sensorially. As flora spread, and thus the possibility of living in trees and living again in daylight, animals had deep-brain integrating and storing ability, created through the interaction of the senses other than vision. The holding of images would in time become the imagination. The kind of temporary storage that made melodies from tones now occurred in vision. But the first step in human-like intelligence, Shepard said, was through the auditory process, the encephalizing or deep-brain elaboration of tissues for storing information.[18]

Whether approached through theory or its own process, audition is a particularly enlivening means of perception. Sound creates a perceived field of energy, making the sounding object seem alive. Auditory energy feels dynamic. The language we use expresses its vibratory and moving nature. When an object "sounds," when someone "speaks out," or when the "telling nature" of something is revealed, we wake up, take notice. Sound is actively expressive, animating, as if an object were bodying forth its essence. Words connected with sound, with a vibratory essence, *sound*

[18] Paul Shepard, *Thinking Animals*, New York (The Viking Press), 1978, pp. 16-17.

vibrant. Sound feels ongoing. Sound runs deep. In our language, expressions like "sounding someone out" or "a resounding voice" or "a telling remark" convey a sense of depth and authority.

Music, the art of sound, is also moving, vibrant. It neither represents the phenomenal world, nor makes statements about it, says Storr. It bypasses both the pictorial and the verbal. Music is based on the experience of, and indeed the human need for, both form and emotion. Schopenhauer thought that music was in a special category. Poetry and drama are concerned with the Idea (Platonic) of human-kind as it manifests in particular situations; but music speaks directly, bypassing the Ideas and copying the Will, which is the dynamic underlying the Ideas.[19]

Sound carries an essence of the creative. As Rudhyar points out, we cannot produce light from out of ourselves. Sound, however, we can. Sound is a basically creative act, full of energy. We hear this in the creative OHM, in the words of creation, and in the truth-telling after the breaking of a silence.

This sense of deeper relationship occurs in part because of the physics of sound. After all, sound *literally* moves what it comes into contact with. When we hear something, we are actually vibrated by it. Producing sound makes the outside air vibrate. The listener who is situated within this air space is in a sense "sculpted" by the vibrations. To listen to someone playing, singing, or speaking is to let oneself be put in vibration with that person. We tend to identify with the manner in which the person addresses us. This explains why in the presence of a stutterer, or someone with a certain accent, we may end up making similar utterances ourselves.

[19] Anthony Storr, *Music and the Mind*, New York (Random House, Ballantine Books), 1992, pp. 140, 65-88 and 139-40.

It works the other way too. Sound is in turn literally moved by its hearers. It is affected by what is around it and what receives it. Sound changes, depending on the medium or media through which it travels. It shifts in response to the substances around it, the surrounding curtains and walls, the clouds, the objects standing around. Sound is highly reactive, and interactive. There is a give and take. And it is palpable. Especially when a sound is at a low decibel or pitch level, it is felt as vibrating, physically and on a conscious level. The auditory process is relationship-making.

Some researchers have related this interactivity of people, objects and sounds to even the geographical features surrounding a culture. The kind of music which develops in a certain culture may be influenced by the physical features of the countryside around it. Musical traditions, says Tomatis, are always in strict relationship with their environment. Polyphonic music develops when the culture is surrounded by forest full of confused murmurs and mingled noises, while desert regions like Chad use the drum as the only instrument.[20]

Unlike light, which can occur in a vacuum, sound requires an elastic medium through which to travel, like air or water or steel. At first glance, air might seem like the best medium for sound, due to its being light-weight. But steel is better. Steel rails carry the sound of a train more clearly than the air. Both kids and railway workers are using this principle when they put their ears to the rail to hear if a train is coming. A good medium, like a good listener, requires the quality of elasticity, and air is actually rather inelastic. A sound will not be audible unless an aura of responsivity surrounds it. This elasticity occurs at a molecular level, in the movement of atoms throughout the object. This move-

[20] Alfred A.Tomatis, *The Conscious Ear: My Life of Transformation through Listening*, Barrytown NY (Station Hill Press, Inc.), 1991, pp. 47 and 80.

ment and vibration is invisible to the eye. Just like psychic "vibrations," it is available only from within the experience, as something which is sensed.

We take little note of our auditory reactions, especially not the subtle and subliminal ones. Many, however, are not far from consciousness. They can offer important and explanatory information, like why we suddenly halted, or what it was exactly that felt so soothing, or what that uncomfortable edge was about. Considering the strong affinity between auditory energy and psychic energy, it is odd that the field of psychology works with so little consciousness of sound and silence and resonance. Few schools of psychology have delved into auditory energy or have, in any depth, addressed audition specifically as a channel for psychic energy. Three exceptions are Neurolinguistic Programmers, Process-oriented Psychologists and Audio-Psycho-Phonologists. It is a strange "oversight." After all, auditory image work is not only a natural channel of energy and communication. It is, simply speaking, the most common one.

In human history, auditory energy has carried the psyche or soul in different ways. There are three obvious angles from which to explore auditory energy. Before addressing sound in the healing arts, there is included some information and thoughts on two of the main ways humans have linked sound with "soul," namely, symbolic and poetic listening and music. Within the broad area of sound bringing meaning and redemption, there is a great deal of overlap, and each field contributes in its special way.

## B. Poetic and Symbolic Listening

> *Imaginal thinking clears the blocked channels of energy that*
> *flow between creatures and things.*
>
> Nor Hall, *The Moon and the Virgin*, p. 89

Jungian analysts are trained to work symbolically. They learn to place the wandering, jumbled, static-ridden reports of everyday events and every-night dreams within the realm of image, dream and myth. Sometimes, Jungians see symbolic work mostly as a way to work with content, using their knowledge of myths and symbology to give context and richness to a client's material. For others, it refers more importantly to an attitude or style. As archetypal psychologist and Jungian analyst Paul Kugler puts it, this means slowly "hearing through" the literal word to its secondary and tertiary meaning, until finally discovering an alternative "axis of being," an unconscious poetic dimension.[21]

For many analysts, it is a basically poetic stance, an ear-based way, from which they listen and respond. They use imagination, resonance and image work in their many forms. A sense of sound, space, vibration and rhythm makes listening poetic. There is a sense of margins, where the space around an image or feeling or event vitalizes the words, the sounds, the images. Listening symbolically, listening poetically, moves experience into resonance, opening out the way that meaning lies under, behind, around its surface levels.

Over the centuries, the deepest, the most musical-sounding and re-sounding of stories have become our myths. They have carried our cultural sense of symbolic meaning, via sound, through the acoustics of story-telling. The human

---

[21] Paul Kugler, *The Alchemy of Discourse: An Archetypal Approach to Language*, Toronto (Associated University Presses), 1982, p. 110.

voice and ear have echoed them on, incubating them, shifting and refining them, along the passages of time. Myths, states Nor Hall, intrinsically have to do with mouths and producing sound. "A myth," she explains, "is not a made-up story, but literally a 'mouthing,' and connects to the first cries, signifying awareness in newborns: "mmm, mem, mum, mu, me.' "[22] Myths have sounded forth our ideas, values, feelings, and thoughts. They voice the lessons we learn, unlearn and then have to learn all over again. They help us comprehend, if only vaguely, the patterns we are bound to follow, as individuals and as cultures.

Getting to know somebody revolves around the telling and re-telling of stories, even if they are of the day's events, or the landlord or even the news. In the psychotherapeutic process too, the work intrinsically revolves around clients telling and re-telling their stories, as therapists listen and listen again. They hear new stories, modified ones, and many too, of the same old ones, and the same old themes, which resonate in different ways in each telling. Whether it is "the family myth" or "my personal myth," there is this singing-out and the listening-in. Their vibrance lies in singing repetition. This central task of re-membering (re-collecting) is accomplished as much by the sound of the words and tones, by their quality of resonance, as by their verbal content or visual imagery. There is a weaving of the story lines of the individual, within the larger fabric of its cultural and archetypal layers.

Nowadays, myth-telling for the general public is mostly in the grip of the mass media, most dramatically, in the spectacular fantasy films of our times.[23] Nowadays, they are

---

[22] Nor Hall, *The Moon and the Virgin*, New York (Harper & Row), 1980, p. 28.
[23] George Lucas said that he studied myths and fairy tales intentionally in creating "Star Wars," a modern heroic myth of space. This film has, without doubt, had great cultural impact.

mostly flickered onto a giant screen, shown on television, to hundreds of strangers. A more personal form is the fantasy and comic books, read by millions of anonymous readers.

Sound – music, voice, resonance, silence – is evocative to imagination. With myths being trumpeted forth with over-whelming dramatics, overpowering high tech effects and high volume sound systems, there is less gently imaginative space to imagine the characters and actions and settings. There is a loss of a more personalized experience of story-telling. No longer are listeners actively engaged in weaving their lives with the story – as happens in good dream or fantasy work.

In modern times, we are overloaded with data and infor-mation, deluged with facts and practicalities, with black-and-white thinking. We are estranged from the mythic dimen-sion of stories in our everyday lives. In the midst of our largeness and even grossness of style, of our hyped-up and mass-minded ways, myths have come to look like an in-and-out, open-and-closed affair. We toss the comic book onto the pile. We flash to a different TV channel or "surf" among channels. After a film, we walk directly out of the theater into the street, into the glare of the city, the rush of traffic. There is little or no bridging or containment of the experi-ence. No wonder Americans often feel disoriented, values-deprived, lost!

It is a necessary part of human experience to live within a mythological level, inside ourselves and inside of our cultures. It is only when we can somehow live within the reality of metaphor, of "as-if" land, that "reality" can ring true. While we do not have to stay in a conscious and philosophic tension, we do need to hear from a place where such complexities can somehow exist, and where we can let them work upon us.

Our cultural difficulties in receiving myth have perhaps accounted, at least in part, for the increased interest in more imaginative, mythological and individually-centered approaches like Jungian analysis and psychotherapy. The popularity of authors like Joseph Campbell, Thomas Moore and Clarissa Pinkola Estés (herself a story-teller) is noteworthy. These authors, as well as many more, are now producing tapes, readings, speaking right into our ears. One reason that sound and myth belong together is that both operate within a natural vessel. Both place a voice, a phrase, a melodic development of events within a larger context of resonance of human patterns. Both require a vessel, a sense of circle or enclosure of listening, which enables contact with their deeper layers. Myth has the repetition, the vocal and verbal patterning, which is experienced, even if it is rarely consciously recognized.

The power of myths and fairy tales throughout time is in part a result of their poetry, their poetic repetition, the sense of resonance heard in their language. The field of poetry has a great deal to teach psychic workers, in a specifically acoustic sense. A writer like Gaston Bachelard articulates such ideas, at the same time as he evokes this sense powerfully in his writing style. In fact, he speaks directly of the value in "a poetic analysis" of humans.

Poetry, symbol and myth are, in the end, inseparable fields. But poets are the real specialists in acoustic effect. T.S. Eliot is quoted as saying that poetry can "communicate before it is understood," working upon the ear the depth of its incantation. Every vital development in language is a development of feeling as well, said Eliot, and words and thought cannot be separated; only the poet, he says, can impart the feeling that he has sunk to the most primitive and forgotten, that his thought and emotions have returned to the origin and have brought back a deeper sense of life.[24]

---

[24] F.O. Matthiessen, *The Achievement of T.S. Eliot: An Essay on the Nature of Poetry*, Boston and New York (Houghton Mifflin Company), 1935. Quoting Eliot in "The Auditory Imagination," p. 81 and 86.

It is the poets who have best developed the art and craft of working with the specifics of images, with the way they are placed, the way they move or do not move, the way they take on meaning through sound and sound association. They are the teachers of how to listen within an imaginal space, with a sense of song and vibrancy in and around words.

Listening poetically means listening in wonder, like a child. Not unlike the Romantic poets, both Freud and Jung advised a vulnerable and open attitude. It is one where the therapist forgets everything previously learned, as he or she listens in the hour. The poet John Keats used the phrase, "negative capability." It occurs when a person is capable of being in uncertainties, mysteries and doubts, without an irritable reaching after fact and reason.

Listening poetically means not being set. It means not being fettered in expectations or needs for certain known ideas or feelings. Most difficult of all, it means not even demanding a meaning or theme that can be verbalized or understood. Whether it involves a poem, a thunderstorm or a client's gravelly voice – or all three at once – poetic listening is poised and alert. It is willing to receive and wonder in a naive way. Poetic listening requires the naked and hairy ears of the animal, who hears acutely, who knows the survival value of sounds and silences. It requires the ears of the youngest Dummling in fairy tales, by definition under-rated, who knows how to listen to the surprising, to the underside. Poetic listening is inescapably open, as inescapably open as conductive hearing through bone and skin. Listening poetically means listening first to the way that words and silences open out meaning, rather than only limit it.

When words are heard as conceptual tools, we talk in terms of "grasping meaning." Words are listened to as if they were objects. They become tools of consciousness, without the "as if" dimension which is really, after all, their essence.

For all words are themselves images, first of all. They stand for something not literally themselves, but only portray a person, place, object or idea. When words are listened to as if they were set definers, they cannot release the layered, the associative level of meaning. They lose that elusive and shape-shifting aspect of psychic experience.

Poets are our teachers also because they work with dimensionality, with the under-tones and overtones of both sound and content. They use onomatopoeia, rhythm, rhyme, alliteration, stanzas, spacing, playing expectancy and structure against freshness and surprise. Just like a good story-teller, just like in the psychotherapeutic hour, poets position images and words sensuously, resonantly in space, in time, in the ear, in the mouth, in silence. When the client is listening to himself in a flat way, with a dull and deaf ear to his own material, his own voice, it is the therapist who must bring in "poetic listening." Then things can reverber-ate beyond the incident itself, beyond the literal level.

Therapists function best as a poetic listeners. They must beware of the scholar, the teacher, the editor or critic. These characters must be put in their places, firmly at the bottom of the page, or even outside the arena altogether. For within the context of symbolic listening, they stop up the resonating space. They go "clunk."

Poetic experience invites strong feelings and emotions. Innately, that is, by its very vibratory nature, auditory work is participatory. Our use of words and silence and sound in therapy, just like in poetry must reach into body and soul, to vibrate us. According to this curious sense of sound and space, words do not so much describe experience. But – through sound and space and silence – they become it. Being moved in an acoustic, poetic-based way means experi-encing moments of participation through sound. It is at some level a union with meaning, with wider layers, even with each other, through vibration itself. It could be said to involve mystical participation. The deepest and most emotionally complete understanding must involve hearing the acoustic call in words and tones, and responding to their vibratory field.

Pat Berry describes listening with a symbolic and imaginal attitude in her essay, "Hamlet's Poisoned Ear." Hamlet, she says, is on a quest for psychological understanding. His "poisoned ear," is his inability to listen to the depths of psychic experience. In the outer world, Hamlet's conflict centers around how to react to his father's murder by Hamlet's uncle, who poured poison in his brother's ear. Hamlet has, in a sense, inherited his father's injury or "sin," his unsolved dilemma. Now Hamlet must respond. What he must learn is to speak and hear properly. Most especially, he must learn not to depend upon the use of platitudes, concretism and empty effulgence. He must learn to understand – and express – himself in relationship to depth. Hamlet requires what Berry calls "vertical bonding," a connection, or even bondage, to depth. He must listen downward, to that psychic space below, to the underworld. In particular, he must remember the guiding, underworld ghostly father, that essence of nonconcrete, imaginal essence.[25]

This image of the poisoned ear points up that symbolic listening is actually a natural state of affairs: it is unpoisoned. It is the concretist and flat use of language, and listening to language, which is out of the ordinary, which is "poisoned." The therapeutic hour calls back this place of unpoisoned listening, of vibrant – uncorrupted – sound and silence. It attempts to create and maintain a rounded, surrounding space, an acoustic vessel. It helps heal the wounded ear, so that space can be given to the sounding the soul.

[25] Patricia Berry, "Hamlet's Poisoned Ear" in *Echo's Subtle Body: Contributions to an Archetypal Psychology*, Dallas TX (Spring Publications), 1982, pp. 127-46.

Listening poetically means hearing the underlying and surrounding resonance of speech and song, sound and silence. It is a way of hearing words as they suggest, associate and open out ideas and feelings, as they sound and then resound. The poetic ear is tuned to the echoes, to the song, moving from specific image into wider realms. It is tuned in the other direction too, where the wider realms of cultural or archetypal image bring meaning to the specific, in one person, in one situation, in one moment. Poetic and symbolic listening is artistic in its invitation to sensitivity, mystery and depth. It moves among the many levels and styles of perception, listening in the moment, in the specific space, to receive the song.

## C. Music

> *[Franz] considered music a liberation force: it liberated him from loneliness, introversion, the dust of the library; it opened the door of his body and allowed his soul to step out into the world and make friends.*
>
> M. Kundera, *The Incredible Lightness of Being*, pp. 92-93

Music soothes "the savage breast." It has the power to calm a restless child or troubled soul. But just as powerfully, it has the effect of stimulating and uniting, as in patriotic, protest or school songs. Music can get people out into the world, into action, propelling them up out of their seats and unto the floor to move, gyrate, glide, to rock and roll. As well, it can bring them into themselves, evoking deep emotional reactions, memories, making access to inner life and spiritual energy vibrant and real. Clearly then, music is a recognized energy in many fields having to do with healing, from shamanism to modern music therapy.

In therapy, essentially musical elements can play a direct role in healing. People may use guiding or centering tones, like a mantra, or a phrase or song or musical theme, or even a certain pitch interval. Central healing energy can come through the musical act of speech-song or through vocal sounds, such as the expression of emotions or primal scream work. Auditory work like this can be understood as employing aspects of music.[26]

In any conversation, it is typical to utilize what are essentially musical elements. Without thinking of it as musical, people naturally accent syllables or words or phrases, making them come forward to attention. They can accent, making something sound lower or higher, louder or softer, slower or faster, or by shifting the timbre or tone quality. Sometimes, they repeat a word or phrase immediately, like a repeated note or phrase in music. Or sometimes, they repeat yet change something slightly, like the accent or pitch or meter. Sometimes the varying is strong and developed enough to sound, musically, like "elaboration," where speakers take words or phrases and re-position them, playing them out in another pitch range or key. Vocally as well as verbally, a conversation often sounds, acoustically, as if a certain theme were being clarified and developed, in a musical way.

And as the sound exchange continues, there are elements of rhythm, returning, like repeats, like codas, like stanzas. Also musical are the "dramatic" elements, where the sounds build, or where silence ripens, creating a musical or dramatic framework of statement, development, suspense and climax. Especially in careful communication, there is a sense of regular return. And indeed, after the exchange, just

---

[26] For a direct description and discussion, see Lane Arye's thesis, "Music the Messenger." Theodor Reik's book, *The Haunting Melody: Psychoanalytic Experiences in Life and Music,* is also interesting this regard.

like after a concert, the tune plays on, in the ear, inside the head.

Theodor Reik also develops the comparison between musical and psycho-analytic "performance" in his book on analytic listening. The analyst, he says, carefully prepares the way for "major melodic statements," first echoing them in softer timbres and less noticed voices – just hinting or giving a faint echo. Or perhaps she uses certain pitch intervals which will later be the building blocks for a central melodic statement. This, Reik continues, can happen within the rhythm of one hour or over many hours. And even after a major statement has been heard, the analyst will probably echo it again and again, weaving it among the different backgrounds and counter-melodies, holding it in relationship to new melodies and sounds which are emerging.[27]

Within the acoustic vessel, the therapist is accompanist to the client in the telling, and in helping them to "sing." Like a musical accompanist, she supports the client's sound and song, helping, first of all, to provide a container. She is audience. She is also partner. In this further layer of experience, she uses an experience of musical accompaniment to provide context, as well as interactional challenge, for the client.

One basic style of accompaniment is largely supportive. It provides a psychically/musically fitting background and base. More in a containing mode, its energy is holding. Thus its interactivity is highly interdependent. This style of accompaniment aims at helping to fortify the song, to help it to become more of itself. It consolidates the teller's voice, saying "Yes!" to its energies. "This is good!" it says, "More!"

This supportive style of listening addresses the task not only of clarifying or strengthening the "song," but also of

[27] Theodor Reik, *Listening with the Third Ear: The Inner Experiences of a Psychoanalyst*, New York (Grove Press), 1953, p. 328.

permitting it. Sometimes, the very right of the speaker to sing out his message is at issue. Listening energy which is surrounding and grounding is not only helpful, but necessary, in order to help the person to "perform" in a true sense, from out of himself. It becomes understood that as the experience builds, these intervals and phrases and melodies will be received, resonated to and possibly worked with. This interaction is not only harmonic; it may contain diverse and conflicting elements. But it is "harmonious-enough."

This containing style of accompaniment is a basic layer of the work. In one sense, it has to do with the establishment and maintenance of the basic vessel. It allows the experience of enough security and trust. In all relationships, as well as in therapies of depth, there are passages which are especially slow and difficult. The accompaniment then becomes more like "company to" – being there with – a partner, rather than elaborating or separating out. The two partners do their work in acc(h)ord.

The other style of accompaniment is polyphonic. The voices of the partners are more individual, more separate. Not primarily in search of unison or acc(h)ord, the two interact as different, yet highly related, entities. There is a strong sense of "back-and-forth." Things are not fixed. The mode is variety of play, interplay and replay. The partners are engaging in repetition, repetitive play, moving perhaps up or down a third in pitch, to a different mode or scale (perhaps major to minor), to a different meter, or using accent in subtly or wildly different places.

In music, such interplay forms the basis for "elaboration." It functions to comment on and deepen, and perhaps expand, the stated musical theme. Elaboration works to explore potential. On and on play the interacting melodies and tones, using the same and diverse patterns of sounds, echoing them, widening and narrowing them, returning, and then ranging out again. The interacting energies are increasing and decreasing differences and thus creating a process of differentiation.

In fugal music, there is a statement of primary and secondary musical themes, rather like speaking out certain important or theme sentences in a speech. The fugal piece then works with, works out, this theme, using separate and interacting voices. If we return this process to the consulting room, first the therapist picks up the theme or song, repeating it, perhaps checking it out, helping it to become well-known. Using an echoing theme, or a similar but different melody, she can re-call and re-echo at a revealing, or revealingly unexpected, moment. The elaboration continues. Perhaps she shifts the sense of interval from major to minor tones, striking an entirely new mood or perspective. Or perhaps she slows down what the client has offered, making it deeper and more resonant.

Or perhaps in trickster style, she reverses the pitch intervals, creating an "upsidedown" echoing. The energy which was going up is suddenly going down, in that same degree of relationship. In "musical imagination," the opposites become audible. They may sound as if they are balancing, deepening each other, offering dimension, as a visual shadow does. Actually, any of these "moves" may as well come from the other partner or client, as he too listens to his own material in new ways, engaging in a play and interplay of energies. There are forays, surprises. The two voices are highly related, the interaction lively. Melody, pitch, timbre, accent, rhythm, all use the interactive space or the therapeutic vessel as their practice room.

It is often the case that a client is unready or reluctant to come out with something. He may be slowly building by "practicing." He will be trying out what he needs in order to realize something in his own psyche, his own reality. In therapy, he may do this by engaging with his fantasies or dreams, by working on his projection on a friend, an enemy, a parent or the therapist, by confronting a situation or issue at work. No matter where it appears in his life, whatever content or feeling is "up," this theme, for example, being under constant criticism, or feeling numbed, will repeat, will appear repeatedly. It will sound itself into being in many keys and meters and styles. The therapist lends her musical ear to recognizing these elements as themes – just like musical themes. Before this kind of listening, themes may be repeating in a mindless, heedless way. They are essentially popping out at strange times, putting odd sounds and words in his mouth. They are playing the client, rather than his performing or functioning in his life with such energies "at his fingertips." In therapy, the psychotherapist helps in the task of hearing energies present, as well as those which are potential, in the unconscious. She helps make sense of the song, the dance, in the interactive space.

Depth psychotherapy is based on working with unconscious contents, and the therapist, in echoing them, will often sound as if she is bringing in something new or strange. A client in the midst of the process will often not understand how centrally he has led in creating in the sessions the particular energies present in the psychic field. He will be apt to hear these energies as belonging to the outer situation between the partners, and perhaps called into being by the therapist. However, a trained therapist will know that, barring byways and distortions, she is searching for and supporting the energies as they emerge from the client. Therapist and client, in practice session after practice session, learn to work, to discover, again and again, how the client discovers and then performs his "song." The therapist interacts "musically" to bring out the client's song and then to reinforce its meaning. And she helps in bringing it into concert with the rest of the world, inside and out.

In both music and psychotherapy, timeliness is of the essence. It is matter of timing, a matter of tact. Reik points out that in its German usage, the word "Takt" carries the double meaning of both "a poised sensitivity to feelings" and also "the musical beat, time or measure."[28] Here again, music is a close partner with psychic and emotional life. In the work, the client sets the basic pace. But the therapist must often exert some influence in setting the rhythm, the pace. Too fast and facile a pace is a common defense. Resonant communication takes care and time and space. In the moment-to-moment feel of things, the therapist must also use considerable tact. Moving too fast, or else moving too coarsely, too slowly, too finely, ruins the feel. If frustration runs too high, or if it runs too low, the energies in the moment will not sound forth in an audible dimension. It will not be heard, experienced, made conscious. If the work is too loud at the wrong time, it will be overwhelming, and thus not received.

Some dissonance is apt to be a regular feature of either style of accompaniment, whether background or fugal. In much of modern music, dissonance is a predominant feature. Some listeners complain that dissonance expresses the conflicted, fragmented and even destructive nature of our times. Rudhyar strikes a more positive note. He describes the ways that the historical periods in music express human psychic development, and posits that the prevalence of dissonance in modern times, that is, the wider range of pitch intervals, expresses an immensely wider range of relations. Earlier and more consonant musical times were narrower relationally. Chords, he says, which are described as dissonant in Western music sometimes generate a far more powerful resonance than so-called perfect consonances.[29]

---

[28] Ibid, p. 317.
[29] Rudhyar, p. 143.

This remark is a valuable acoustic reminder in regard to both kinds of accompaniment. Avoiding dissonance in the therapeutic hour, as in music, as in relationships, avoids a kind of life energy that carries powerful resonance. Therapists, friends, family can be sing-song in wanting healing or positivity to happen. This kind of acoustic and psychic experience does not hold to a many-angled, full enough relatedness.

The client uses the therapist's ways of listening to learn to hear himself. This self-listening must be present to increase consciousness, to help him perform from more of himself. Consciousness is often fleeting and refractory. But the auditory channel forms a natural bridge of interacting experience and consciousness, with its vibrant, flowing and layered nature. A musical sense, with its ear for rhythm and style help hold the attunement and rhythmic necessities, as the partners are audience to, as well as engage in, the necessities of a soulful life.

## D. Sound and the Healing Arts

> *The world we live in is one long vibration emanating out of silence.*

> L. Garfield, *Sound Medicine,* p. 93

Before the auditory chaos of modern life and before we isolated the experiences of poetry, myth and music from our common and shared lives, sound held a more beneficial place in our culture. In human perception, sound is linked with essential life energy and creativity. Sound is closely connected with the basic life force, with creation, with breath and speech. Sound brings things into motion, and gives them form.

In its very roots, sound is associated with health. This idea was widespread in different eras and geographical locations throughout human history. This linkage between "sound" and "health" is resoundingly present in our language. "Sound" literally means "healthy," as in the phrase, "sound mind, sound body." The roots – or we could say, the unconscious layers – of the word "sound" come from the Old English and modern German word "gesund," meaning "healthy," "legal," "unbroken," "thorough." "Sound" also refers to more specifically psychological words like "stable" and "trustworthy,"[30] as in a "sound personality."

This deep connection between "sound" and "health" is present in the word "tonic" too. Medically speaking, a "tonic" is a substance which has the power to make healthy, to invigorate or build up strength. And in music, the "tonic note" is the fundamental tone in a musical scale, the central pitch around which melody and harmony are organized. Acoustically speaking, it is like a center or base, around which the structure of the song develops, like its core.

That sound is involved with soundness in health must have been more obvious before the Industrial Revolution. With mechanical power and high productivity as its god, the Industrial Revolution sounded forth with metal sounds, mechanical sounds, loud and repetitive. In both quality and quantity, sound changed. Metal beating on metal, with no variation, beat after beat, is clanging and intrusive. It is auditorily boring. The rhythm, the pace of life, became more machinelike, and much busier. In cities and factories, the air rang with hissing, chugging, roaring, pounding, sounds that transformed the auditory world into unrelenting thrust and bustle. In the burgeoning cities, the teeming activity of people and vehicles dominated the narrow streets.

---

[30] Funk & Wagnalls Standard Dictionary, P. Barrett and C. Cohen, et al, Eds., New York (New American Library), 1980, "sound," p. 770.

*The Annunciation*
*Master of the Retable of the Reyes Catolicos (15th century, Spanish)*

Pre-industrial days and rural life were a radically different auditory experience. Sound was a manageable and meaningful experience. People used to have to listen carefully, as most animals still do, to the wind, the trees and grass, to a sudden quiet, to other animals' sounds. These were basic cues regarding food and safety. Ears were hungry – not overloaded – and listening brought necessary information. Words were rarer, more attended to, more valued. After all, in the olden days, most societal contact was oral. Both commercial and governmental information was communicated by way of the ear. Town criers periodically called out announcements, from officials and rulers and governments. Street vendors sang and chanted out the marketplace news. Indeed, some of these calls and chants are still echoing down to us, as musical and poetic motives in kids' songs and chants and in different art forms. In those times, information arrived by way of a human voice. It arrived at a human pace, as a welcome, comprehensible part of living life together.

Story-telling by way of ear and mouth, used to be vital, a core societal activity. People told stories and poems and played music to communicate and celebrate their collective values. Evenings were spent listening to tales told round flickering firelight. In crowded enclosures made of wood or earth or stone, heated by fire and body warmth, surrounded by the silence of the dark night, people sounded forth their stories, poems and songs. The words rolled off well-schooled tongues into wonder-filled ears. Oral tradition, its stories and poems and songs, were a lifeline to social contact and meaning. It created a space where people could relax, remember their social identity, and re-experience their shared values. Stories, poems and songs must have been a great comfort in the arduous and bare lives of the everyday person, in the midst of the long and hard labor that almost everyone, even children, had to endure.

We have lost this ear-based center of reception. Fewer and fewer people, it seems, love language. Perhaps our loss of language via the ear is one reason. Reading language, seeing it on the written page, or hearing it in its jarring role of the staccato companion of commercials and sound bytes, has made us shut off our ears and hearts. Now, language appears in an orphan role, separated from the sound roots that give it resonance and depth.

Before medieval times, written language was always spoken aloud, a practice that modern-day students are taught to avoid at all costs. In classical Greek times, it was a rare accomplishment to read without speaking the words out. The language of oral tradition, of the fairy tales and myths, songs and poems, vibrates with the body, pulses with the heart. It is easy to love, listening in this way. Such language is full of symbols and poetry. It sings with lovely, haunting phrases. Its repetition affirms our listening, as we deepen our contact with its meaning and its sounds.

We are subtly and profoundly moved by the language of resonance, the language of the ear. For many modern people, being read fairy tales and children's books is their only memory of this kind of experience. Nowadays, it is mostly children who are permitted this hunger for stories. The sound of repetition, rhyme, rhythm and the language of symbols are simply enjoyed, their sounds lending familiarity and aesthetic completion.

## Sound in Religion

Religion has been one area which has kept sound at the center of its activities. Hymns, chanting, and rhythmic, resonant liturgy, accompanied by the poetry of holy texts and prayer, have, for most churches and temples, remained the core of religious observance. This is no coincidence, for religion has intrinsically to do with being "sound," whole, with a return to the spiritual roots of being. It offers a "tonic," a return to the core sound, to the central, redemptive soundness.

Religion addresses that logically impossible place between the "body" and "spirit," which we have split up in Western culture. It ministers to that area in the middle, called "soul." The traditional place for "psychological healing" used to be religion. "The soul" used to be synonymous with "the psyche." Likewise, in earliest times, the body was united with the soul and spirit. In early traditions, healing, the healing of the whole person, was firmly in the hands of medicine men and women, shamans, witches, holy people, and all of the many types of healers. "Mental health" was inseparable from physical health.

Modern mental health practitioners would not have to stretch their understanding far to admit that they hear confessions, and work with forgiveness and faith. In modern times, with its emphasis on psychology and individualism, a major controversy is whether "god" or higher powers are inside or outside. But whether outside, inside or both, the search for healing and wholeness has continued in human history. Rather than to engage in this either/or conflict, it makes sense simply to acknowledge and reflect on the ways religion has parented the search for soul, to understand some of the ways it parallels and informs psychological work. Sound is an evocative force in psychological healing and in religious observance.

There is a long, rich acoustic history in the religions in both preliterate cultures and modern world religions. This is testimony to the depth levels of meaning that auditory energy can convey. Sound carries a spiritual essence. Apparently in all eras, people have used sound – singing, chanting, playing instruments – to worship and celebrate religious events. The cultures of the American Indians, says Newham, used the cathartic talking about guilt and worries to the willing listener, as well as voice and song to heal. In many of

the northern tribes, the right song, a medicine song, must
be found from certain "chosen ones," perhaps in a dream.
The singing of such songs is often accompanied by chanting
by the family or tribe and the rhythmic beat of the rattle.
Medicinal use of music, song and voice is reported in
cultures throughout the world, for example, in the Aborigi-
nes of Australia, the tribes of Papua New Guinea and the
nomadic peoples of the Sahara and the Sudan.[31]

Energy, states Beaulieu, is sacred sound. Not only is there
"the Word" in Christianity, but "Kung" in ancient Chinese
or the cosmic tone. There is also soundless sound, the key
note, the cosmic sound, OHM. In India, it is said that the
universe hangs on sound, a cosmic vibration so massive and
subtle and all-encompassing that everything seen and
unseen (including humans) is filled with it. Audible sound
is the road to sacred sound[32]. In the mythologies, for
example, of Hinduisim, in Indonesia, in Japan, sound is
associated with creation and with the bridge between
humans and the divine. D. Campbell singles out the African
American gospel church, African drumming, Central American shamanic singing, Balinese dancing, and the North
American sacred harp as aspects of culture which particularly invite the inner and outer worlds to blend and harmonize simultaneously. Indeed, in our times, we might particularly need acoustic techniques. We have, says Campbell,
developed "such strong, logical, left-brained constructs to
control the outer world that we may have lost our natural
awareness of how to harmonize and work with the inner
world[33].

---

[31] Paul Newham, *The Singing Cure: An Introduction to Voice Movement
Therapy.* Boston (Shambhala), 1993, pp. 47-48.
[32] John Beaulieu, *Music and Sound in the Healing Arts,* Barrytown, NY
(Station Hill Press), 1987, pp. 32-36.
[33] Don Campbell, *The Roar of Silence: Healing Powers of Breath, Tone &
Music,*Wheaton IL (The Theosophical Publishing House), 1989, p. 60-70.

From the resounding gongs and haunting muzzah cries in the Muslim and Eastern worlds to the pealing church bells and chants and hymns, ascending in Western cathedrals, people around the globe have used sound as a call to worship. The bells and gongs have sounded, ritually calling, re-evoking the awareness and profundity of larger and more powerful energies. They have re-minded people, every hour, every day, every week, of spirit and soul, as they have lived their earthly lives. There is a fascinating difference between the Eastern use of the gong and Western use of the bell. Their auditory realities are similar: a blend of a heavily resounding totality, an overwhelming sounding of all the pitches and overtones – or at least it seems so. Eastern religion is introverted, and thus its gong expands outward, its spiritual life balancing and compensating (in Jungian terms) its conscious mode. The bell, however, reflects the extraversion of Western religion, its direction outward, into outer life and outer acts. Its pealing bell has an enclosing shape, carrying the energy inward. The bell and gong express the need for inclusion of the opposite energy that leads to wholeness.[34]

On listening back in fantasy, how much more vibrant the Jewish and Christian messages must have been for the people in past times! They heard "God's Word" as it rang out, primarily via the ear, reverberating through synagogues, churches and cathedrals. "Hear the Word of the Lord!" intone pastors and priests still today, holding in ritual sound the link with God as creative and redemptive force. The healing power of sound still rings in the powerful African American spirituals, now sung and played in a many American churches. In evangelistic services of all kinds, powerful phrases and hugely oratory sermons take on

[34] Rudhyar, pp. 16-24 and 52.

strongly musical[35] and hypnotic rhythms and sounds. Their sound may be more important than their content.

The theme of creation, and its related theme of redemption, is particularly important in the healing process. Creation and creativity are closely related themes, helping us to recognize and be guided by energies larger and wiser than our too personalistic selves. Both require the ability to connect, and re-connect, again and again, to the initial core of being. For believers and nonbelievers alike, for those who take them literally and those who live by their symbolism, the central themes and meanings of Judeo-Christian teachings remain important roots of our value system, even as it may shift. These stories and myths (even if heard only outside of religious institutions) have structured and informed our lives.

Listen, one more time, to the Old Testament creation story in the Judeo-Christian Bible. First, there is a state of initial darkness, formlessness and emptiness. We are used to thinking that creation began with light. But in this story, it is not seeing, or light, which begins creation. It is sound. This god-energy becomes creative, a creative force, only when God speaks – only when this Spirit gets sounded by means of the voice which says, "*Let there be light!*" (Genesis 1:3). Sound comes before light and, in fact, brings it into being.

This message is echoed in the New Testament. In the beginning, it says, was "the Word," which was both with God and itself God (John 1:1-3). The main theme of the New Testament is "redemption" through the Son of God. Its Latin roots mean "to buy back," to reconnect to the initial value, in this case with the God and the forces of creation. It is an affirmation of the human bond with the creative or healing energy or with God.

---

[35] To hear to an impressive example of evangelistic speech used as music, listen to John Adams "Christian Zeal and Activity" (see Bibliography).

In this new listening, God as Father and Son is sound-centered, first as initial speech and then, as "the Word." The central redemptive figure, the Son incarnated to heal the human soul, was not only "Light of the World." He was first, in his aspect as the creative father, "the Word." Both Father and Son take the image of creative and redemptive sound. The Holy Ghost also had to do with this theme of sound as creative. In a story from Medieval times, it was said that the Holy Ghost entered the ear of Mary to conceive Christ.[36] In one of his few comments on sound in his writings, Jung noted the association of sound with creation, not only in Genesis, but in two alchemy texts and a Greek papyrus.[37]

Sound is often linked with light, especially in its creative aspect. The light of the stars is all that is visible, said Jung, but we still speak of the music of the spheres and of celestial harmony. The Greek god, Apollo, is a sun-god as well as a divine musician with his lyre. "It probably no accident," declared Jung, "that the two most important discoveries which distinguished man from all other living beings, namely speech and the use of fire, should have a common psychic background. Both are products of psychic energy, of libido or mana."[38] Berendt too points out that this intermingling of light and sound is archetypal. It is a deep and recurrent pattern in human history. In the Indian spiritual world, Prajapati, the primal creator, is "singing light," "a singing sun," and "the sound of light." And "Radiant Light" is transformed into sound in the *Tibetan Book of the Dead.*

[36] J.C. Cooper, *An Illustrated Encyclopaedia of Traditional Symbols*, London (Thames and Hudson), 1982, "ear," pp. 58-59.
[37] C.G. Jung, *The Collected Works of C.G. Jung*, H. Read, M. Fordham, G. Adler and W. Mcguire, Eds. (Bollingen Series University Press). *Vol 5*:56; Jung also includes sound with breath and fire in discussing creation and the beginning of speech, for example, in 5:237 and 8:665.
[38] *CW 5*:163-65.

Light, he comments, is often a passing manifestation of
sound of creation.[39]

*Science as Healing*

In some ways, it is no exaggeration to call science a
religion. Science receives a great deal of emphasis in our
culture. In fields like medical science and psychology, its
link with healing is clear. In Western culture, especially in
the last century, science has taken over what are essentially
religious functions. It has posited a belief in a higher order:
natural laws. And it has attempted to explain and ease
human difficulties in the world, as a religion does. "Believers" in science abound. Indeed, perhaps they dominate.
Even those who understand little about science manifest
devotion to it and, if you ponder the matter, what can only
be called a "leap of faith" in its efficacy. When an individual
needs more credibility, he or she will call on the name of
science to give authority to a fact or an idea.

There are sometimes biblical echoes in scientific texts
and essays. One of the most interesting is in the scientific
account of Hans Jenny, a Swiss medical doctor and engi-
neer. Jenny worked directly on the relationship between
sound and matter. He experimented with subjecting some
relatively formless materials, such as liquids, sand, clay and
fine powders, to the effects of continuous sound vibrations.
What he discovered is that, apparently, sound organizes
matter. Photos of these substances, vibrating on metal
sheets, show that extended sounds produce patterned
shapes. And the longer the sound is maintained, the more
defined the shapes become. On video tape [see the bibliog-
raphy], the substances began forming four-sided shapes, as
well as three- and five-sided ones, and sometimes mandala-

[39] Joachim-Ernst Berendt, *The Third Ear: On Listening to the World.* Tim
Nevil, Trans., Longmead, England (Element Books), 1988, pp. 32-33.

like forms. Some sounds produced shapes like mountain ranges. This process bore a striking resemblance to the events in Genesis!

Sound, by its very essence, occurs in the realm where matter and energy meet. Jenny's discussion of the phenomena is similar to the way that physicists describe quantum particles. Matter in the world seems to be a product of both pulses or waves, particles or form. There is no clear separation. Actually, one of the major theories, that of "The Big Bang," directly advances the idea that creation was sound-centered. It posits that the universe as we know it began with a giant explosion. Again, science and religion display affinities, despite their historical conflicts and opposing mental modes. Unlike a religious person, who would hear this creative sound as expressing divine will ("And God said…"), scientists understand it as a mere "bang." Science's viewpoint is secular, with no human or godlike meaning or intentionality behind creation. What science does believe in, the final proof, is measurability, quantification. The scientific description of this creative force is in terms of its megatons of explosive power. In science's parlance, this is a Great Noise, this "Big Bang," lordly in its secular magnitude.

According to the Big Bang theory, we could speculate that our world is moving out from, or exploding away from, this vibrant, auditory energy, this initially creative – and ever re-creative – sounding energy in the universe. In current times, we could say that we are seriously disconnected; we are acoustically "unredeemed."[40] We are zooming farther and farther away from the creative and redemptive sources of life.

[40] My favorite typographical error occurred at this point: "unredᵣeemed" for "unredeemed." Errors in transciption often point up, via the fingers and then the ear, fascinating relationships, which are based not only in content, but in rhyme or other kinds of sound relationship as well, just like in poems.

Berendt posits that it could be our filtering, limited consciousness with its miscomprehension of space and time that reduces to a "bang" all of the following: Jakob Boehme's divine "resonance," the Indian tradition's primal Nada, the eternal primordial sound of the Sufis, the Logos of the Gospel according to St. John, the voice of the Creator moving over the waters in Genesis, and Sikhs' Naam. Creation is misperceived as an explosion lasting only a fraction of a second because Western scientific consciousness is incapable of perceiving "the whole."[41]

So science, like religion, understands sound to be the primary force which brings the world, and indeed the universe as such, into being, making life possible in its present form. The Big Bang, like the voice of God, is the creator. Dane Rudhyar notes that we repeatedly associate sound with creativity and creative will. He speculates that the reason is that, after all, we experience ourselves as producing sound at will, from our own selves. This we cannot, for example, do with light. We can create sounds with our own bodies, whether by humming, playing an instrument or speaking out, even in the most mundane of circumstances. We can do so from an energy which has to do with our will, with some central expression of ourselves. And this is an energy that we link, at the deepest level, with creativity, with our experience of the existence of larger powers, with divinity or God.

*Sound Medicine*

In present times, the most conscious use of sound in healing occurs in alternative healing methods. There is a range of healing methods which employ singing, cathartic and expressive theater, chanting, humming, crying, screaming, drumming and the playing of other musical instru-

---

[41] Ibid, p. 104.

ments, to name the most common. One such healer is Jill Purce, who offers inner sound and voice workshops in England and elsewhere. She has studied the interrelationship between what she terms "inner sound" and feeling. She calls her work "Musical Medicine," and employs mystical sound techniques, and especially Mongolian and Tibetan overtone chanting, to break through "the chattering Mind," induce meditation and reduce anxiety. "The world is a vibratory unity plus language," says Purce. "Liberate the voice, and you liberate the tensions. Trying to find your own note is an attempt to find yourself."[42]

Another healer and composer is Kay Gardner, who teaches how to do drone baths, musical drones, different kinds of toning including different vowel sounds and key notes of the planet, chanting, mantra work, and Tao sounds which relieve the organs. She also discusses the healing possibilities in music elements: harmonics as a stairway to the spiritual, rhythm as pulse, the moods and shapes of harmony, melody as heart and soul, form and divine proportion, and the instrumental spectrum, including the human voice.[43]

There are many more kinds and combinations using sound as a force of healing. However, modern mainstream Western medicine also partakes in sound more than we might be aware. For one thing, it has its roots in sound. The modern day symbol for medical practice, the physician's rod of healing, or "caduceus," consists of two snakes intertwining around a rod. This symbol comes from Greek myth and is directly associated with sound or, to be more precise,

[42] Jill Purce, "Sound in Mind and Body," Reprint in *Resurgence* No. 115 (March/April 1986), p. 1.

[43] Kay Gardner, one-day workshop, "Sounding the Inner Landscape," Sept. 9, 1991, Minneapolis, Minnesota. And *Sounding the Inner Landscape: Music as Medicine*, Stonington, Maine (Caduceus Publications), 1990, pp. 28-59.

music. The caduceus (the gift of healing) was given to Hermes by Apollo after Hermes had offered Apollo his gift, the first lyre (the gift of music). Beaulieu comments that the image of the caduceus with its central staff and two intertwined snakes resembles a high-speed photograph of a vibrating string.[44] Indeed, the careful use of sound and the healing process have long been in a relationship of interchange.

Our medical forefathers, Aristotle, Galen and Hippocrates, were cognizant of the healing effects of sound. It is known that the classical Greeks prescribed rest and dreaming for healing. They also prescribed certain kinds of music or musical scales to soothe or stimulate the soul. Each of their seven scales was recommended for a different mental purpose, according to strict rules. It was thought that using the right mode (or key) could calm or stimulate, in different ways, the souls of the sick, and maintain balance for the healthy. In a long tradition in India, there are over 4,000 ragas or scales, each designated for a certain time of day, mood, or ritual. Certain intervals seem to be linked with certain feelings or states of mind in different cultures, and there is some speculation that these intervals reflect levels or patterns of development of the collective psyche. In everyday Western musical experience, people often recognize only the major and minor keys, only two modes and a limited range of intervals. Some speculate that this musical loss might be linked with a lessened range and subtlety of emotions in contemporary Western cultures.

Even in the mainstream medical establishment, sound has some place. It is not only a vital part of careful observation, but of communication. In "seeing" a patient, a good medical doctor needs to be a careful listener and questioner, with a sharp ear for many aspects – the history,

---

[44] Beaulieu, p. 44.

timing, and description of symptoms, as well as genetic and environmental factors. She or he must have the ear to hear those certain themes or dissonances which are so telling. In direct examination of the body too, a doctor uses listening and sound for both diagnosis and treatment. One of the first things a physician does is listen to the heart and lungs, and often as well to the bones, organs and other body parts as they function. Sound in its ultimately silent form, ultrasound (or sonography), is used to obtain pictures inside the body, of fetuses and also abnormal masses like tumors and gall stones. In dentistry, it is used to clean teeth, and in physiotherapy, to ease pain and stiffness. Silence too is a recognized, if too little attended to, aspect of modern healing. Although in reality, hospitals are often extraordinarily noisy, they are zoned to be in quiet areas. Sleep medication, one gets the impression, is supposed to be the "silence-inducer," promoting rest and healing.

In the field of mental health, there is one school of therapy which places sound and listening clearly at the core: "Audio-Psycho-Phonology" (APP). This method, first developed by a French medical doctor, A.A. Tomatis, works with psychological and other problems by "re-educating" the ear. APP therapists believe that if a person can learn to hear the full range of sound, and this usually means the higher frequencies, that the psyche will open up – hear – what is corrective or what has been missing. Using highly refined apparatuses and tapes, APP therapists work with retraining the middle ear bone mechanism to pick up the frequencies it has learned to tune out. The theory is that in order to guard themselves emotionally, some infants and children never learned to receive some types of auditory input. With this retraining of the ear, a person can learn to receive the full range of necessary auditory input. Tomatis's machine, the Electronic Ear, allows the subject to progress from a weakened power of listening to a better adjusted one[45].

Tomatis has also worked with applying such methods to language-learning. People can supposedly learn any language, and also after adolescence, if they open up their listening capabilities. Speakers of different languages have sensitivities to different frequencies. For example, it is difficult for a French ear (1,000-2,000 Hertz) to hear British English (2,000-12,000), while North American English presents few problems, with its lower basic frequency band (peaking at 1,500 Hertz). The Slavs, who have a reputation for learning languages easily, have a broad frequency band of sensitivity, ranging from 50 to 8,000 Hertz. Tomatis claims that he can superimpose on a person's original listening pattern a way of hearing which compels it to focus on sounds according to the frequency band of the chosen language.[46]

Tomatis also suggests that listening patterns have a great deal to do with how well people get along with each other. Using the Electronic Ear, he gave two subjects, who happened to be monks, an identical listening pattern and had them discuss a thorny theological problem. Next, he gave them incompatible listening curves and had them talk about the rain and fine weather. In the first case, they agreed on every point; in the second, they quarreled in less than 15 minutes.[47]

Among those who "sound the depths" in psychotherapy, it was more often Freudians than Jungians who were at home in the auditory mode. (Note for example the contributions of A. Margulies, T. Reik, O. Isakower and E. Schwaber.) Perhaps classical Freudians are more ear-attuned because of their practice of working with the couch.

---

[45] For a description of the work of the founder of APP, Alfred A. Tomatis, read *The Conscious Ear: My Life of Transformation Through Listening*, New York (Station Hill Press), 1991. See especially pp. 57-59
[46] Ibid., pp. 72-75 and 78.
[47] Ibid., p. 47.

Sitting behind a patient lying supine on a couch is visually boring, for both client and analyst, and encourages non-visual modes of contact and fantasy. Unseen, an analyst may operate with more consciousness of her or his own vibra-tions, with more cognizance of the psychic material itself. Immediate, face-to-face, relational demands are in abey-ance. Perhaps the face-to-face mode that Jungians use encourages a more visual orientation.

The way that Jung talked about sound, if infrequent, and the ways that sounds impacted on his life make an interest-ing study. Jung was a "seer," and not only in the visionary sense. Vision, it appears, was his dominant mode of percep-tion. Jung centered his work around the idea that symbols and images were the language of the psyche. "Everything of which we are conscious is an image, and that image is psyche," he stated. Although discussing images mostly from a visual aspect, as a viewer looking on, his writings show a recognition of the many kinds of image work. Jung pointed out that images occur visually, auditorily and kinesthetically, and some people work best with their hands, others with bodily movements or automatic writing.[48]

A number of workers, especially in theater and psychol-ogy, have found Jung's ideas stimulating in their work with sound and the voice.[49] Throughout Jung's *Collected Works*, there are brief descriptions of voices, like of the utterances of schizophrenics, women's harsh voices, a childishly affected tone of voice, the soft and modest (Eastern) Indian voice, and the British "macho" voice (see the excerpts in "The Evocative Voice" chapter). In only two areas did Jung discuss sound at length. The first was "Klang," one of the

[48] Jung, *CW* 13:75, 8:608 and 170.
[49] In his book, *The Singing Cure*, Newham has put together a full line of development of vocal and psychic work, including Wilhelm Reich, Alex-ander Lowen, Paul Moses, Alfred Wolfsohn, Peter Brook and Jerzy Grotowski. Also, see references to Noah Pikes.

most important complex indicators on his Word Association Experiment, which was designed to prove the existence and explore some of the contents of psychological complexes.

"Klang," which means "sound" in German, occurs when a test subject, in response to a stimulus word, gives a response word based on its similarity in sound, like alliteration or rhyme. The presence of Klang means that a word has been indirectly associated to, that is, that a complex, or an unconscious constellation of energies, is interfering with a "natural" ideational link. For example, most people would recognize "blue - sky" or "son - daughter" as natural ideational associations. But Jung believed that a Klang response like "blue - do," linked "indirectly" through sound, meant that an energy field was touched, involving certain disturbing feelings having something to do with "blue." Most often, Klang occurs as rhyme; but it may also occur through looser auditory relatedness, such as half-rhyme, alliteration, or partial repetition (for example, in pair like "change - chain" or "happily - happening").

Since that time, however, Jungian analyst Paul Kugler has made a link that Jung was just beginning to explore. In his book, Kugler states that Jung was connecting the sound of words with the archetypal, or deepest patterns of the mind. He credits Jung with recognizing the fundamental role of image and sound in the formation of dreams and unconscious fantasies. It is not only the "seeing through" that archetypal psychology describes, (that is, the transforming of the literal and naturalistic perspective into an imaginal one, centering in image and imagination); it is also "hearing through" which he finds important. Kugler is not speaking of the vocal aspect of speaking as itself expressing auditory image, as emphasized in this book. What he does explore is the way that images are associated phonetically. In Kugler's words, the "phonetic associations are precisely where the archetypal presents itself."[50]

Kugler states that, in keeping with Jung's work on the Association Experiment, the meanings of words cluster according to a fundamental law of imagination. Its mode of operation is sonorous, acoustic, phonetic. "Words," he says, "are fantasies in sound!"[51] For example, Freud traces an analysand's dream associations to a flower which bled, given to her by her fiancé. In terms of their sounds, these words stay in the same clusters across three example languages, English, German and Hungarian, despite the fact that the words are not etymologically or historically connected:

| *English* | flower… | deflower… | defloration |
|-----------|---------|-----------|-------------|
| | carnation | carnal | carnage |
| | violet | violate | violent |
| | bloom | bloomers | blood |
| *German* | Blüten | bluten | Blut |
| *Hungarian* | vera'g | ve'res | ve'r |

In this and in further examples, Kugler shows that the archetypal image is presented in the acoustic "family resemblance" between words, in phonetic similarities. The acoustic image is the crucial intersection between the external and internal, between the literal and metaphoric.[52]

Later in his career, Jung concerned himself with his second area concerning sound: the inner voice. Repeatedly, and with considerable power, he articulated the therapeutic possibilities in inner voices. For Jung, inner voices carried great potential for bringing in the more unconscious side, and thus a healing wholeness. Hallucinatory voices, he said, sometimes "correct the complex." If a person with a conciliatory temperament becomes unaccountably "possessed" by biting sarcasm (energy from an unconscious complex), that

[50] Kugler, pp. 108-09 and 28.
[51] Ibid., p. 17.
[52] Ibid., p. 52 and 113.

"negative" energy is balancing or compensating a too-adaptive identity. But these hallucinatory voices usually compensate in a manner unacceptable to the ego.[53] Jung also spoke of vocation, or calling. Neurotic symptoms sometimes conceal a "vocation," he said, a hidden attempt to lead toward wholeness. Inner voices, he stated, can reveal "an astonishing common sense" and a "profound philosophic import."[54]

Surely in the auditory realm, Jung's forte was the inner voice. He advocated not only listening to voices within, but actually "talking back." Thus Active Imagination (or dialog with an inner figure) came into being, becoming a basic Jungian tool or method. The inner experience of the voice was "a necessary aid to psychic development." Developing the personality is a gamble, Jung proclaimed, and the tragedy is that spirit of the inner voice is at once our greatest danger and an indispensable help." He called seeing visions and hearing inner voices a true primordial experience of the spirit. "Only the man who can consciously assent to the power of the inner voice becomes a personality," Jung solemnly intoned, "but if he succumbs to it, he'll be swept away."[55] Voices are powerful in dreams ("passive imagination") too. Jung said that a voice which has no known source, "ringing" from some unknown place, and music as well, arrive at decisive moments [psychically]. For the dreamer, it may have "the final and indisputable character of … some truth or condition that is beyond all doubt."[56]

However, Jung did not write about inner voices in their specifically auditory manifestations. It is clear that he concentrated on the verbal or ideational message. Jung wrote little on music and when he did, he spoke in a brief, modest and generalized manner, suggesting it as an area for others to develop (see excerpts).

[53] CW 3:180 and 459.
[54] CW 17:313 and 11:63.
[55] CW 17:321, 11:535 and 17:308.
[56] CW 12:294 and 12:115.

## Jung on voices in general:

*Voices are treacherous; they reveal far too much. You marvel at the fantastic efforts people make to sound gay, fresh, welcoming, enterprising, jolly, benevolent, full of good comradeship, and so on. And you know it is merely an attempt to cover up the real truth, which is very much the reverse. It makes you tired listening to those unnatural sounds, and you long for somebody to say something unkind or brutally offensive.* CW 10:997.

## Jung on Music:

*Music certainly has to do with the collective unconscious – as the drama does too; this is evident in Wagner, for example. Music expresses, in some way, the movement of the feelings (or emotional values) that cling to the unconscious processes. The nature of what happens in the collective unconscious is archetypal, and archetypes always have a numinous quality that expresses itself in emotional distress. Music expresses in sounds what fantasies and visions express in visual images. I am not a musician and would not be able to develop these ideas for you in detail. I can only draw your attention to the fact that music represents the movement, development, and transformation of motifs of the collective unconscious. In Wagner this is very clear and also in Beethoven, but one finds it equally in Bach's "Kunst der Fuge," etc.*

Letter to Serge Moreux, Jan., 1950.
In *C.G. Jung Letters*, Vol. I, p. 542

## Jung on Music Therapy

*In old age, in 1956, Jung had an apparently isolated yet emotional meeting with Margaret Tilly. As she played for him, with the intent of showing him what music therapy was like, she said that he appeared deeply moved. They discussed what she would do in different types of cases. Finally, she said, he burst out with this speech:*

*This opens up whole new avenues of research I'd never even dreamed of. Because of what you've shown me this afternoon – not just what you've said, but what I have actually felt and experienced – I feel that from now on music should be an essential part of every analysis. This reaches the deep archetypal material that we can only sometimes reach in our analytical work with patients. This is most remarkable.* (p. 275)

*A note by Alan Watts explained that Jung's "musical" daughter, Marianne, had later thanked Ms. Tilly, saying her father had never understood her love of music, and her coming had changed all of that.*

Margaret Tilly, "The Therapy of Music," in *C.G. Jung Speaking*, pp. 273-75

It is not in his *Collected Works*, but in his autobiography that the auditory world comes alive. It is, in fact, quite striking to notice how some of the most dramatic and decisive moments in Jung's life involved auditory events. Of central significance were three auditory events which were apparently synchronistic (meaningful through coincidence). Two occurred within two weeks of each other. One, "a report like a pistol shot," happened when the dining room table suddenly cracked. The other, just as sudden, involved the loud cracking of a breadknife in the sideboard into several pieces. Jung related that these sounds were fateful events in his life. He was in the throes of choosing a profession, and they pointed him irrevocably in the direction of researching parapsychology[57] and later, studying psychology.

A third major auditory incident involved his painful and disorienting break with Freud. After several years of stimulating interchange, their differences, and apparently their complexes as well, began to rankle. Jung reported that during a discussion in 1909, Freud was "shallowly" dismissing parapsychology and precognition. Jung began to feel a sensation like a "glowing vault" in his diaphragm region. At that moment, there was a loud report in the bookcase nearby. Freud called this experience as "bosh" and relegated it to a "catalytic exteriorization phenomenon." Jung then predicted a second loud report. And it did immedi-

---

[57] *Memories, Dreams, Reflections of C.G. Jung*, recorded and edited by Aniela Jaffé, New York (Random House), 1965, pp. 105-07.

ately occur. Freud, he commented, always regarded him with some distrust after that incident![58]

Since highly charged unconscious energy often seemed to take the form of auditory energy in Jung's life, it is no surprise to learn that his most steady auditory work was during his period of intense "confrontation with the unconscious," from about 1912 to 1917. He was doing active imagination (or inner dialoging) with several major inner figures, including Elijah, Salome, a black snake, his artistically seductive anima and perhaps the most central, Philomen, who taught him psychic objectivity and the reality of the psyche. Jung wrote: "Sometimes it was as if I were hearing it with my ears, sometimes feeling it with my mouth, as if my tongue were formulating the words; now and then I heard myself whispering aloud. Below the threshold of consciousness everything was seething with life."[59] Auditory energy returned to plague Jung's old age. Like many elderly people, he suffered from "otosclerosis," a stiffening in the mobility of the middle ear joints, resulting in repetitious noises within the ears.

Jung manifested a state of relative unconsciousness and vulnerability and yet a moving responsiveness, in regards to sound. He was rarely consciously moved by sound from the inside or outside, but when he was, he allowed his life to be profoundly guided by the messages he heard. For Jung, auditory energy was a basic and creative life force which reaches toward potential wholeness, creating a vibrant bridge between the unconscious and consciousness.

Reverberating within these companion areas of religion, healing and medicine, the acoustic vessel of psychotherapy, in its small and individual way, partakes as a potential microcosm for awareness, creativity and healing, as we will

[58] Ibid., pp. 146-56.
[59] Ibid., pp. 170-99.

*Jung on Otosclerosis and Auditory Synchronicity:*

   *(A Letter to a friend)*

   *I see with regret from your letter that you are suffering very much from your noises in the ear. The unconscious often uses symptoms of this kind in order to make psychic contents audible, i.e., the symptoms are intensified by a psychogenic afflux and only then do they acquire the proper tormenting character that forces your attention inwards, where of course it gets caught in the disturbing noises. Obviously it should turn inwards but not get caught in the noises; rather it should push on to the contents that are acting on it like a magnet. The little word "should" always means that one doesn't know the way to the desired goal. But often it is at least helpful to know that on top of the organic symptom there is a psychic layer that can be lifted off. I know from experience that the demand of the unconscious for introversion – in your case the ability to listen inwards – is unusually great. And equally great is the danger that instead of being able to listen inwards one is compelled to listen inwards. My own otosclerosis has presented me with all manner of noises, so I am fairly well informed on this matter. You are quite right to remember the storm that interrupted our conversation.[1] In a quite irrational way we must be able to listen also to the voice of nature, thunder for instance, even if this means breaking the continuity of consciousness. ...*

To "Dr. S," Aug. 8, 1951, C.G. Jung, *Letters*, Vol. II, pp. 20-21.

---

[1] It is interesting to note that this incident of auditory synchronicity occurred between these two men who shared similar auditory symptoms.

address in the third section, "The Acoustic Vessel." But first, we will make a brief foray into the human way of accomplishing hearing and speech, listening to the facts and images of the voice and the ear.

# II. The Human Ear and Voice

*The intangible that is invisible as well as untouchable can still be audible.*

T. Reik, *The Haunting Melody*, p. 12

# 1. The Enigmatic Ear

The human ear has an intriguing shape, with its shell-like curves and symmetries. It suggests a spiral, the shape of DNA, the mystery at the center of life. People have wondered at how the shape of the ear is interactive with the very shape of sound, its coils and incurves having formed, over time, by sound waves. Its curves have a beauty. Its whorls take a fragile turn, with translucent bendings and inturnings. It has a stubborn delicacy, like a shell. The ear is special. It is, in every way, beautifully suited to receiving sound.

When we think of the ear, we tend to think of the outer ear, the part that protrudes on either side of the head. Of course, the human hearing apparatus also consists of the middle and inner ears, connecting to the auditory nerves and auditory sections of the brain. Indeed, the ears are a many-faceted organ. In many cultures, people decorate them with jewelry. In some, people have them re-shaped in the form of rings, loops or disks. In our culture, the ears are often considered erotic. People may arrange their hair up on their heads or behind or around the ear, making them more enticing. The ears are vulnerable. In the cold or wind, we keep them covered with hair or scarves or hats. In cold weather, they can get cold, even frostbitten. Especially with children, the ears can get painfully infected. Due to their

proximity to the semi-circular canals, which control orientation and balance, and to the brain itself, ear problems can
be serious.

The ears are expressive, rather like a subliminal part of
the face, just off to the sides. Sometimes, they reveal aspects
we would prefer to keep hidden. They have an earthy
quality. The ears are hard workers, and the wax they produce is actually the ear's "sweat." Its smell is pungent. The
ears also attract dirt, slough off skin and sprout unwanted
hair. Often out of sight and usually out of mind, they harbor
the hairy, the smelly, the unclean. While their shape can be
beautiful, it can also be humorous or bizarre, and even
shocking. We have stern rules regarding how much they
dare protrude. Large ears or ones that flop or stick out are
comical or embarrassing. "Cauliflower ears" shock us, and
pointed ears take us aback, suggesting the devil or some
other being from the "other side."

Perhaps part of our ambivalence about the ears has to do
with their being experientially connected with lack of control, with hot flushes of shame or desire. In moments of
exposure, we dread their flaring up, their red heat publicly
revealing an enflamed state of embarrassment or shame. In
their sexual role, the ears reveal all, heating up, enlarging
and turning shades of pink and red to expose erotic stimulation. In some groups, piercing the ears signal puberty for
a girl, and a gay sexual orientation for a man.

Basically, there are two ways to hear. The first is *conductive
hearing*, which utilizes the whole body. In comparison to its
counterpart, selective hearing, it is a relatively simple process. Whenever there is a sound, the air around begins to
move or vibrate, to "bombard" or "caress" all of the body.
Conductively, we hear through the whole body – skin, tissue,
and in particular, the bones. It is a bit like being in a bath
tub and experiencing the agitation of the water.

Conductive hearing is a given, a part of the experience of the air or water around our bodies. A person cannot escape it. For the hearing impaired, this factor is helpful, for even in cases of total hearing loss, conductive hearing remains. Beethoven was the most famous person to use conductive hearing to help his selective hearing loss. He put a wooden board between the sounding board of his piano and his mastoid bone (at the base of his skull), in order to hear the sound. His bones conveyed the vibration. Conductive hearing is an important way that the body as a whole functions in vibratory space. As a given of existing in an environment, there is no way to turn off conductively transmitted auditory sounds. They can only be reduced or decreased, but not eliminated. We are, very simply, subject to conductive hearing.

In contrast, the second type of hearing, *selective hearing or neuro-sensory hearing*, is more controllable. This is what most people mean when they speak of "hearing" (passive) or "listening" (active). Selective hearing is based on cochlea-to-cortex (inner ear to brain) messages. It auditorily receives, focuses and then transmits what is heard, which is then registered in the brain. The parts of the hearing apparatus, the outer, middle and inner ears, function together to gather and process what is heard, and then guide its interpretation.

In any vocal communication, people sound forth to each other. On the conductive level, sounds vibrate directly into bone and skin, creating a "bath" of energy. On a second level, the selective hearing level, auditory energy vibrates into the complicated mechanisms of neuro-sensory reception, with its guiding auditory pathways. Human beings are audio-sensitive "instruments." Communication, and especially depth communication, with its levels of meaning, requires attention to both kinds of hearing. We need to

maintain awareness and work from a sense of the simultaneity and interchange of these two levels.

Audio-Psycho-Phonologists [see the previous chapter]
use instruments designed to test and compare these two
kinds of hearing. They claim that in a "well-adjusted" person, the tracings are congruent. Well-adjusted people have
the ability to swim, but not drown, in the surrounding
"pool" of sound conveyed as conductive hearing. They are
neither possessed by this conductive atmosphere nor cut off
from it. Simultaneous with conductive hearing, the selective
hearing process focuses, filtering out distracting stimuli and
reducing it to subliminal perception.

The combination of these two kinds of hearing means
that on the one hand, people can listen in a focused way,
which is in Jungian terms, more conscious and "one-sided."
On the other hand, they can *also* listen in a way that is
contained, but not overcome, by its environment, the larger,
enveloping atmosphere of sound, resonance and silence.
For people interested in the unconscious, this combination
offers the great advantage of being able to listen and reflect
on the animating field of energy surrounding them, including it in a conscious listening experience.

What is the human ear like, including its inner terrain?
What does it look like, and how does it work? The actual
mechanical parts of the hearing apparatus are inconceivably
complex and delicate. Actually, all of the sensory processes
have these qualities; auditory perception is, in one sense, no
exception. But what is moving about the auditory process is
its specific imagery. Audition involves a participatory style of
consciousness. Its nature is resonant with receptivity. Auditory awareness perceives in a moving and direct contact with
an experientially vibrating base.

How auditory energy moves and transforms along its
pathway to the brain reads like a mysterious sojourn. It
sounds like a myth or fairy tale. Its realm is labyrinthine,

watery, and its "journey" of energy involves reverberating cavities and evocative shapes. Sensibilities are acute. And there are three dramatic transformations, utilizing three types of energy – and all to hear one sound! The following description of the auditory process uses mostly the words of audiologists. However, some phrases and emphases would admittedly ring oddly in their ears, being full of psychic echoes and overtones. In a phenomenological and poetic sense, the pathways of hearing echo the image pathways of the soul's journey.

When we hear something, sound waves travel to us. Sounds are received into flesh-covered, shell-shaped outer ears. Unlike the eyes, which are frontal, the outer ears are to the side, on each side of the head. They are cupped forward. They are not positioned to focus on one forward-looking place, but to gather in an entirety all around. The outer ears not only gather in sound. They also amplify it. Their cupped shape guides the sound into the narrowing ear canal, which is also flesh-covered and somewhat hairy. Its narrowing shape amplifies the sound – auditorily, not psychologically – as it travels to the eardrum or *typanus*. Sound energy has entered human "materiality" – or flesh and cartilage. It has "incarnated" and begun moving along the path of "mattering." This is the first of three transformations: mechanical energy moves from air into the body, into matter.

The eardrum, which is about one-third of an inch in diameter, is extremely sensitive. Numbers alone confound. It can "hear" a vibration of air so slight that it depresses the eardrum less than one half billionth of an inch. And the amount of auditory stimuli in any one millisecond is in the hundreds of thousands.[60] When two people talk or make

---

[60] Arthur S.Freese, *You and Your Hearing*, New York (Charles Scribner's Sons), 1979, p. 16.

vocal sounds, there are four tiny eardrums vibrating. There is a minute, inner, native drumming in every interchange.

The process of amplification continues. Vibration intensifies as it moves from the air into the narrowing outer ear cup, and then into the smaller-sized membrane which is the eardrum. After further amplifying the sound, it channels the energy into the *middle ear*, a space about 3/16 by 3/8 of an inch. Here, the auditory energy travels down a bone chain of three tiny interconnecting bones, the hammer (*malleus*), anvil (*incus*), and stirrup (*stapes*). The stirrup is the smallest bone in the entire body. The middle ear bone chain amplifies the sound by about 100 times.[61]

The minute foot of the stirrup fits into what is termed, elegantly enough, "the oval window." It is 25 times smaller than the eardrum, which results in a still stronger intensity of vibration. This auditory oval window provides the transition from the middle ear, with its vibrating bone chain, into the watery labyrinth of the inner ear. The inner ear, say audiologists, is the central organ of hearing.

The *inner ear* is the innermost chamber, full of mystery. Naturally, it is invisible from an outer perspective. It is set into the head by about 1 1/2 inches on each side. The foot of the stirrup functions like a piston, pressing into the inner ear "cochlea." This vital organ consists of a closed, fluid-filled tube, curled up like a snail. Since the cochlea has rigid, bony walls, the vibrating stirrup foot creates pressure waves in the cochlear fluid. It is the amazing task of the inner ear to take the amplified mechanical energy (here, the moving of flesh and bone and cartilage), and transform it into hydraulic pressure waves. This is the second transformation of energy, into a watery, inner world.

The cochlea is about the size of the tip of the little finger. Actually, it is made up of two spirals within one; one is bony

[61] Ibid., pp. 16-18.

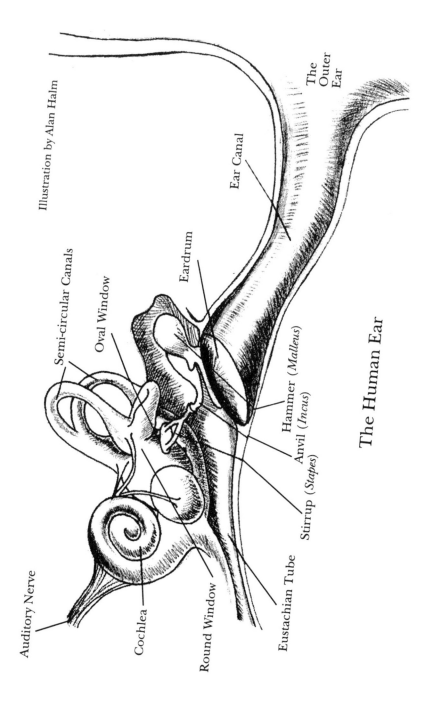

Illustration by Alan Halm

The Human Ear

The Outer Ear

Ear Canal

Eardrum

Hammer (*Malleus*)

Anvil (*Incus*)

Stirrup (*Stapes*)

Eustachian Tube

Round Window

Cochlea

Auditory Nerve

Oval Window

Semi-circular Canals

and suspended in a complex of ducts and sacs, and the other is membranous. The cochlea is termed "the labyrinth." "*The organ of hearing*," intone audiologists, "*is in the labyrinth*" [emphasis mine].[62] Here, within the cochlea's coiled complexity are minute acoustic hair cells, together termed "the Organ of Corti." In minute fashion, they move in response to the auditory waves in the fluid, and it is this movement which the brain registers. There are about 17,000 acoustic hair cells, supplied with about 30,000 nerve fibers. Their sensibility is highly refined.

In audiological terminology, the function of the Organ of Corti is "to differentiate" and "analyze" the auditory stimuli. It picks up and interprets the complex frequencies of the sounds. This task is mind-boggling, for it includes not only the tones or sounds heard consciously, but all of the unconsciously registered overtones of complex sounds, which are most sounds. These tiny hairlike forms minutely wave in contact with their base, called the basilar membrane. This motion produces electro-chemical changes, which excite the Eighth Cranial Nerve or Acoustic Nerve, which then sends messages to the interpreting brain. This is the third transformation of energy.

It is a lively, sparked pathway to the brain. A series of coded signals, the neural impulses, race through the brain, firing signals at the rate of 1,000 messages per second. The auditory process can distinguish time differences between 6 and 12 millionths of a second.[63] When a person locates a sound or recognizes it from previous experience, it is this interpretive process which is occurring, at an unconscious, lightning-fast pace. All of these steps which make up our auditory processes take up only fractions of seconds.

[62] Ibid., pp. 18-21 and 34.
[63] Ibid., p. 39 and 52.

In moving along the Auditory Nerve, auditory energy enters the realm of electrical energy, that is, of neural responses which control the body. Positive and negative electrical charges occur in matter of all kinds, in atoms, quarks, and on down the sub-atomic line. As already mentioned, modern physicists, as well as Jung, have studied the place where matter and energy most clearly – and incomprehensively – come together. Contrary to the Western notion of matter and energy being split, here it is apparent that matter and energy are one.

Electrochemical energy has to do with the play of opposite energies, which in Jungian terms are the stuff of psychic differentiation. What the opposites do on the psychic level – make psychological differentiation or consciousness possible – atomic particles do on the physical level – differentiate the forms of matter. No wonder then that in audiology, neurology and Jungian psychology, all three, the same terminology describes similar functions: *analysis, differentiation* and *interpretation.* Such is the journey of auditory energy, with its three transformations through the outer, middle and inner ears.

D. Campbell links audition with the four basic elements, which are used as conduits in the journey of sonic vibrations. First, auditory energy moves from the outside *Air,* into a cave where the eardrum resonants with the bones, the element of *Earth.* From there, it moves into the cochlea, into *Water.* Then the auditory energy makes the long chemical and electrical journey from the inner ear, into cranial nerves to the brain centers, entering the element of *Fire,* or electrical charges.[64]

To guard against overload, nature has provided shielding mechanisms. Structurally and functionally, the middle and

[64] Don G. Campbell, *The Roar of Silence: Healing Powers of Breath, Tone & Music,* Wheaton IL (The Theosophical Publishing House), 1989, p. 85.

inner ears are especially vulnerable and are thus protected in several ways. One safeguard is another "auditory window," this time termed the "round window." Positioned at the far end of the cochlea, it acts as a safety valve to protect against too strong a hydraulic pressure wave. The round window bulges back into the middle ear area if the pressure gets too great. "Yielding is the function of the round window," pronounces one audiologist, sounding remarkably like the *I Ching*. As further safeguards, the perilymph and endolymph fluids within the cochlea, as well as certain supporting tissues holding parts of the middle and inner ear, act to prevent auditory overload, while at the same time, further enhancing auditory discrimination. And the inner ear, as befitting its importance, is sturdily protected. It is set in the body's hardest bone: the densest part of the temporal bone.[65]

Actually, the inner ear is not only for hearing. It also houses the semi-circular canals. They too have a vital function, being the major organ of balance and orientation in space. When their functioning is disturbed, a person becomes dizzy, nauseous, unable to walk or move through space. Like the cochlea, the semi-circular canals consist of a double spiral, with the same "bony" and "membranous labyrinths." Likewise, they are filled with fluid. Head movements up or down, right or left, or back and forth, are registered by means of the tiny hair cells inside. Within the inner ear, the cochlea and the semi-circular canals are highly similar structures, in both their shapes and modes of functioning.

"Balance was the original function of the ear in the evolutionary development of animals," as one researcher points out; and still is "the chief and only function of the ear in many creatures."[66] This basic sense of physical and spatial

---

[65] Freese, pp. 31 and 34.

orientation is intrinsically involved with the hearing process. Apparently, hearing evolved directly from it. The affinity between these two organs suggests that there might be a connection between a person's sense of "placement" in the world (where he or she is physically situated in the environment) and how a person auditorily selects and interprets that environment.

Psychoanalyst O. Isakower had a similar idea regarding cochlear and semi-circular canal functioning. He stated that for humans, what was psychically involved was primary identification and certain characteristics of the relationship between the ego and external world in the early states of mental development. The ear, he suggested, is related to this basic development of ego and also super-ego structures, especially due to its relation to speech.[67] It is in the inner ear, in the cochlea and semi-circular canals, where the basic sense of balance and position in the world is experienced.

So hearing involves a cupped reception of vibration, a channeling inward, and resonance into matter and mattering. It employs intricate, tiny bones, labyrinthine vibrancy and a spiral-shaped journeying. And its movements include vibration of flesh and bone, a watery, wavy reverberation, the back-and-forth of sparking energy, and the shift and flow between different kinds of energy. The facts and images of the hearing process are full of potential, as both fact and image. Literally and imaginatively, the ears carry us further, deeper, in the ongoing exploration of depth communication.

---

[66] Ibid., p. 36.
[67] O. Isakower, "On the Exceptional Position of the Auditory Sphere," *International Journal of Psycho-analysis* 20 (1939), pp. 340-48.

# 2. The Evocative Voice

People use their voices as a major means to express themselves, as well as to impress themselves upon others. Vocal expression bears a direct relationship to the emotional and psychic spheres, as well as the physical. And thus it offers a rich source for working on the psyche. The voice, says P. Newham, more than any other part of the body, is essentially used to communicate the state of the mind.[68] Most people's reactions to voices are vivid and strong. Jung was no exception, as expressed in the accompanying excerpts.

An important part of our sense of being resides in the voice. When we as individuals find our own voice, it is a resonant metaphor, as well as core experience, for finding a center of ourselves. The voice defines and expresses the personality in its many dimensions. Politically as well as individually, the voice is vital: "having a voice" in public affairs is a democratic right. The human voice has a remarkable capacity for richness of expression. Its potential for communication is remarkable. It is a consummately "telling" part of our personalities, on both a conscious and unconscious level. And this truth holds, even when its messages are not consciously willed.

[68] Paul Newham, *The Singing Cure: An Introduction to Voice Movement Therapy*, Boston (Shambhala), 1993, p. 138.

*Jung on the British "macho" voice:*

> You cannot help noticing how a great number of perfectly nice and decent Englishmen elaborately imitate a he-man voice, God knows why. It sounds as if they were trying to impress the world with their throaty rumbling tones, or as if they were addressing a political meeting, which has to be convinced of the profound honesty and sincerity of the speaker. The usual brand is the bass voice, of the colonel for instance or the master of the household of numerous children and servants who must be duly impressed. The Father Christmas voice is a special variety, usually affected by academically trained specimens. I discovered that particularly terrific boomers were quite modest and decent chaps, with a noticeable feeling of inferiority. CW10:998

*Jung on the childishly affected tone in the voice:*

> This veiled reproach a child levels at her mother ... [is] unjustified, and to the trained ear this is betrayed by the slightly affected tone of the voice. One often hears similar tones even with grown-up people. Such a tone, which is quite unmistakable, does not expect to be taken seriously and obtrudes itself all the more forcibly for that reason. CW 17:15

The fields of the expressive arts, politics, public relations, as well as psychology, all teach us that what a person is heard to say is determined most of all by *how* it is said. What matters to interpreting meaning is the way the person sounds while speaking. Linguist J. Lotz stated that based on the quantitative analysis of the acoustic signals emitted by the human voice, only 1 per cent would prove to be of linguistic use and purpose. *Ninety-nine per cent* of meaning comes entirely from vocal or phonics.[69] In a therapy encounter too, what the client says (verbally) is less important than the sound of his voice as he speaks, as well as the resonances and silences which surround it.

By the way, to speak of *vocal expression* and language together is not a given. It is a generally accepted fact that humans are genetically set for some sort speech and for grammar, apparently to fulfill the function of generalizing and symbolizing. Since most of us are used to a vocal base for our language, we think of language as vocal, developing from and refining on, the primal hums, grunts and groans of pre-lingual creatures. However, language may as well be conceived as growing from any channel of expression, for example, kinesthetic or gestural expression in the case of American Sign Language, or from visual signs in the case of written language.

Also, outer speech, that which is actually spoken, is not the same as inner speech, or the "voices" that go on inside our heads. Eastern cultures, which are mostly older and more introverted than ours, approach this matter of listening with a great deal more differentiation. There are five levels of listening listed in India: singing aloud, whispered signing, mental singing, subconscious singing and super-conscious singing.[70] It is generally agreed that we cannot in

[69] Paul Newham, *The Singing Cure*, p. 212. The Lotz reference is paraphrased from *Linguistics: Symbols Make Humans*, New York (Language and Communication Research Center, Columbia University), 1955.

any facile way equate outer vocal speech with the basic experience of inner speech, or the inner language that goes on inside of our heads. L.S. Vygotsky, a Russian psychologist writing in the early 1900s, believed that inner speech, which is indispensable for further development, is not the interior aspect of external speech, but a function in itself. In inner speech, he says, the words die as they bring forth thought. It is speech almost without words. It is "thinking in pure meanings," he says.[71] More recently, Oliver Sacks said that our real language, our real identity, lies in inner speech. Its ceaseless stream and generation of meaning constitutes the individual mind. "It is through inner speech that the child develops his own concepts and meanings," says Sacks. Through inner speech he achieves his own identity and finally, constructs his own world.[72]

In this chapter, we are speaking of vocal manifestations, a majority of them verbal, that make it into the outer world. Few people have consciously trained or modulated their voices, at least consciously. We tend to pay little attention to the sound of our own voices. Exceptions occur when a person makes the effort to cross social or professional classes, like Eliza Doolittle in "Pygmalion," to learn a new skill, like assertiveness training, or to learn a new language and culture. Otherwise, we tend to speak, to voice things, in our typical ways, without thinking. The human voice is highly revealing. And it tends especially to express unconscious qualities.

This idea is recurrent, that voices are closely connected with the unconscious and the repressed, also outside the

---

[70] Lane Arye, "Music the Messenger," pp. 26-27, quoting P.M. Hamel, *Through Music to the Self,* Longmead, Shaftesbury, Dorset (Element Books), 1978, p. 64.

[71] Oliver Sacks, *Seeing Voices: A Journey into the World of the Deaf,* New York (HarperPerennial), 1990, pp. 73-74.

[72] Ibid., p. 74.

area of depth psychology. Revealing as it can be, vocal experience lies at the center of cultural communication, socially, politically, and artistically. The voices of people around us are inescapable experience. They literally enter our heads and bodies, whether we want them to or not. We must deal with them, and with our own reactivity to them. The more awareness we can bring, the better, in all areas. But it is especially important in therapy and in psychoanalysis, "the talking cure."

For all our potential for scientific study, we do not really understand what exactly accounts for the capacity of the voice for expressivity; neither do we understand exactly what makes so impressive our ability as listeners to differentiate voices. We do know that, from the start, our neural and sensory systems are fully set up for highly differentiated responses to the voice. Just as it is necessary for a grazing mammal to be able to walk within hours after birth, so too are human newborns able to make sensitive interpretations, from the start, regarding vocal expression around them. We are appropriately hard-wired, from birth on. Apparently, vocal and verbal abilities are a human capability from early on, necessary to becoming a functioning member of the species.

Scientific investigations have never been able to account fully for the unique characteristics of a voice. Nonetheless, most people recognize, with great accuracy, vocal features of other people. This vocal recognition occurs even when listeners have heard these voices only on the radio. Perhaps it is because we are naturally, unconsciously, so good at receiving vocal communication that we rarely make the effort to deepen the experience of listening; we rarely bring the vocal aspects of speech more clearly to consciousness.

Speech therapists and foreign language teachers know this law: that what we hear is what we are capable of speaking. So when listening is underdeveloped, so too is vocal expression. We are not really "in" our voices. We do not even begin to use them fully, freely, expressively. Noah Pikes of the Roy Hart Theatre rails impressively against the highly trained classical voice, which has so narrowed our conception of vocal art, as well as vocal reality. Under the sway of Apollonic fantasy, he says, Western science, as well as vocal artists, do not recognize sources of the voice in the body below the very upper part of the chest. Other cultures, like traditional Vietnamese musical theater, have a number of voices located in parts of the middle and lower body. Pikes calls this more complete voice "The Body Voice,"[73] associating it with the body and the body's energy. The bias against the voice's being "whole," both psychically and vocally, is due in part to Christian conceptions, which call the body diabolic. He also calls this voice "The Whole Voice."[74] We are hungry for this wholeness of voice, seeking it in both real and imaginal sound.

Indeed, it is the dark and shadow sides of the voice which fall into the unconscious. Pikes, in his work with wholeness in the theater and the theater of the psyche, defines his task as exploring just these kinds of untamed shadow places in the voice. In this wholehearted approach, the voice is considered to have a potential range of at least four octaves, and with work, as many as seven. The voice has a potentiality of textures, colors and dynamics which is literally unending.

The VOLUME of a person's voice is a basic acoustic experience. It expresses how much energy the person pos-

[73] Noah Pikes' tape, "Vocations," (see bibliography) contains compositions and improvisations on the art of voice, as well as demonstrations of some of its potential – its pitch range and timbres, in particular. Feast your imagination on these titles: Side A: 1. Geology, 2. Female-Male and in between, 3. Motor Harmonics, 4. Flying High, 5. Oiseau de l'arbre, 6. Dirty Dennis, and 7. Poem 73. On Side B: 1. Aux Cinq Coins, 2. Vitres de son, 3. Vowels and Body, 4. Be Not Afeard, and 5. Poem 30.
[74] Noah Pikes, "Giving Voice to Hell," *Spring 55: The Issue from Hell*, Putnam, Conn. (Spring Journal), 1994, pp. 57, 61 and 51.

sesses and especially, how much is being put out at the moment. Its effects are dramatic: shouters literally flatten their listeners against the backs of their chairs, while whisperers necessitate a careful leaning forward. However, it is in no simple sense that a low volume is necessarily less energetic or powerful. A soft voice may carry a strong sense of intensity or authority, while a high volume voice may sound empty or insecure. People with "volume disturbances" lack the most basic sense of being received by the people and environment around them. They may be out of contact with their own resonance, with the way that they can and do affect others. Because finding the appropriate volume is so basic an aspect of communication, sometimes the issue seems to be getting heard at all. Then it is a search for affirmation of existence, at its most basic levels.

VOCAL PITCH is a second basic characteristic. High voices are usually associated with children and women. They may carry qualities of purity, clarity or innocence, or on the negative side, shrillness and insecurity. High voices sound as if they have less substance. Acoustically, they are heard to fill less space. Since it is a common goal to gain more security and maturity, and also, within the rules of patriarchy, more masculinity, people often view it as positive when a person's voice becomes lower in pitch, whether in a man or woman. A lower voice is usually heard to be more powerful, more authoritative. Perhaps this reaction has in part to do with the gain in resonance, which makes listeners more, and more deeply, responsive.

The high voice or falsetto in men has fascinated people, since the times when boy sopranos were castrated to maintain their boy's voices. With pitch, we hear speakers to be in, or tantalizingly out of, basic human categories, like male/female and adult/child. Perhaps for that reason, incongruities are strongly experienced: a heavy-set man with a high voice or a small woman with a bass voice are unexpected –

and fascinating. When an impression has been created via auditory energy, on the phone or in another room, a face-to-face meeting can produce a shock. The "incorrect" aspect is likely to be carrying the person's energy too, in discovering the wholeness of that individual.

Exactly what determines the third vocal characteristic, TIMBRE, is unknown, scientifically speaking. A combination of many forces play a part in giving each person's voice a unique quality. These forces include the mass, frequency, tension and shape of the vocal cords, the shape, mass and constitution of the resonators, the skeletal structure, a constantly changing chemical constitution, as well as the muscular architecture. Anything that affects the psyche will influence chemical, neurologic and physical operations, and thus affect the voice.[75] The amazing range of timbres in the human voice express a wide spectrum of individual personalities and moods.

The voice is the richest and most various of all "musical" instruments, communicating with great sensuousness a myriad of feelings and qualities, both subtle and powerful. As already heard, it is in regards to the voice in particular that we are, from birth on, exquisitely sensitive. We recognize the specifics of the various voices of family, and friends. And we are almost as accurate with the voices of mere acquaintances or people we've heard just once, on the TV or film or radio. The ear is very finely tuned to vocal elements like timbre.

For many people, timbre offers the clearest invitation to do auditory image work, that is, to notice and deepen contact with a piece of auditory meaning. We speak easily of a gravelly quality, or an angry edge, or a honey smoothness in a voice. Perhaps this reactivity to timbre is because it tends to be so closely – and tantalizingly – related to the other

[75] Newham, pp. 127 and 132.

senses, especially the tactile and visual. Timbre encompasses an intermingling of the senses, leading quixotically in and out of the purely acoustic realm. Consider the breadth and variety in the following list, taken from one voice classification system used to "diagnose" a client's voice:

> dark/light, soft/hard, warm/cold, tender, relaxed, empty, dry, wiry, pointed, colorful, sonorous, sparkling, clear/blunt, raw, covered-over, muffled, husky, hoarse, breathy, nasal, oily, grating, silvery and metallic.

We could continue on and on. Hairy! Greasy! Gutteral! Wispy! Haunting! Blasting! Somehow, the imagination is easily drawn in by the timbre of a voice, just as it is by the rich and shifting tone qualities of an orchestra or band.

A fourth quality of the voice is FULLNESS. A full voice sounds very much like itself: it is filled with its self-ness. In the right context, it evokes a sense of reverence and awe, being strongly impressive, or almost emotionally or spiritually overwhelming. Sometimes, a voice that is very full can sound too full of itself. It sounds inappropriate to the everyday situation. Like a high priest intoning in the kitchen, it is too heavy, too voluminous. It quickly becomes too much, sounding vain-glorious or extreme, like a caricature. Unless its context is declamatory, elaborate, to "carry" it, like in a cathedral or on stage, this level of fullness sounds exaggerated, even ludicrous.

A voice that is too thin is more common. It gives the impression of lack of substance, of only partial relation to oneself or to what is being expressed. This thinness may suggest a lesser or inferior relationship to listeners and the environment. It communicates a sense of too little energy having been gathered together, too little reverberating outward. Listeners may disregard a voice that is not full enough, reacting with non-engagement or easy dismissal. Resonating too little within itself, it also produces a lack of resonance in others.

In general, vocal characteristics are not separable, except intellectually. Experientially, they overlap and flow into each other. Volume, pitch, timbre and fullness relate to mental or psychic vitality. According to a chart of vocal characteristics, MOVEMENT in a voice is considered to have to do with the expression of feeling and temperament. It contains within it the aspects of tempo (quick, headlong, calm, measured, dragging, lulling, etc.), rhythm, with the subcategories of 1) *uniformity* (regular, restrained, variable, etc.), 2) *flow* (lively, rigid, hesitating, etc.), 3) *undulation* (short to wide wave, little swing, etc.), 4) *tension*, and 5) *melodiousness*. Finally, a last category of vocal characteristics moves into the verbal parts of speech: ARTICULATION and ACCENTUATION.[76]

The characteristics listed above are a straight-forward, academic description of the range of vocal expression. However, once in the actual working and playing field of voice, the range of possibilities expands. The great trickster qualities of the voice make their appearance. Some startling descriptions of these little-considered aspects of vocal expression come from philosopher David Appelbaum. He includes a wide range of natural vocal expression as part of the study and experience of the voice. The cough, he says, is "the detonation of voice." It is devilish and chthonic, inter-rupting God's sermon of phonetic abundance and the soul's self-iteration. It dwarfs us, as we bend double in its gutteral thrust, and breaks us away from the delicate affair of speech, shocking the cognitive apparatus in its brute

---

[76] August Vetter, "Hauptgesichtspunkte für die Beurteilung der Sprech-weise" ("Major Points in Judging Vocal Characteristics"). From "Merk-malsschema aus den Seminarübungen an der Universität München, Winter Sem., 1960/61," in Rudolf Fährman's *Die Deutung des Sprechaus-drucks*, Bonn (Bouvier and Co.), 1960.

reminder of organic experience. While the cough stays low to the ground, says Appelbaum, the laugh rises, heaving, changing shape like an escaped balloon; it thus betrays its origins in the trickery of Hermes' laughter at fooling Apollo.[77]

Add to this cast of characters, says Appelbaum,

> *the sneeze, the grunt, the wheeze, the clack (of the tongue, of dentures), the hiss, the cackle, the gasp (a vocal inspiration), the squeal, the squeak, the screech, and the peculiar unnamed sound of clearing the throat. When the phonation is broken in the assault by this rogues' gallery, the body of the body issues audible vibration. The defense line collapses. The walled citadel keeping guerilla sounds out and cognitive ones in is overrun. ... The breath, unmodulated by broadcast articulation, bursts forth.[78]*

As Appelbaum stresses, the breath is vital. Deep breathing encourages contact with emotional centers, body centers. In the midst of strong emotional energy or great stress, we need to breathe, to recontact a center in ourselves. Indeed, breath is vitality itself. "As long as I have life and breath," we say. Indeed, the word "psyche" has its origins in "breath." Doing voice work brings participants back to spirit, back to breath itself. Some people include voice emanations that consist mostly of breath, with little or no vocal sound, like in sighing, yawning or whispering, or hisses and clicks. There is as well overtone work, where "forcing" air or breath produces the very highest of tones, much higher and breathier than most people would conceive possible of their voices.

Sighing, humming, babbling, crying. ... The origins of vocal sound are deep, both collectively and individually. Paul Newham links pre-verbal cultural sound-making to animism, where every object and being was believed to have

---

[77] David Appelbaum, *Voice*, Albany, NY (State University of New York Press), 1990, pp. 2, 6, 9, and 16.
[78] Ibid., p. 38.

a soul or spirit. The fundamental essence of something, he said, was transcribed into sound and movement for the purpose of communication, to contain this spirit. "Therefore when people sang of the bear, they became one with the animal's soul. In the same way, through their song they partook of the sun and the moon, the earth and the river." Slowly it became unnecessary to experience this essence in order to express and identify it, and that was when abstract understanding came into being. Humankind, says Newham, had ceased to express through sound and begun to describe with words. This ability to abstract, of course, expressed and further created the cognitive mind, the very ability of humans to be "homo sapiens," knowing beings. However, something was also lost. According to Newham, the ability to abstract eroded the sympathetic relations between the essence of natural elements and people. It increased the distance between people and their emotions. And it restricted the tonal range of acoustic qualities into a comparative monotonal system of words.[79]

Releasing vocal sound from words is liberating, returning us to original creativity. Vocal exploration returns us to infancy and childhood. In the first three months of life, the infant cries only as an expression of hunger and distress, using a melody which rises and falls like a siren. Its unique cadences and qualities of rhythm and melody can be detected by its mother. At around three months, a new quality of crying emerges, with a rising and falling melody and slightly higher pitch range. This development signals the emergence of the pleasure cry, the ability to express hunger, tiredness, physical discomfort, irritability, distress and pleasure, all decipherable. These will later be the vowel sounds of speech. The baby, not yet familiar with such a scheme, makes cooing sounds, arranging them according to

[79] Newham, pp. 23-24.

an innate intuitive and creative sense of pitch, melody and rhythm, akin to the composition of music. Babbling begins between the ages of three to six months. It contains the raw material for the consonants.[80]

Psychoanalyst Paul Moses suggested that the move from vocal playing to speech acquisition is not only difficult, but highly restrictive for the individuality and creativity of a child. At birth and soon after, the preverbal sounds a child makes are extremely pleasurable and liberating, associated with suckling. Unhampered by any external restriction, they follow the baby's own whims, feelings, and responses, as well as involuntary physiological events. Thus the acquisition of speech is a traumatic experience, limiting this free-functioning vocal expressivity, involving the small child in a traumatic game of punishment and reward.[81]

Many schools seek to release vocal function from constriction. Paul Newham's Voice Movement Therapy uses natural vocal sounds, "sculpted" by working with muscle tone of the body, breathing, massage and manipulation of the body, as well as suggestion of moods and images. They form and animate the voice, which can increase radically in range, tone and substance. A client devoid of lower pitches can be given the opportunity to locate lower pitches in his or her voice; upon hearing that its timbre sounds generous and warm, the negative associations between depth and aggression can be depleted Such work can have effects which are psychologically uplifting, physically invigorating, and creatively rejuvenating.[82]

Newham credits both Freud and Jung with giving the voice a central place. Freud, he points out, emphasized that a hysterical symptom cannot be relieved by rational recollec-

[80] Ibid., p. 25-26.
[81] Newham, p. 80, quoting P.J. Moses, *The Voice of Neurosis*, New York (Grune & Stratton), 1954, pp. 15-20.
[82] Newham, 17-18 and 201.

tion, but only by recalling a traumatic event in the greatest possible detail and with the greatest emotion, which includes the stored somatic reaction. Freud understood that words alone do not "ex-press" the energy, and encouraged nonverbal letting off of steam, like crying or screaming. But he did not consider that sufficient, without verbal content. Newham credits Jung and his work on the Word Association Experiment with connecting words with unconscious preoccupations (complexes), which produce affect or emotion (revealed in complex indicators). Jung, he said, also listened to the voices of inner personalities and schizophrenia, and explored other sensory and artistic "channels" for working with images, which can stimulate and interweave with specifically vocal work.[83]

Most in keeping with the Jungian spirit of discovering a relationship with the mysterious "otherness" of unconscious contents is the work of Alfred Wolfsohn. Wolfsohn, a medic in World War I, was fascinated by the vocal emanations of the wounded and dying. These voices, the "voice in extremis," plagued him in his traumatized, guilt-ridden survival, bringing him to the point of aural hallucinations. When extended psychiatric care yielded no relief, he began to search for his own cure. He came to formulate this "cure" as the finishing of the release of accumulated terror and guilt. Every day he worked with his voice, keeping in mind the extreme emotive vocal sounds he had heard in the trenches. He greatly extended his vocal range to over eight octaves, wider than the range of the grand piano. He discovered that the voice could express not only untold suffering, but a wide range of joy and pleasure. In this strange and tragic beginning to his work, he did attain a cure to his own mental state.

---

[83] Ibid., pp. 51-52 and 68-69. See also the part on Jung in "Sound and the Healing Arts."

In fact, he became a renowned singing teacher and "father" to the modern-day Roy Hart Theatre.[84]

In asking his students to record their dreams and express them orally, Wolfsohn could be understood as exploring in the aural realm what Jung explored mostly in the verbal and visual realm. Wolfsohn also liked Jung's emphasis on the shadow or dark, neglected side of the personality. For him, it was the "non-beautiful" voice which cut to the bone of expressiveness, and especially reached the unconscious. Wolfsohn, like Jung, was also interested in "the androgynous voice," expressive of the contra-sexual energies that most people keep hidden, even from themselves. He understood that these expressions were connected to the collective unconscious.[85]

Learning to listen well and help people work with their voices can have many angles of approach. The voice is innately and profoundly expressive of ourselves. In learning to receive and work with the images in the voice, and with the voice as image, exposure to the world of artistic, mythic and archetypal images is necessary, as well as grounding in the realm of societal and personal levels of images.

[84] Ibid., pp. 76-82 and 176-77.
[85] Ibid., pp. 81-86 and 90-92.

*In her diploma thesis entitled "The Singer and the Voice," Jungian analyst Barbara Bliss compares the process of developing a singer's voice with the Jungian individuation process, or the process of psychic development. Describing different ways of producing vocal, singing-related sounds, she offers possibilities to attune oneself to one's own psychic and somatic states and also to the world around. "Elementary breathing and humming exercises done in a meditative fashion," she says, "can permit the voice to emerge in acceptable coordination with the personality and the psycho-somatic climate of the moment" (p. 88).*

*Bliss suggests giving feedback to clients on their voices, as well as advising therapists to pay attention to their own voices. Learning to sing with one's authentic voice is like developing the wholeness of the personality. Like with the four Jungian functions, one sung vowel tends to be superior, and another inferior, needing "redemption." In the Jungian framework, it is wholeness which is necessary, not perfection. The voice's "shadow" must be integrated into the voice as a whole, says Bliss, its brilliance sacrificed for "vocal wholeness" (p. 26).*

*Breath cavities amplify the voice, in a similar way to Jungian amplification, which creates psychic space and enhances a sense of the psyche. Space, resonance, "a living space full of vibrations and resounding with vital breath," are experiences of the voice (pp. 50-51).*

# III. The Acoustic Vessel

# 1. Sound as Shape

*Did not Pan summon Echo on his reed pipe without either words or gestures; was not Apollo, with his lyre, the progenitor of all the chorus of the Muses; did not Orpheus move Charon by the eloquence of his lute; and did not Bach venerate the Divine Being in his Passions in such form as no preacher could have imitated? I tell you that beauty captivates not by what it has to say but by the form and manner in which it said.*

*The Unbearable Lightness of Being,* Kundera, p. 171

Acoustic work is a necessary, indeed an inescapable, part of listening in depth. Psychotherapeutic work requires a vessel in order to contain what is occurring. This vessel holds and clarifies the experience, encouraging sensitive awareness within the reverberation and flow of energies. The therapist's listening attitude evokes a resonance, a deepening and containing response, while at the same time, the client begins to hear new things, richer things, in himself and those around him. He begins to listen in different and more differentiated ways. In the field of psychotherapy, listening is a central activity.

It is generally acknowledged that doing psychotherapy requires special tuning skills. In our everyday lives, we are used to an atmosphere of too little space around words, too little resonance. Words have lost their essential quality of resonance. In describing his work, Joska Soos, "sound shaman" from Brussels, said the following: "You have to grow beyond the word. You have to strive to be inside the sound. … When I'm in the sound, I'm apprised of the vibration of things around me whether I'm on the street or in a train. I also observe the vibration of my own spiritual problem."[86] Psychoanalyst Theodor Reik warned that psychoanalysts lack "ear training," the kind given in a musical education. He also expressed regret that language has developed so far in the direction of objective communication, of denoting things and acts, which impoverishes it as an expression of emotions. The verses of great poets, said Reik, are the most appropriate manifestation of emotional life. In fact, he called the language of scientific psychology "the lowest point in describing and portraying human feeling"![87]

The different types of psychotherapeutic work reveal many assumptions about sound and words and silence. In the field of depth psychology, traditional psychoanalysts create an atmosphere of "poised attentiveness," where the analyst usually remains silent and receptive while the client talks. Reik describes psychoanalysis as surrounding clients with "benevolent silence," inviting the unheard.

Jungians usually work face to face, also using words. Together with the partner, they seek to explore the images and symbols of the unconscious. Unfortunately, nothing can reduce an image to meaninglessness faster than talk-talk-talk. Verbalizing, indeed even clarifying, has its dark, its simplistic, flat side. Even when it comes out as "beautiful" or exhilarating – the kind of talk that soars – that does not always help the partners deepen contact with the material or

---

[86] Laeh M. Garfield, *Sound Medicine: Healing with Music, Voice and Song*, Berkeley, CA (Celestial Arts), 1987, p. 133.
[87] Theodor Reik, *The Haunting Melody: Psychoanalytic Experiences in Life and Music*, New York (Grove Press), 1953, p. 12.

with each other, especially not in terms of differentiated emotional connection. Neither does emotional flow which is too flowing or too slippery. Resonance is a space which allows for both connectedness and space.

Sometimes, words are intoxifying. Up and away, the soniferous expanse of verbiage becomes irresistible! However, the flashy usage of words is misleading in its brilliance. It keeps the speak-speak-speakers back from darker and dumber dimensions. Too much verbosity, too much verbal agility, is like a Siren Song. It seduces psychic voyagers from the deep sea journey at hand.

Naming is a potent act, presented in myth as the provision of the gods. Words are powerful tools. They define and differentiate, giving us "handles" to express and manipulate ideas and experiences. In a more poetic and reflective vein, they suggest and associate, creating a vibratory web. Whether used to define concepts or open out images, words are instruments of craft and instruments of art. Words e-voke, re-sound, in-tone. Words may home in on something or they may radiate out meaning. They may encompass vastness, striding across huge stretches of space and time. Or they may touch the exquisitely precise, the consummately subtle. Words hypnotize, calling forth the gods and demons.

In my analytic training, I did much of my supervised work in a language foreign to me. It was also somewhat foreign to my clients, who for the most part spoke Swiss German in their usual lives, and high German with me in the session. We had to speak slowly, carefully. Although difficult, this experience suggested a certain kind of advantage in not being able to use words too well. Again and again, it was important that words *not* be too finely tuned an instrument of conscious will. Often, it is the stumbling, resoundingly awkward moments which are the most important. Only when an inarticulate-enough atmosphere is created can the deeper levels of experience be touched. Then the grand repertoire of articulateness cannot gloss over the deeper, slower, murkier elements of experience. Indeed, they are often the most resonant.

Sound-based work is a prime element in transforming talk-talk-talking into what Breuer and Freud termed "the talking cure."

## A. First Forms: Initial Contact

Like the stirring "Once upon a time" or "Ladies and Gentlemen," like God's voice in the Judeo-Christian story of creation, the opening tones of an event sound forth, setting things into motion. From the first moment of contact between client and therapist, sound is central. Usually, initial contact occurs acoustically, by telephone. Little harkened to, this is an important event, the first and freshest contact. Consciously honored or not, it is an experience of sound's creative and shaping energy. It is an encounter full of vibratory potential, sounding the first tones, the first forms for a new space of soul encounter.

This first auditory exchange probably involves considerable energy, especially for the caller. She or he might well have given much thought and emotion to starting an analysis or therapy. Choosing a therapist is an important decision, and it can be fraught with conflict. The caller's attitude might well be complicated. Hopes may be running high. Difficult feelings, or shades of them, indeed the very ones which bring people into therapy, will be lurking. Many people have anxieties, as well they should, in trying to deal with who they are and what is wrong. And many have strong projections, or unconscious ideas, both positive and negative, regarding therapists and what they might see or hear or do. All in all, planning and then making that call may well involve considerable tension and effort.

This first phone contact is far more than the factual exchange of information or the practical setting of an appointment. It is a first perception of the potential partner, received on an auditory wavelength. The first energies sound, meet, mingle. The first tones and rhythms are struck. From this moment on, auditory fantasies of the work to come have been evoked. Each partner has been vibrated, moved, if minutely. Each has begun to reverberate to the energic realities of the other, and the vessel.

The telephone is a powerful medium of acoustic exchange, and it can create strong impressions. Some people have described telephone contact with a therapist or answering machine as a major determinant, as if their choice were based primarily upon this auditory experience. They may say a therapist's voice sounded "mechanical" or "friendly" or "too happy" or "nasal" or "just right." Therapists too express initial, and often strong impressions of clients from initial telephone conversations, as well as from the messages left on their voice mail or answering machine. It is a good idea to record these impressions in case notes, for indeed, the case work has begun. Sometimes they may appear incorrect initially. But such acoustic impressions may well express an angle of truth. They may have to do with a first appearance of transference/counter-transference.

Initial phone contact is, in one sense, a pure auditory experience of the other person. Telephone interchanges are an excellent indicator of the field of energy between the two potential partners, to how each one responds to the sounds and silences of the other. On the telephone, there are no visual, gestural or tactile cues. It is uniquely clear, acoustically speaking. Consciously registered or not, it is an experience, mutual for client and therapist, of how the other person sounds, and how he or she listens, or resonates to what has been said – and left unsaid.

The energy sounding across the line is also formed by the caller's inner and outer experiences of trying to get help. There is an underlying fantasy present, in acoustic form. It may be audible in layers of the voice and the silences. It may be audible in the rhythms, pitches, and repeats. Some fantasies or ideas about what help consists of, as well as what elicits help, are unconscious. They result from personal experience, as well as the archetypal images of healing, that is, our human heritage of all of the images and stories about what help consists of. It is essential to get at least a feel for what help means to the client, to judge if the client and therapist are a good match, and also to begin to define the task at hand. In these moments of initial contact, these energies may be heard, vibrating their potential.

First comes the bell. For the caller, the therapist's telephone, heard over the line, may sound like a clear ring or raspy buzz. It may have long or short pauses, and occur in varying rhythmic patterns. This impersonal, telephone-to-telephone connection, this mechanical, metered ringing, first places the therapeutic process into "real time." For the caller, the contact, up to now only imagined, has now entered the realm of measured, ticking time. Things have been set into motion, and any split second the therapist will "answer the call." The metered buzzing on the line is suddenly punctuated by the sound of the receiver being picked up. Personal sound connection is established, voice-to-voice. It is a creative moment, moving from silence, to mechanical count-down, to electric vocal connection.

But wait. In modern society, the caller may well meet with immediate frustration. Few therapists are easy to reach by telephone, at least at first try. Callers may well have to deal first with a receptionist or answering machine. Even if the voice they encounter does not belong to the therapist, it will be associated with him or her. How messages are taken and the call handled will influence the work, as a prelude

experience. If a receptionist is used to set first appointments, the therapist is not apt to get this first acoustic
experience of the client's voice. The recorded voice on the
answering machine, as well as its message, will also shape the
fantasies of the caller. It will form part of the field of energy,
the thoughts and emotions and fantasies emerging, about
the therapy and therapist. These initial auditory experiences are like starts and stops in the essentially profound
attempt to communicate between client and therapist.

Being answered by an answering machine is an increasingly familiar experience. In America, people do not necessarily expect to find "a real person," in any sense, on the end
of the line. Getting a machine or an automaton, or a
machine-like, bleary-eared person, is a common experience,
whether in the medical or business world. Having gotten in
synch with the technology surrounding us, beeping and
humming, processing data, many people act more and
more like machines. Increasingly, callers are speechless at
getting "real voice" on the telephone. Startled, they suddenly have to pull together what they had planned to leave
as a message and switch into "interactive mode."

Disgruntled clients sometimes refer to therapists as "therapy machines." Everything a therapist hears, they complain,
is with an ear to applying the 12 steps to recovery or the five
stages of grieving or Jungian shadow work. Machinelike
mechanics kills the music and poetry, the experience of
image. In one sense, most clients are already suffering, both
inside and outside, from the relentless mechanics of their
complexes and neuroses. They are seeking a receiver that
can listen without a taped response or set responsivity,
without the defensive shifting of the program into "how-
to's." The response they want is one of resonance and
creativity.

But enough delay! Back to the live acoustic drama! The
bell has sounded. The first vocal note is struck by the

therapist, answering the call. In working with telephone exchanges, the therapist may be busy, perhaps between appointments. Somehow, she has to discover a "poised attentiveness" for this brief exchange. During the call, there are practical demands, as she gives information or sets an appointment, besides the relational demands on her conscious functioning in responding to the caller. But as in the actual session, her therapeutic ear is already engaged. Hopefully, she is beginning to catch the vibrations, with some consciousness, listening to the waking dream. In the voice alone, even without verbal content, there are meaningful vibrations. There may be over- and undertones of doom, clangs of excitement, a whanging of fear. There may be an edge of panic, a trumpet call to challenge, a flute tone of seduction, all of which might be heard in the most mundane verbal exchange. As a depth worker, whether on the telephone or in the hour, she bends an ear to both the surface and the dream.

When the therapist picks up the ringing receiver, there is the sudden stimulation of a new voice, a new line sounding – sounding her out – from the first moment onward. To the caller's ear, a crisp, professional ring to the therapist's voice will call up a very different response than, say, a more lilting, inquiring tone. This electric voice may be high or low; it may be melodic, monotone or percussive in style. Its rhythms and timbres will vibrate within the ear of the listener in distinctive ways.

With a first "hello," some type of vocal exchange, some meaningful pattern of auditory back-and-forth, has come into being. The receiver voices pace one another: the duet has begun. Some exchanges are flowing and rhythmic, carried along like smooth improvisation. Sometimes one partner keeps things going more than the other, or in a different way than the other. Is there much echo? What is being echoed, and with what kind of echo? The therapist must have the ear to hear herself as part of the duet too, in order to notice the part she is playing.

Frequently, there needs to be a pause, perhaps in response to a question or impactful statement. How does it sound? Often, due to the rhythm-stopping checking of calendars, silences, a sense of *missed* beats, occur. What is that like? In this new musical drama, many kinds of moments can occur, of various duration and intensity: rushing flights forward, a sudden blankness, a noisy distraction, or a certain hollowness in the timbre of the voice. They will probably be reacted to unconsciously. But if responded to consciously, these auditory elements can deepen and expand perception. They can resonate into the layers of awareness, and the process of wondering at their meaning, their necessity, can begin.

And silence! Silence on the phone is apt to sound strange, flat – through the spaceless receiver. On the telephone, there is so little room between receiver and ear. It is as if the silence vibrates along a more direct, a more material vibratory pathway, from receiver right into the body. Telephone impressions are often strong, and we need to allow them their full reverberation.

In this first exchange, the mutual need to care for something is already present. On the surface, it is as limited as asking about credentials or specialties or payment, or making a first appointment. A great deal is going on. It is difficult to concentrate on sound. Without even thinking, it is easy to fall back on listening exclusively to verbal content, to land back in that place of verbality, where the meanings of words drown out their meaning through sound and acoustic exchange. Receiver to ear, it is important not to focus too exclusively on words. Lending an ear to the "basics," to *how things sound*, is attention to the fundamental song. It invites perception of the play of energies from inside and outside the interchange. This perceptivity is essential to depth communication.

There are many more possible questions about how things sound. What is the conversational "pitch"? Is one person slower? lower? Is one activating and one responding? Is one chasing and one being sought? What sensory fantasies do the timbres invite? Is there an interactivity of timbre, perhaps one raspy and one soothing? Are they metal on metal? Countertransference images are common, and rich. Are there any silences? What are they like? If not, what is their absence like? Questions such as these give image to vague auditory impressions and lend them clarity. If therapists could become more conscious of auditory perceptions, and record them as a natural part of case notes, they might discover that many of their "hunches" come from auditory perception. What we call an intuition or a "sense" of something can often be traced to an auditory perception.

As the therapist listens to herself, to her own voices and silences as part of the exchange, part of the echo, she has the chance to hear herself, and re-hear herself, here as in the hour. Only on the telephone are there no visual demands for interaction, no attention to how her own face or posture or gesture might be expressing something. It is a unique opportunity to concentrate on the auditory dimension, the acoustics of the exchange.

The idea that auditory energy gets below the surface is a recurrent one. Indeed, most people spend a great deal more energy on the appearance of their clothes and face than on the pitch or timbre or rhythm of their voices. The ways in which people use their voices are relatively unconscious, revealing striking aspects of personality, and often ones which are not well integrated.

Auditory fantasy often takes shape only after the telephone exchange. As the call echoes on in the ear, ideas and fantasies are evoked. They are worth some time and attention. They may be clarifications of aspects of the experience, or an impression of the whole. The therapist might realize there was a sense of steady performance, which felt highly controlled. Clinically, a sense of a person's defenses might be clearly audible, in a sense of over-control, or in a subtly demanding tone, in a too quick over-accommodation in pacing. Perhaps, as the call echoes on, some meaning in the rhythm clarifies – the ways that the partners created patterns or variations. Perhaps the pitch in the voice comes to the forefront, strangely high, or an incongruent fullness in the voice, compared to verbal content. Often, such elements reverberate into conscious images only slowly. They come around in their own time, when ears and minds are open to fantasy.

In fact, whether invited or not, auditory-based impressions may well have an afterlife. Their echoing presence may reinforce or else shift their meaning as they re-sound imaginally in the ear. Certain moments of "solo" occur, moments which, when reheard inside the head, seem distinctive or suddenly important. Sometimes in auditory fantasy, human or animal figures, musical instruments, sounds from nature or society or memory, suddenly make a visitation. The realization enters that that sounded like the wail of a hungry child, the rhythms of an insistent salesperson, the timbre of a growling animal, the wheezes of an accordion, a laugh like water running, the resonance of a silent presence. Such auditory images enter the listener's ear, for future evocation.

Sometimes acoustic impressions become clear only next to incongruences, especially in meeting person-to-person, after the first acoustic impression. The face, the gestures and style of movement, the clothes, the experience of the handshake now enter the scene. Meeting the rest of the person provides contrast, making auditory impressions emerge more clearly. In fact, many people become aware of having had an auditory fantasy only when they encounter discrepancies. Comments like "I thought you would be much older" or "You are nicer than you sounded on the phone" have come from just such half-conscious auditory fantasies.

There are charts of vocal characteristics which, like symbol dictionaries, associate vocal characteristics with generalized traits [as cited in the previous chapter]. A constant strong rhythm might indicate a powerful persona or else mania, or dramatic variance in vocal melody might indicate strong emotionality. But like any image, each auditory image occurs in its own time and space, with its own essences and variances. Auditory imagination allows images to come up, revealing the musicality, or cacophony, of each individual exchange.

Impressions during initial contact have the wisdom of fresh perception. They are like the pure moment in a poem, before the need for congruity or structure. They are outside of those elements which come from ongoing contact and the need for structuring in the old familiar ways. During initial telephone contact, the client and therapist are hearing each other, possibly for the first time. Whether consciously registered or not, they are joining, in some fashion, in an experience of tone, meter, pitch and melody, complementing, opposing and echoing each other in an auditory reciprocity. This "duet" is the real beginning of the work. Each has auditory perceptions and fantasies which begin right here. What are they? And what will follow? A few desultory phrases? a brief melody? a song in blues style? a jazz improvisation? or an entire opera? And will it be solo, duet, quartet, or an entire symphony – or a wild menagerie of sounds? What are the combinations, the modulations? Whatever happens, it is yet to be heard.

I experienced a strong auditory fantasy in response to one such initial phone call. I was asking for an appointment with an unknown analyst, and I was full of anticipation and trepidation. Amidst my hesitant, yet constantly catching-up tones and rhythms, it seemed to my ear that the analyst suddenly sang out:

/     ^     ^     /
Let's / Take a chance!

The sound of this phrase, ringing and re-ringing in my head afterwards, sounded like the first strains of a waltz. It seemed firm, engaging, and somehow old-fashioned too. This proved to be an apt auditory image in retrospect, for our work did indeed begin in a whirl in which – to my amazement – he led with some firmly structuring steps. My acoustic fantasy had proved meaningful.


## B. The Ritual Shape of the Hour

> *anyone lived in a pretty how town*
> *(with up so floating many bells down)*
> *spring summer autumn winter*
> *he sang his didn't he danced his did.*
>
> (e.e. cummings, "anyone lived in a pretty how town,"
> first stanza)

Sound shapes our lives. We hear the bells which toll the hours. We jump to the clang which begins or ends a class or work shift. The sound of footsteps or of arriving or departing vehicles make auditory transitions, giving us the sense that "now, it is time." Even when subliminally heard, such sounds offer a familiar sense of entry, ongoing-ness, stopping. They lend shape. And they also provide a holding structure, which offers not only meaning, but also security. However subliminally, they "organize" individuals who are out of sight and touch and smell of each other. They sound, into the shared air, a resonating meaning, a common experience of rhythm and form.

The sounds we use create a sense of place, helping move our being and doings toward meaning. In his book, *The Songlines*, Bruce Chatwin tells of peoples who practice rituals of sound to define and praise the land that they inhabit. He describes "invisible pathways," "ancient tracts made of songs," which connect with each other all over Australia. It is the religious duty of the Aboriginals to offer these songs as they travel the land, singing to the ancestors and spiritual forces. These rites are conceived of as a vibratory exchange through song, between the gods, earthly territories and human energies. In his closing paragraph, Chatwin links this singing with our very origins:

> *I have a vision of the Songlines stretching across the continents and ages; that wherever men have trodden they have left a trail of song (of which we may, now and then, catch an echo); and that these trails must reach back, in time and space, to an isolated pocket in the African savannah, where the First Man opening his mouth in defiance of the terrors that surrounded him, shouted the opening stanza of the World Song, I AM!*[88]

Here, Chatwin is describing song as spiritual map, a topography of singing soul. It is a religious observance, through songs, from the different geographical areas expressing a vibratory interchange with the humans who live there. These songlines, create a "map" of patterns and connections. They connect people with their territories, with each other and with spiritual forces.

Actually, echoes of such practices are not so far-fetched. Our neighbors, the birds, are a species which defines itself and its spaces according to song, "establishing territory" with their songs. Historically, human societies have layers of songlines. In a culturally diverse country like the United

[88] Bruce Chatwin, *The Songlines*, London (Pan Books Ltd.), 1988, p. 314.

States, different strata of cultures and subcultures, through time, have inhabited its areas. For European-based cultures in the upper Midwest, "A Mighty Fortress is Our God" might still, in ghostly fervor, be sweeping the old immigrant prairie. And before that, the drums and chants of indigenous peoples. Some people still hear these echoes. What a chorus of racial, class, national, generational, and historical times have all sounded forth! In the United States, we have a great profusion of songs, with their distinctive rhythms and timbres, melodies and meters. Many sound, especially in cities, within relatively small areas.

In present time, certain sounds and songs belong to certain territories, within the spaces of country or city, or ethnic groups within larger aggregates. There are a myriad of songs on the airwaves of our radios, C.D.'s, tape decks and P.A. systems, which function to establish our own auditory territories: old rock 'n' roll music in this place and classical music in that, Latin jazz out of this car, and the clipped tones of the BBC Radio from that. As we move through these territories, we vibrate with or against these auditory worlds, these "songlines," avoiding this store or home or restaurant, and going to that one instead. However, as cultures mix, electronic possibilities intercross and multiply; families disperse. Our songs and sounds have, in many ways, become less discrete auditorily. In this cyberspace of lightning-fast interlinks, there is, increasingly, a confusion of territories.

Other "songlines" are more subtle, to be found not within our music, but within the music of spoken language. A few people have a sharp ear for the accents in our language, formed by grammar, intonation patterns and pronunciation. In some cities, people's accents change every few blocks, and in some buildings, in every apartment. In hearing a certain accent, we register the presence of a larger energy. And we often "sing back," picking up the accent, the intonations, without even noticing.

Chatwin's words sound a call to notice the way that sound structures our lives, acknowledging the specific vibratory realities of wherever we are. In part through sound, we "sing back" our energies, which create a back-and-forth echo in these spaces, in these areas larger than ourselves. Through this interchange, it can be heard how people and their surroundings exist within a complex interchange. Through the ear, we can enter the larger reality where humans do not create their environment, as we are wont to believe, but where places and things and beings are created by each other. Here we experience the reality of vibratory interchange, the very world, in fact, that modern physics describes.

In a psychotherapy session, sound structures the hour and the interchange. Sound and silence provide form for what Jungians call the *temenos*, that special, even holy, space, set apart and protected, which is necessary for therapeutic work. Every hour is shaped by its ritual sounds. This shaping occurs in both a collective and individual sense. Some sounds are common to every hour in that room, some to certain seasons of the year or certain periods of the work. Some are present only with certain clients. And some, defined by constants, are always present. These sounds and silences form a natural part of the "ceremony" – rather like the cyclical Liturgical Year in the Christian Church. They form a vital part of the observance of psychic or "soul" work.

Because sounds are usually a subliminal or vague experience, we rarely register consciously the sounds that structure us. We would notice them only if they were suddenly absent, the way a newly deaf person misses the most simple sounds, the clock ticking, bells chiming, doors opening, breaths taken, of the shade rattling in the door's draft.

The ritual shaping of the therapeutic hour might begin with the sound of the file cabinet drawer rolling open and a file being slid out, the pages shifted and shuffled. Or it might begin more dramatically, with a door-bell, or door-buzz, like an electric herald of the start. In coming into the consulting room, there are one or more doors, an opening and closing ritual of sound and gesture. And then, the sound of literal steps into the space, of footfalls across the hall or waiting room. Then there is the actual entering into the inner room, the consulting room itself. This is the literal entry into the acoustic vessel, with a latch-click, the swish of a door opening, ushering in the work. The therapy hour has begun.

Sometimes, few words are spoken during this entry phase, or none. However, there has already been a "musical" interchange. When the client rings, the therapist might already have rung back, "buzzing" them in. The door has swished open, and then swished closed. Or perhaps a verbal back-and-forth has begun. Verbal beginnings are ritually engaging. At this entry stage, the therapist might well be more responsive in a social sense than she will be during the most of the session, as she assists in the bridging from usual social exchange into the peculiar space of "the talking cure."

Sounds like footfalls, the door handle clicking, leathery soles rubbing on bristled doormat are the regular "opening tones" heard every session. So too are verbal greetings, the "hello's" and name-saying's and "come in's," with their distinctive, and repetitive melodies and rhythms. These phrases shape the acoustics of the hour and carry it forward. Ritual sounds even lie in the sounds of the furniture, the comforting squeakings of a certain chair, the ticking of the clock, the passing footfalls in the hall. In settling in, a coat hanger may rattle, a purse jingle or crackle, a briefcase latch snap. There may be swishings and rubbings of materials, the rustle of paper (the first signaling of a written offering?), the zip of zippers, a violent Velcro rip. There may be breathing and blowing and throat-clearing, and the creakings and groanings of chairs, sofas, voices, or even bones!

By their regularity, or by their small changes, their variations on the theme, participants are moved into the hour in a meaningful way. Some clients say "howdy," some say "well…" and make a weekly report, and some, in lively fashion, try to amuse or joke. Some rush forward, sliding headlong into the theme of that hour. Others typically shift and shuffle in awkwardness. A few simply sink into profound silence. These are their ritual styles and sounds, as client and therapist enter the therapy space, physically and psychically. The hour has begun to take its shape.

The ritual form of the therapy consists of all of these aspects together. The usual sounds of an hour are its ritual "re-petition": literally, they are a re-seeking of the meanings, present, past and potential. Their repetition is meant to set up and move into the known space of the hour, once again. They re-establish the therapeutic space. Such sounds form the sensuous setting, just as happens in any meaningful ritual. Like in a church or synagogue or a family holiday observance, this therapeutic space, created anew in the present, is shaped by the sounds which define it as a known place. They recall the presence, the vibration, of the known, reminding us of its specific details, be they familiar, comforting, or rankling. They recall its value too. When a good enough vessel is in place, we are reminded of its being a container, a space especially made for our psychic work. We remember that it can hold our confusions, our passion, our impossibly difficult aspects, whether too renegade or simply tiresome. We remember. We recreate. We resound. The hour has begun its distinctive acoustic pattern.

Especially for some clients, it is a long step from the pop song energy of the street into the therapeutic vessel. Actually, this is probably true for any client currently engaged in deep levels of the work. Entering is heavy with overtones. The power of this experience may be subliminally registered, with only indirect manifestations of inhibition or anxiety, or awe or relief, marking its presence. Many times, therapy hours remain quite low key. For some clients, and at some phases of the work, this feeling of potential, the sense that powerful truths or emotions, if only vaguely contacted, can be quite overwhelming.

The potential could lie in the repressed, the painful and confusing past, descending. Family scripts could come alive, all too alive. The ghosts from the past could seduce, horrify, howl. Fearfulness can plummet, become overpowering. You never know, especially when the mysterious unconscious is to be honored. The endless realm of the unknown, the call of the underworld, the death experience of changing, and even death itself, all could await the unassuming client who bops in off the streets, just looking for a little insight, a little growth, a little help with one step. At least in one sense, it is no different for the therapist in her companion role. While training, intuition, experience, self-knowledge and even diagnostic prowess can help, nonetheless, any good therapist knows – at least potentially – that any client might end up taking her into any kind of material, any emotion. Seated in mystery, rituals help us with that sense, especially palpable in working with the unconscious, that larger forces are at work, and mystery prevails.

In collective life we find ritual, and often formal ritual, as a binding and reminding force, all the way from poker parties to Girl Scout meetings, from business meetings to discussion groups. But most noticeably, ritual occurs in spiritual life, where potentially powerful spiritual energies are being engaged. There are many kinds of therapy which recognize in some manner that therapeutic work requires the help of larger-than-personal energies. For Jungians, a resonant layer of the work is the collective energies of subgroups, society, culture, and archetype. Jungians are especially attuned to the way that the spiritual dimension interacts with psychological meaning. Indeed, Jung called the human thirst for spirit an *instinct*. In understanding modern psychotherapy to be in the tradition of shamanism and religious care of the soul, Jungians are close to a sense that the therapy hour is a ritual. Entering the hour is like entering a religious or ritualistic space, one already infused with collective, archetypal meaning, re-called through sight, sounds and movement.

This ritual coming together is not only desirable, but necessary. As Jung so eloquently clarified, the sacred possesses destructive powers equal to its healing powers. The gods have a dark side. And it is not only demons, but false and empty gods who present dangers. Humans have the need to take care, to find a pattern that will make things safe and right. We use rituals of sound and movement and sight to recall ourselves to this place of contact with the spiritual. We use them to contain and form ourselves and our world. The human relationship to spirituality requires a dignity of humility, a sense of associative links with different levels. It is a way of being little understood in our impatient, logic-minded, workshop-mad times.

These human patterns, rooted in the archetypes, resonate in our souls, creating meaning and contact. When something moves us suddenly, mysteriously, that is the resonance of deeply-layered meaning. Around events like Christmas or a baptism service (birth, hope, faith), in the middle of a high school graduation (adult initiation) or Mozart's famous "Requiem" (loss, death), we might discover ourselves reduced to tears. Intense emotional reactions like these are more than sentimentality. They well up from chords of meaning deep in the human soul, from the basic structures of psychic meaning: "mother," "father," "rebirth," "death," "child," "awakening." Tey vibrate with the energy in our most deeply meaningful images and symbols. Entering into archetypally powerful places, even if only vaguely sensed, we require at least a modest ritual entry. It functions to connect us, slowly and truly enough, with these larger energies. And at the same time, from what has become a "holy" place, they echo us back to our human-sized selves.

Entering a ritual space can be difficult, and it is done slowly, step-by-step. In the therapy process, especially to the tune of many dollars per hour, there is the urge to plunge in, get right down to the main business, be efficient. But our bodies and souls need the right timing, the right space, the right resonance around them, if the experience is to be real. At first, there may be awkward pauses, shufflings, tense vocal sounds. They are a necessary prelude to deeper connection. They help the partners move through superficial enactment to depth. Preliminary "smalltalk" or cover-chatter is often a necessary pacing. Its auditory components may include "flighty" sounds, a quick meter, high vocal pitches, shrill or sharpness of timbre, or different kinds of implosive sounds, snuffings or laughter. It is easy for any underlying profundity easily to escape the ear. However, the therapist and client are slowly calling into existence, once again, that deeper level of contact. They are seeking it both within their own selves, as well as with each other.

This first stage in the hour is rather like musicians in their places before a concert, warming their instruments with their breath, re-checking mouth-pieces and reeds, keys and valves, bows and strings. They re-try the agility of their fingers, re-try their range, testing the vibration in the air and in the stretch between high and low. In every session, the client as well as the therapist is in a new, as well as a recalled, space. Both are feeling out the newly constellated, newly shared space of this hour. From the background of their previous work, they are discovering this new hour, bending an ear to this old/new space that they will together be filling with their sounds and silences, and with their mutual "listening" too.

Whether the "theme of the day" involves a dream, a story from "real life," a complaint about the last hour, or the tale of how he got to the hour, this warming-up enables a closer and deeper attunement. It is, most especially, a warming-up of the client to his own self: to his range that day, his tempo, his timbre, his key. It is an attunement of himself so that he can perform in enough relationship to the space around him. It is also a tuning to the vibrations of his therapist-that-hour, as she at the same time tunes to her client-that-hour. For some clients in particular, enough responsiveness or "playing back" is vital to this warming-up process. Each turns an ear to the other, finding the vibration level, the volume, the pitch, the meter, the rhythm and the timbre which they can play to – and with – the other. They establish a meaningful consonance and dissonance. When their base is safe and sound enough, they can enter into deeper psychic levels, into a deeper experience of the psychic process at hand. They can again be *in concert.*

Ritual sounds carry the participants into, through and out of the hour. Meter is a prime mover. For example, it may be nervously fast for a couple of minutes, then slow into deeper contact, a grounding and remembering mode. It may shift into a more start-and-stop meter, which expresses the energies of an approach/avoid-dance. Vocal aspects may make regular, that is, ritual shifts, as the hour moves into itself. Some clients begin the hour speaking in a shrill and high-pitched voice, and slowly, lower and soften their voices. Others begin in a low-key style and become agitated, dramatic, intense, or excited. Besides expressing their own process, they will also be reacting in a duet sense to the space in the session, and the therapist's voice and style. Her energy might be more relaxed, lower in pitch and softer than theirs. Or it might be stimulating, challenging, that is, sharper, clearer, more melodious or faster in sound.

We are highly reactive, in a relatively conscious way, to intonation patterns or the melodies in each other's voices. Monotone sounds nondramatic, steady, usually dull, while a strong contrast in melodic pitches may indicate drama, and a call to dramatic response. Changes in meter, timbre and pitch level, as well as the intonation patterns of the client's voice, reveal the places of increased psychic energy and tension. They are a "song-map" showing where the psyche has the greatest motion or emotion. That map often has a regularity, a typical pattern that moves it along. Therapists, sometimes unconsciously, are often following a crescendo of energy, and a familiar one, as they respond to which image or thought or feeling to focus on and follow through a session.

Meaning also lies in the sounds of breathing. Sounds of entry are often breath-oriented. At the beginning especially, deep breaths are taken and expelled, noses blown, throats cleared – the spirit pathways are opening. Sighs occur, energy which is perhaps just beginning to find vibration and voice. Some are eloquent, expressing a longing, an emotional moving-toward. And sometimes, there are large-chested exhalations of air, a great gulp of relief which signals something of great import, felt in the bone. Breath is a spirit-force. Breathing, as both rushing sound and its many vocal variations, provides a vibratory path, an airborne song, reaching toward the depths of things. It vibrates the Kundalini snake inside, singing to it, charming it, as it rises from the depths, with its life- and spirit-giving energies.

Often, as the hour takes shape, issues find their first form as fragments of content. At first, they are mere hints or suggestions, like an emerging motif. Sometimes a typical entry into a main issue will be more dramatic: a "flashing" of contents or feelings. This is a brief and superficial revelation, quickly retreated from. It is the necessary surface contact, a first attempt. It may sound vague, desultory, shrill, loud, stark, gaudy or comic. A deeper statement, a slower and more naked contact, is yet to come.

Sometimes an entry into difficult material is surrounded by silence. Like the hush before a musical concert or the start of a new movement, this quiet lends it emphasis. For the client within such a hush, it may be an experience of grounding, of tuning, of gathering the energies together for the movement. It may occur in a slide, easy or hard, sudden or slow. Often it occurs in halting stages, with layers of approach and entrance. In time, patterns like these become recognizable as typical, and even ritual, to the attentive ear.

Silences are important, as an experience in and of themselves. Indeed, periods of silence are present in most rituals. The quantity and quality of the silences, as well as their regularity, can vary a great deal with each client. In fact, the way that silence is placed within the hour creates a vibrant sense of what is important in this movement of the work. It reveals what contents, what moments, need the profundity of resonance around them. Conversely, a different kind of silence can echo into emptiness. Contact (or lack of it) is occurring in this space and time, both between the client and his own inner ear and between the listening ears of the two partners.

Towards the end of any meaningful coming-together, even in the lightest melody or the most perfunctory social encounter, there is a striving for some sense of resolution. A *descrescendo* or a lessening of intensity, is called for, out of the space of heavy engagement. It is a move from deep conflicts and deep values, back into the everyday action of the sidewalk or roadway. In a musical piece, primary melodic themes are often repeated in brief at the end, as in a *coda*, which replays a fragment of the central theme, often in a faster or lighter style. In the ending of a therapy hour too, the main theme will often be re-sounded in the manner of a coda. This coda makes it possible to bridge this deeper energy, to carry it along into the street. With its lighter and faster style, it is possible to remember and hold this energy as the demands of transporting oneself, of re-entering the outer world anew, become uppermost.

One example occurred with a woman whose most intense energy had been in telling me about her weekend women's "self-experience" group. One of their exercises had entailed jumping, fists clenched, shouting "ME!" "ME!" at each landing. She was a rather isolated woman, and in a femme fatale style, had concentrated mostly on relation-ships with unresponsive men. She had had little experience, especially positive, with other women. It was her first try in a women's group. Understandably, she had not dared to do this jumping activity herself. Instead, she had experienced it, with considerable emotion, in watching a particular woman, "a small woman," doing this. Only later, in our more familiar and personal vessel, did she get to her feet and try it for herself. In a surprisingly early slide into excitement, she had shown me the exercise, jumping and gesticulating, and shouting "ME! ME! ME!" at each landing!

We did not stop to talk about this jumping moment. We simply shared it and enjoyed it. As we talked on about other topics – her workload, her colleagues, her boyfriend – we returned to this "ME!" as a audible theme a couple of times, as the theme of affirmation from herself and others circled around again. At each return of the motif, as the work had circled around, one or both of us had jumped a bit in our seats, saying "ME! ME!" The theme receded in the second half of the hour, and the closing of the hour pulled us abruptly into time and money practicalities. As she left, before the ritual good-byes, the ritual vocal sounds and gesturing, we found ourselves in a coda. Spontaneously, in unison, once again we made "me"-like grunts, making a last round, a final coda, on this theme. Only then did we say our usual good-byes. Such closings have the energy of an "Amen," as the spoken or sounded re-affirmation is re-sounded. Therapist and client are making a circle of knowing and safety around the awareness they have gained in that hour.

Only with the closing tones, like an auditory "Amen," can the containing vessel be left. The ritual phrases of "Good-bye" and "See you next week" are sounded. And the session auditorily unwinds. It moves back and around itself. The same footfalls sound, the same rustling of clothes and carpet, paper and leather are heard. The same latch clicks, the door swishes the same way against the carpet. All of these sounds occur again, moving in reverse time, as acoustically the hour makes another full circle. But in keeping with the quality of resonance essential to the work, each partner has heard or vibrated to some energy which is deep. Each has, hopefully, expressed and responded to the harmonies and disharmonies in their separate and shared spaces.

## C. Rhythmic Patterning

> *Constant repetition, as inexorable as the movement of the
> ocean, yet each wave different from the last. ... The ocean
> and time move on and on and no two tones, though they be
> the same, ever sound the same. We change, our notes
> change; the emphasis, the length, accompanying harmonies,
> rhythms – all vary from couplet to couplet. Even the rests are
> various. There is a special pleasure in it. The tension builds
> from the recurring, endless recurring bass. We are comforted,
> we know what to expect and yet the transformation amazes
> us and makes us smile.*

(*Resonating Bodies*, Lynne Alexander, pp. 216-17)

Rhythm is a constant and vital part of our lives. The
rhythms in therapeutic work are echoes to the rhythms that
are everywhere in life. Rhythm is present in the meter of our
hearts, our breaths, our footfalls. It resides in patterns of our
everyday actions, the leavings and returnings of work and
school and weekend worlds. It sounds forth in the ticking of
clocks, in the opening and shutting of doors, in the starting
and shutting off of motors. Technology too is rhythmic, in
the digital blinkings of watches, the steady, pulsating throb
of machine sounds, and all of the intermittent beeps and
clicks that surround us. These make up the pulse of our
minutes and hours and days.

There are also the larger rhythms of day and night, of the
weather and seasons turning, of moisture taken up and let
fall as mist, dew, snow, rain. There are the rhythms of the
oceans' waves and tides. There is the rhythm of the moon
waxing and waning, and of the planets and stars as they
make their rounds in space and time. So assumed are these
basic rhythms, and so much a part of our felt lives, that it is
almost impossible – and somehow frightening – to imagine
life without them. Rhythm is a subtly powerful force.

On a conscious level, we notice rhythm most when it occurs as the moment-to-moment pulsing of energy. But its most important function involves a larger capability, the way it offers shape to experience. Rhythm provides a meaningful pattern of back-and-forth. Without it, life could be a dull and constant hum, or chaos. In its very nature, rhythm partakes in a regularity of accent and non-accent, carrying things along. It makes them interesting, satisfying. Rhythm also provides meaning by changing its pattern, for example, by intensifying the established pattern, or setting up an opposing accent pattern (as in syncopation), or otherwise shifting its places of accent or crescendo. It usually operates in conjunction with other elements, like meter, pitch, and timbre.

Thus rhythm focuses and generally facilitates awareness. It prevents experience from being lost in a sea of same-nesses. Rhythm creates structure by creating a basic, although malleable, pace. It is like the physical breathing or heart-beats of a body, around which the movements and positions of that body take place, as it functions and creates meaning. The rhythm of each partner and the rhythm of their interchange in a therapy session, once established, provides an auditory background. Along this felt contin-uum, they will be positioning things auditorily in more or less prominent places, making palpable the relative impor-tance of these elements, and their relationship with each other as it moves along.

The rhythms within one session provide a sense of going onward, yet returning. Rhythm helps make memory possi-ble, that essential re-membering (or putting together again) of those parts that have been lost or separated out. This sort of shape-giving is central. There is in fact no more vital a description for much of the work of psychotherapy.

Rhythm helps things to take on a sense of soundness, a sense of importance. Through the ear, from within the natural meters of the body, it becomes palpable that psychic processes have meaningful curves, waves, phases. Rhythm evokes and shapes in subtle and unconscious ways, helping us to perceive, from within the flow of things, some structure, in a sounding of undulation, an ebb and flow.

However, this is not to say that rhythm always assists in finding meaning. Its very power to create shape can also detract from it, destroy it. Some rhythms deaden meaning or consciousness. A rhythmically sing-song voice or a machinelike, mindless repetition has a dulling or irritating effect. Such rhythms are rigid, automatic. They blunt experience. Their effect is either to bludgeon or hypnotize. Machinelike rhythm reduces consciousness by killing the natural flow of relatedness. Psychically, it defends against an uncomfortable or unbearable situation. It may occur in the endless self-rocking of an abandoned child, in the pacing of a caged animal or in an obsessive or compulsive pattern. In its extremity, such a rhythm has turned into an autonomous force rather an expressive one. In doing so, it defends against the psychological impact of the moment.

However in its usual form, rhythm is a moving element – in more ways than one. As rhythm moves along, it makes the creatures and objects around it, in it, move too – echo, dance, vocalize. Perhaps through no other means can the activity of different psychic and life energies be so naturally experienced as having a shape and meaning. Too much concentration on verbal content will lead the therapist into timing mistakes and feeling errors. It is rhythmic cues in particular which can help the therapist to sense what is happening, to hear the relative importance of something, where it belongs in the client's process and also, within the container of the hour. When she is in rhythm, in attuned response, then her style and intensity can be fitting, evocative, moving as it does out of a felt musical or poetic response.

Moving constantly between their samenesses and differences, rhythmic speech and sound somehow lead to more than their sum. They create an experience which re-sounds beyond life-in-the-moment. In Jungian terms, rhythm involves sensing, if only in the broadest, vaguest way, the pulse of unconscious realms, including collective and archetypal ones. It is one way in the microcosm of individual experience that this resonance with the macrocosm, or larger world, can occur. There is, in Jungian terms, a vibrant connection between all of the levels of the psyche or soul, between inner figures within, between individual souls in outer relationship and some of their inner figures, between an individual and her family and other groups, between an individual and culture, and all are related to the broadest and largest of all structures (or pre-structures), the archetypes.

Difficult as it is sometimes to face, the psyche seems to have its own timing. In acknowledging the power of the unconscious, depth psychology recognizes that our conscious wills have limited control over the pacing of the work. In fact, an administrative attempt to push the rhythm may well interfere with the process. The psyche demands that things ring true. Somehow, even when the content is "true," a premature revelation, like a premature ejaculation, provides partial relief, but mostly frustration, unfelt at any depth by either partner. Anxious flight forward may move forward; but it is, first of all, flight.

However, the natural self-pacing of the psyche is not by any means always slow. Sometimes, a lightning bolt of truth descends, like "I am in love with my worst enemy" or "I, not my mother, am the ravenous beast." Although they have forced us into revelation, such intense experiences cannot be forced into being by us, at least without losing a core resonance. When the rhythm, the pacing, has been right, they can be received in a way that can be deeply received and integrated, so that its meaning radiates out into all aspects of life.

However, in many analytic and long-term processes, it is more the slow rhythms, the seemingly endless returns of psychic work, which are in the forefront. In approaching instinct and archetype, the natural interplay of forces is central. Its pace can be influenced, but not directed. The rhythm of this kind of work, in its solidity and substantiality, can seem so slow, so endlessly sunken and belabored, that this feeling itself becomes part of the suffering. Things turn leaden, dim, for weeks and months, and even years. The process fits, all too well, the long, arduous alchemical work that Jung researched and described. The field of psychology, in its brashness of youth, has turned away from its great historians and teachers of soul work, previously found in the fields of the arts and religion and philosophy. We are sadly out of tune with such long-established melancholies, the documented and eloquently trustworthy turnings of the soul. In countries like the United States, economic and political forces, as well as the state of the national psyche, stress speed, rationality and immediate results. It is to the detriment of a naturally occurring and thorough process.

Many images suggest themselves for the rhythmic pattern of the work. Some work is galloping, some loping. Some rhythms feel like brakes on, some with sudden plummets into a wild pace. Some are tentative tip-toeing, some heavy stomping, in varying patterns and paces. These rhythmic patterns are telling to the way that the client is moving in response to his own psychic life. They are also telling to the way that the work occurs in concert, between client and therapist.

Noting, feeling, reflecting on the regular rhythms of a session creates an imaginative awareness of the client's usual mode. Rhythm is meaningful in both its regularity and irregularity. An atypical rhythm calls attention to itself. If one stretch of the work moves out of its usual rhythm, that change is part of its meaning. When the rhythm begins to sound more controlled or less, when it slows or freezes, when it speeds up or careens out of control, these elements alert the therapist to something happening, changing – and often before its content is clear. The usual way a client places emotions, ideas, sounds, movements, images within the pattern of his hour gives a felt "weight" to them, defining their relative importance. It suggests their relationship to each other within that time-space.

The most common auditory perception of the pattern of a client is the crescendo, a rising to a climax of energy. This peaking of psychic energy centers around intensity, and is expressed through elements of pitch, meter and timbre changes, as well as volume. There may be accompanying new accents, along with new or shifting verbal content.

The rhythm of the hour, or lack of it, is mostly a product of what the whole psychic organism allows, including the unconscious. For many clients, this moment of highest intensity typically occurs at approximately the same moment, for example, halfway into the hour or ten minutes before the end. Just as in an effective theatrical or musical piece, as in the telling of a joke, a "sound structure" must be solidly laid underneath to take the load of the "big moment." Only then can the top of the crescendo, the climax, be reached. Some clients have a highly changeable pattern, and a few have none, allowing the rhythms and climaxes come as they will. In my experience, most clients have typical rhythms and climactic points.

The point at which this intense moment is placed, early or late in the hour, is important to the experience of its impact. However, a growing intensity in psychic material will not always be expressed through an auditory crescendo. A descrescendo (a steady decrease in volume), a silence – or even no change at all – are also possible. These elements will have an audible meaning to the sensitive ear. But most often, a building of energy behind a story or description or image will literally sound forth.

When therapists are describing their "sense" of something, or its felt importance, when they are "feeling for" a client's connection to what he is saying, rhythm might well be the most telling aspect, even more than verbal content. The fact that the felt weight of a moment or image is so rarely described in terms of its rhythmic placement is, again, evidence of a less conscious attitude regarding auditory elements. Their impact is significant, but we do not consciously perceive it, nor think to name it auditory energy or rhythm.

Often in the hour, a client's crescendo is very gradual. Indeed, it may be so slow or uncertain that it is difficult to pick it up. Then, in order to get the moment not merely "talked about," but re-experienced, the therapist has to repeat and intensify. She might try to replay the crescendo, giving back into the client's ear the content or story or ideas as she steepens the rising energy, amplifying the crescendo so that it can be heard more clearly. She might "replay" or restate the main point or points, moving at a faster or slower pace. In auditory terms, she will be echoing the client's pattern of pitch or timbre or volume changes, but with increasing emphasis. She might also use gestures or repetition or an enlivening of content, in response to what has sounded like too vague or too shaky a "theme."

Most of these essentially musical moves would occur quite naturally, in questioning, reflecting and re-experiencing in an empathetic, reactive mode. Working with the acoustic image returns to the client's ear his own sound. It creates resonance, so that he can begin to supply his own "empathy," so that he can discover his relationship to his own images. Then the moment becomes "psychological." Through listening, the person becomes resonant to a sense of self and other, inside and outside. It becomes a moment to re-experience and reflect on.

Attention cannot be held forever. The 50- or 60-minute time limit bears a weight, a pressure. It is part of the heaviness of felt time – the end of the hour looming – which pushes toward a "climax." The rhythm of time passing, the end approaching, necessitates the arrival of the most psychically vibrant moment. D.W. Winnicott describes what amounts to crescendo and descrescendo in different scenes in his book, *The Piggle.* He says his client, a 5-year-old girl, only slowly builds to "the main business of the hour," that is, to what is most occupying her. When this goal has been reached, heard, felt – whether directly or obliquely – the crescendo has been reached. Then the energy can recede. Then the "business" of separating or leave-taking occurs (musically, the decrescendo).[89]

As already noted, rhythm receives more conscious attention in its irregularities than its regularities. It is the sensed changes, the absences and additions, which make us take notice. There may be a disturbance from the beginning. A usually soft-spoken client barks a staccato greeting and strides to his chair. Or a usually brisk woman gives a limp ritual greeting, shuffles unevenly to her chair and sits humped in a throbbing silence. These "disturbances" or changes in the assumed rhythmic pattern of the hour call out a special awareness in the therapist. She finds herself in a newly created space, in strange territory. There is a need or a new attentiveness, a need to react acutely (if often silently), as an animal would prick its ears in the dark.

---

[89] D.W. Winnicott, *The Piggle: An Account of the Psycho-analytic Treatment of a Little Girl,* Ishak Ramzy, Ed., London (Hogarth Press and the Institute of Psychoanalysis), 1978. Winnicott's descriptions of the sessions generally include this sense of climax, interpreted in terms of verbal, symbolic and behavioral cues.

Moments such as these occur regularly, and usually fairly consciously, in the normal experience of the therapy hour. They are a usual part of the reactive field between a therapist and client. Although we react constantly to such energies, when we become more conscious of them as auditory or rhythmic elements, we gain useful images. Speaking of them directly to the client, using musical or auditory language, may be useful. Such images enliven reactions and suggest possibilities. Perhaps a client rushes forward in surges. Perhaps he hits his way through a story with the metal unstoppability of a piston. Perhaps he drags at the introduction, is erratically stop-and-go in the middle and drags again at the end. Such rhythms may suggest a great deal about his relationship to the material at hand, to the way that he moves through his inner world or his life in general, to the way he experiences the analytic/therapeutic process, the therapist, and/or other relationships in his life.

To my ear, elements of rhythm provide especially valuable clues regarding the type, degree and pattern of defenses that a client – as well as a therapist – is using. Perhaps the sense is thrusting ahead, evasion sideways, collapse backward; it may be flight forward, or panicky galloping around in the outskirts. Or it may be a recurrent, irregular rhythm, or a nonrhythm, a stasis. Again, the therapist might want to bring such an auditory image into the hour verbally, offer it as image to the client in some way, direct or indirect. Its having entered her ear, she might even replay it out later, just for herself, to try it on, deepen her experience of it, and see what happens. Sometimes this kind of auditory "working through" occurs without any intention or even invitation, like a song that goes on in the head, in the ear, until its energy is finally over.

Patterns, I suppose, are most necessary when orientation is difficult. In my analytic sessions with one client, I often became lost in the fog. Her content was disconnected and furtive. Her thinking often seemed convoluted and there were long lost- and vague-seeming silences. During much of the hour, she would speak sporadically, her eye contact minimal. It seemed I was hearing isolated fragments popping up along a largely silent – and very easily derailed – train of thought. Through the smoke-screen of her diffuseness, it provided some welcome orientation to become aware of her auditory pattern. It offered meaning and shape to how she was using the hour.

The rhythmic pattern of this woman's sessions was as rigid and fixed as the meter of a metronome. Upon realizing this, my first and immediate thought was that it strongly compensated her diffusiveness. As I reflected further, as I checked it out in ongoing sessions, the pattern became more definable in its particulars. Beginnings were somewhat chaotic. Often she would mention, in a rush, often in humor, the content of what was to become "the main business of the hour." This first mention would occur in a light, playful patter of smalltalk or else in a loud sudden "flashing," often accompanied by a sharp slap to her thigh. This was the percussive prelude of things to come.

As more intense contact ensued, her verbal content and train of thought would get more dispersed – but not her energy level. The sense of "fullness" or energy intensity would increase. More erratic-sounding speech would occur, and also longer silences. Apparently, she was not aware in any clear sense of these silences, which, after all, did seem like busy times for her. I was clearly not to interrupt them. Any attempt on my part to ask about where she had gone, or to return to what she had already said – even if I used the softest volume or the slowest, lowest of tones – was rejected. It was either sharply rebuffed or, more commonly, dully or spacily not responded to. I was allowed no access to the inside of her space. It was clear that I was simply *to be there.*

Her control of me, apparently unconscious, felt as rigid as her control of the time and pattern of the hour.

Her diffuse meanderings would resume after such silences, as the session progressed. Then, towards the end, this "main business" would come back with a shock, suddenly, often after a pointed glance at the clock. This was her "climax point" in the hour, about three minutes from the end. BAM! She would strike and then retreat. She would drop an emotional "bomb," an extremely distressing moment or memory or fact, and then get up to go. She initiated cutting off her sessions on the stroke, like an executioner, every hour, leaving things – herself and often me as well – in an out-spilling turmoil. This woman's hours were a rigid, chronically sabotaged enactment. After the confusing rush into and around issues, and the lost but somehow necessary middle, then finally on came the inescapably ruined attempt at the end.

Becoming conscious of this difficult rhythm, of this machinelike "un-success," brought some clarity to my often confused and tortured reactions to this client. I felt, in working with her, that I was subjected to this pattern. Nothing I did, or did not do, could change it. As I suffered in it over the months, it began to get clearer that it was exactly this rigid pattern which was *itself* the experience which needed energy and attention. And actually, if obliquely, it had been getting it, in the form of frustration, patience and suffering. We – together – had to experience, again and again, this prisonlike encasement in the rigidity, in the somehow vague but heavy impossibility, which must have been her experience of human contact all along.

Our awareness grew slowly, measure by measure. This pattern was the means by which she pulled me into her experience and also maintained what was for her a necessary control of my attentiveness and accompaniment. I believe that enduring and then becoming more clearly conscious of this pattern made "being held" possible – in the only way that she could then tolerate it. I was "tested," hour after hour. I had to be ready to "catch" and try to hold what she would, oh so reliably, drop. And I had to be made to fail, again and again. And from my side, I had to endure knowing it was coming, again and again.

This client's split-off isolation from her own self and from others, and her mixed positive and negative mother transference to me made this "testing" necessary. Despite the intense frustration, my response to her was mostly containing. As her auditory images made clear, her lostness, her diffusiveness, was profound. It took about 20 months of struggle for enough ground finally to be built under us. She then moved, in an oddly quiet, yet for me, dramatic, slide into a space of noticeably more trust. The 57-minute climax all but disappeared. Her rhythm became a more flexible phenomenon which not only allowed, but sometimes sought and even demanded, that her emotionally difficult and confusing stories be heard and resonated – *within* the hour. The way that this woman had "shaped" her sessions rhythmically, in their regularities and transformations, were central carriers of meaning in our work, as she learned to risk, and risk again, getting attention and care.

Living with such patterns, being alive to the way that they echo, inside and outside of the hour, offers increased contact to images and feelings, clarifying what might otherwise be a vague "sense" of things. It suggests many questions, some widely philosophical. Does the pattern express the client's relationship to some specific material at hand (or at ear)? to the therapeutic process itself? to the transference situation? How essentially reactive is it to the therapist's patterns and energies? Is it a wider life pattern? Is it from the past, too? What might be its relationship to the future? Does it belong to a complex or to one part of the client's psychic realm? And the questions can range even wider: What part is it playing in the symphonic expression of the culture, the species, the universe? Such questions as these, of course, do not belong exclusively to the auditory sphere. But auditory imagery offers a distinctive, and at times especially evocative, way to approach them.

# 2. Sound as Revelation

## A. Sound Accent

*Hey, what do I have to do*
*To make you feel the tingling too?*

Laura Nyro, "The Bells"
(*Gonna Take a Miracle* album, no date listed)

"Accent" is an auditory word, coming from the Latin *cantere*, "to sing," and *ad*, "to." "To accent" means "to sing to." People sing out certain syllables, certain words, certain parts of a phrase or sentence, to make them understood. And they accent the moments which carry the most meaning. We "sing to" what is important. We make it vibrate, as it has made us vibrate.

While its roots are auditory, accent can also utilize elements of vision, movement, space, tactile texture, etc. People use spotlight or shadow, bright or enticingly subtle coloring. They accent with "dance," using many variations of gesture and movement, jabbing fingers or clenching fists or sweeping their arms. They use varying and sometimes startling textures and surfaces, a sudden shiny smoothness, a slice of gravelly matte. And they use a sense of balance or imbalance of composition, whether auditory, visual, spatial or kinesthetic. There are a myriad of possibilities. Accent offers variety and direction to expression. It moves attention along and shows what is more important.

Auditory accent involves elements of volume, rhythm, pitch, timbre, and also pause and silence. Its specific qualities make it especially effective. Acoustic accent reaches right into things. In fact, it reaches right into the hearer, making him or her literally vibrate. Auditory accent makes an experience immediate. Its effectiveness is probably one reason why it is so very common: we raise or lower the volume of our voices, vary the pitch, shift the timbre, change the meter or pace. We may snap our fingers, slap our thigh, or pound the arm of the chair as we sound forth the important words and sounds. Sound accent often involves more than vocal elements, and can give a highly effective percussive shock.

Auditory accent in speech is a vital element. Without it, our speech would be not only mindlessly boring, but unintelligible. Accent is a natural part of English speech, as it is in most languages. It must be practiced as a necessary element when teaching foreigners to speak English. Without proper syllabic and phrasal accent, they will be only poorly understood. So in speaking, accent involves basic understanding. As people go about expressing what they want to say, in the way that they want to say it, they further accent words and phrases to clarify and add emphasis. They may speak more loudly, vary the meter, add gesture or facial expression, shift the timbre of their voices, or even add sounds with their hands or feet. Sometimes, people accent something with pauses or silence. They surround what they say with "pregnant silence." By not sounding, by something not being said at all, something can gain peculiar intensity. In these ways, vocal speech is like music, creating accent by varying elements such as volume, rhythm, pitch, timbre, pauses and duration.

In the therapeutic hour, clients use auditory accent to pull the therapist right into their experience. They use it make the therapist vibrate, and vibrate with *their* meaning, *their* experience. Psychoanalyst A. Margulies describes just such a moment. His client is reporting an important, numinous dream in which his father tells him to go and stand in the ray of light, coming into the church from above. When the dreamer goes to do this, suddenly there is a clap of thunder and – the dreamer rises into the air. Margulies vividly reports the way that this normally pensive man tells of this thunderclap:

> *[to my surprise, the patient smacks his hands together loudly – clap!] Dr. Margulies, it was just like that; in fact, I actually heard it and woke up – but I kept dreaming, strange. It was very powerful – it was a lightning bolt that hit me.*[90]

Margulies heard this thunderclap as being the most compelling sensory element of this dream. This was so for his client and, due to this auditory accent – the re-created clap – it became so for Margulies.

Margulies continues:

> *Sound has a palpable presence here. With sight you can close your eyes or turn away, but hearing comes at you. In this case, sound is literally hurled like a lightning bolt. It feels as if he has awakened me from my detached and somnolent listening. With this noise, he jolts me into a more vivid awareness. I have a sudden change in my affective state and with it an excited, higher level of sensory attention: I am acutely in 'present-time.' ... Loud sound is no longer out there: the background envelops us and makes our skin and even our bones vibrate as we fuse with the beating surround.*[91]

This handclap, suddenly and dramatically, insisted on a vibrant responsivity to the client's dream experience.

---

[90] A. Margulies, "On Listening to a Dream: The Sensory Dimensions," *Psychiatry 48*:371-81 (Nov., 1985), p. 373.
[91] Ibid.

Accent is a linear phenomenon in that it lends emphasis to psychic elements in a time flowing forward (that is, the telling of a story, going onward). The heightened attention to the accented part of the word or phrase or story takes place along a story line, just as musical accents occur along a line of musical time, within musical measures or spans of measured time. But accent also makes time stop. Or more exactly, it makes that thunder continue to resound, thus making time stand still. Time, as it is re-lived, seems to stop. Margulies' patient still felt the clap of thunder as he awakened and vividly recalled it to his therapist as if it were still there, thunderous in his ears.[92]

As Margulies illustrates, sound used as accent functions not only to re-create literally the important moment, but also to make it resonate in time. It sounds onward in the meter of our lived time, like a "re-captured" moment in a song re-sung. Through this re-sounding, some important moment or meaning can be reached to again. We accomplish the same timing, and timelessness, in film, in mimicked gesture, photograph, sculpture, painting, and even in the private auditorium inside our own heads.

Among the auditory aspects mentioned in this book, acoustic accent probably receives the most uncomplicated response, and the one most easily made conscious. For the most part, the therapy hour revolves around what the client initially accents. From there on, there is an ongoing process, sometimes with a re-accenting, or an accenting of different things. This accenting is central to focusing, and understanding what is important. It also forms a part of the relational aspect, the feeling that the therapist can understand the client, and vice versa.

Re-reacting with the client, as Margulies did, is ordinary human interaction. Especially in the therapist's role of

[92] Ibid.

bringing in the unconscious, she may have a very different reaction to that same accented element. Accent does not always create the same reaction. What it does is to create a situation where the chosen element is reacted to anew. It is a kind of re-run, yet sounds forth as fresh and new, offering a wider experience for the speaker too. Accent can also evolve. It can change during repetition, whether during the session, in the next, or the next week or month or year. Accent then becomes an aspect of how something echoes (see the chapter on echoing).

Such accents are important to a basic sense of accompaniment and resonance. The therapist's reactivity shows that she is moved and takes the client and his material seriously. For some clients, such responses may be vital, even primary. If a person's ego state is too unformed or insecure, he is working toward a basic sense of himself. The therapist's being highly reactive and furthering the client's own sense of accent, his own sense of what is important, offer support, a sense that whatever the client is doing or being, *that* is important. Further, it lends definition to the shape and meaning which may be expressing itself only unclearly. It helps him realize that he does have ideas and feelings, that he is a person coming into more definition and shape.

For such a client, with a relatively unformed sense of himself, the resonance to the accent *is* the core of the work. Reacting to accent does not just provide focus or deepen experience. The accenting is itself the actual process which the client is seeking at the most important level. He is asking for it loud and clear: to be heard, validated and moved by the emerging shape of his own meaning.

One of my clients used her therapeutic hours to report faithfully the events of her life between sessions. It was noteworthy how commonly she used a variety of acoustic accents. They were often playful, onomatopoetic sounds like "boof" or "zak" (from Swiss German, her native language). "He acted just like my father," she might say. "So cold and clever. I told him he was really a jerk, and not really as smart as he thought. Boof! I really told him off. Boof! Boof! I could still just hit him!" Exactly as in Marguilies's description, these vocal accents, also accompanied by a clenched fist sideswipe gesture, functioned to startle me and pull me deeper. Just like with theater, I landed right into the middle of the story she was telling, right with her, as she herself was re-living it. These dramatic accents sounded her experience to life again, giving them importance and literally re-creating their reverberations for us both. It sounded into being an experience we could have together.

It was obviously vital, indeed, it was the main thrust of her energy, for this woman to "re-live" these moments with me in the hour. The lack of such an individually empathetic reaction was central to her psychology. Her background was one of emotional neglect, with both parents only partially functional. It was palpable from her presentation that she was demanding response to her particular accents, both unconsciously and consciously. If I was unresponsive, her face would fall, just like a disappointed child's. Then she would often repeat or heighten her accents or enlarge her gestures.

This woman was filling her inner emptiness, making her inner world an important-sounding place, which it was. She was creating a custom-contoured space from which to discover her individual reality. At the same time and very importantly, it also affirmed her value. This reproduction of life events in the hour and just as importantly, her control over what was important seemed to offer a sense of reality and affirmation to her life. She was sounding forth, accent for accent, tone for tone, building up a world she could herself believe in. It was her world, and like a young child, she sought affirmation, that this certain thing was exactly in this place, right at this moment, like an exact arrangement of necessary objects or toys. This immediacy was so important to her that she asked me not to work on her dreams when she was not there. This request made sense. Reactivity to her accents was the main work.

In the above example, accent functioned to "make things right." But, like everything, accent can be misused. Accent, whose purpose is to increase comprehensibility, can also disappear in a frenetic lack of focus, for example, in an overexcited or hysterical atmosphere. When *so much* is important, *so much* is dramatic, nothing sinks in, nothing can really be fathomed. To the listener, blasted with accent, nothing means anything. Rather than evoking response, it creates a state of numbness. Accent can mislead into melodrama or drama for drama's sake. Too much accent, for example, is like the child who always cried, "Wolf! Wolf!" just to see the excitement. The meaning is lost in exaggeration and manipulation.

Giving accent to a story or description is a natural process of self-expression and ultimately, communication. It ranks high on the list of indicators when a person's communication is being unconsciously sabotaged. In such interactions, when accenting is too strong or frenetic, too subtle, or too thrill-seeking, listening becomes an experience of impatience, confusion and numbness. At the same time, the client, quite unconscious of his own sabotage, will probably feel the therapist (like everybody else) is cold, stupid, nasty, or deaf.

In its essence, accent can reveal a great deal about how a client elicits attention from others, or fails to do so. Perhaps the client is a dramatic performer; or perhaps he is a subtle, gentle enticer or muffled, lost soul. The subject or topic being accented is of course important, indicating what the client deems important. But, at the same time, the style of accent has many images to offer, for example, regarding assumptions of how recognition and care happen. It may be by fanfare, by firm rhythms with calculated drama, by a series of controlled accents at off-guard moment, to unbalance the listener, or a constant stream of accents, in constant interplay. Or it may be by sounding accents so subtle, that the listener has to move close, to be curious and help.

Indeed, accent can also occur by way of subtlety. A sudden dropping of volume is an effective way of gaining the attention of someone who is within hearing range. In fact, it requires more of the listener than in normal listening. She has to exert effort, become more active, concentrate more intensely, moving closer or asking for repetition. A subtle accent has many reasons and forms.

Accent might be especially important in working with depression. The withdrawal or loss of accent is a good description for depressive symptoms. Their "affect" or emotion is flat, dull or blunt. In this state, either nothing matters, or else everything overwhelms. Thus no important point can emerge. Finding meaningful accent, in any of its forms – acoustic, visual, gestural, postural – becomes the central search. It takes a special ear to stay alive to frustration and difficult feelings when they apply to everything! Within the dark and fog of depression, accent is an obvious choice in trying to find some contour and meaning.

When plumbing the depths of depression, therapists and clients alike can take heart by thinking about some process-oriented psychologists, who painstakingly search for signals as minute as a eyelid twitch, in states as extreme as coma and catatonia. Whether it results from depression or timidity, shapelessness or just complexity, it takes a certain kind of ear, and a wealth of patience, to listen to the complexity and subtlety of some accents.

Accent, and especially acoustic accents, are a primary means of basic expression and emphasis. But just as important, it is a major means by which a person evokes reactivity. It makes the listener, the world at hand, and herself in her own ear, take on the meaning, and exactly that meaning, that she is in the process of discovering and experiencing.

## B. Sound Synchronicity

> *In a quite irrational way we must be able to listen also to the voice of nature, thunder for instance, even if this means breaking the continuity of consciousness. …*
>
> from a letter from Jung to "Dr. S" (1951)

Synchronicity is meaningful coincidence. It describes an event, experienced as mysterious, which brings two or more events or people together in a way that appears random, but is embued with meaning. For example, it was synchronicity when two people celebrating their 30th wedding anniversary in a restaurant found themselves seated within greeting distance from the old priest from another state who had married them. Another example occurred when two people were talking about a hummingbird in a dream, and a hummingbird suddenly hovered outside the window.

Western culture has for the most part understood such phenomena as "mere coincidence" or "pure chance." People shake their heads at the strangeness. However, Eastern philosophies have long considered synchronicity a source of meaning. They have accepted it as a valid source of information, and regularly ponder what synchronicities might mean. There are many different kinds of practices, not only from the East, which regularly interpret or "read" energies expressed through seemingly random events, for example, the shape of tea leaves in the bottom of the cup, the way that straws or coins fall in the I Ching or the laying of Tarot cards.

As Jung pointed out, synchronicity is not totally random. Apparently, it expresses unconscious patterns of meaning, and thus we cannot fathom the connections. Synchronicity appears to express or reinforce meanings of which we are unconscious. From this broader perspective, it is the limits of consciousness that make connections appear random. No matter how a person racks the brain for a causal explanation or willed act behind the event, none can be discovered. The event has simply "struck," and left behind its mysterious resonance.

In their disinterest and disbelief, Westerners may not notice even synchronicity when it happens. If they do, many stop at saying, "Wow!" discounting its capacity for any depth of meaning. However, for those who have begun to respect synchronicity, it is not so uncommon. It is possible that synchronicity impacts and guides our lives more than we are aware. According to Jung, synchronicity functions to give a particular accent or impact to a situation, often reinforcing its direction. Sometimes too it might function to set things moving in a new way.

It is not uncommon for synchronicity to center around auditory phenomena. The three times which Jung reports in his autobiography, which shocked him and then influenced his thoughts and actions are good examples (see "Sound and the Healing Arts" chapter in Section I). A certain sound, or a resonance or silence, may enter the scene, without causal or rational links, and connect things up in some way that is meaningful. For no discernible reason, the conjunction of energies reveals some mysterious meaning. Events occur in strikingly everyday ways. Upon driving past a former lover's street, a man hears the song they used to call "their song" on the radio. A woman dreams about a mosquito getting caught in her ear, and it occurs the next evening.

In psychotherapeutic work, sound synchronicity usually occurs in the form of sounds which unexpectedly enter the hour. Such occurrences are often related to surrounding events, like happenings in the building, the sounds of traffic, sirens, animals and insects, the weather, things falling or breaking and some involuntary body sounds. It is easy and, on the surface, even "sensible" to ignore such sounds. Especially if they are unpleasant or repetitious, and if they interrupt something important, it seems necessary to push them aside. They sound irritating, disturbing, when they are heard as mere interruption, meaningless "noise." However, with more open-minded attention to ear-perception, it becomes clear that these "noises from the outside" can make important contributions. It is well worth it to give them attention and ponder the ways that they could be carrying meaning.

In the course of one of my cases, there was an extended series of acoustic synchronistic events which gave me ample opportunity to ponder such matters. During one phase of work with a Swiss client, the body therapy group, which met regularly upstairs, would begin thumping, pounding, and hee-hawing their way into our sessions. This was noteworthy because, not only were they usually quiet, but also, because their sounds followed us through three schedule changes of her regular sessions. We just could not shake these sounds. This was a highly persistent specimen of synchronicity, in the auditory mode. Due to their insistence, we could not ignore or discount these sounds.

Perhaps it is difficult to imagine how such a phenomenon could produce anything but irritation. But oddly enough, our three schedule changes had had nothing to do with escaping this "noise." Perhaps we were, on some level, cognizant that it was helping our difficult work in some peculiar way. This woman's childhood had involved a basic disregard of, and sometimes even scoffing at, her individual reality, and especially her emotional life. She had internalized these attitudes, and in her adulthood was busy ignoring and scoffing at her feelings. She was apparently maintaining a myth of a warm and close family, hoping still that she might be offered the support she so craved. She saw herself as ungrateful and unfair to the family. She remained crucified between her real feelings about the family and their disrespect, and her defensive guilt-taking, trapped between feelings of inferiority/arrogance and compliance/rebellion. She felt despised, inside and out.

The thumping and hee-hawing would typically come when this woman had pulled back, withdrawing eye contact and falling silent. She would appear to be remote from her feelings, as well as from me. Then these sounds would insert their way into our work. Any attempt on my part to "help," to ask or wonder or offer a response, only seemed to move her farther away from consciousness of her feelings. However, these noises woke her up. They expressed, I believe, the very energies which she so badly needed to shake her out of her romanticizing and stuckness. And sometimes they did just that, jarring her into reaction. She would jump nervously and clutch at her heart area. We began calling them "devil-noises," expressing their connection with nasty and disruptive underground energies.

Although I too found these sounds startling, I slowly realized, to my surprise, that I experienced them as dramatizing and stimulating energy in our work. Nor did she ever protest. This evil-sounding hee-hawing and thumping from above gave image to the distanced, and often arrogant, ceiling of her own discounting and superior attitudes toward her own reality. They were – again and again – synchronistic events, sounding forth the energies which were trying to be felt and recognized, amidst great frustration.

And by the way, such events were by no means uncommon in her life. Dramatic events occurred frequently around her, often involving anger. These events from "the outside" appeared to be synchronistic energies which mirrored her own inner anger and frustration. Such events, constellated also in social situations and even in nature, were similarly volatile and sometimes even violent. Socially, she regularly elicited anger and frustration in friends and colleagues, because of her difficult personality. Reportedly, without her saying a word, fights would occur on trams and at group events. Once, a volcano erupted during a visit climb to the edge with a friend she was having a passive struggle with. Such synchronistic events corresponded with her state of being walled off to a volatility in herself. They occurred in what Jung called the *unus mundus*, the mystically unified world.

This recurrent synchronicity of "devil-sounds" did stop. But, again synchronistically, it was only as some of these energies inside of her began to get clearer, and get humanly responded to, in the hour. At first, this woman had not been able to bear any confrontation – or even clarification – from me, a human agent. She described as "aggressive" even my gentlest questioning of her, when I was not understanding what she meant. The noises stopped at approximately the same time as she began risking more emotional clarity about her hurt feelings, and less often, her aggressive and arrogant feelings too. This "release" coincided with her beginning to endure the knowledge that I perceived, and also somehow respected, these difficult sides in her – and still supported her. These synchronistic sounds had the quality of lightning rod energy, channelling this difficult energy into the vessel. The work now moved to a human channel, the relational and transference energy, allowing warm and gentler back-and-forth energies.

This example of acoustic synchronicity involves fairly dramatic acoustic phenomena. Perhaps more often, sounds are subtle. This less dramatic quality can mean that they are easily bypassed. However, it is sometimes this very quality of subtlety which lends them special impact. A client told me of awakening during the night while her husband was away and hearing a soft, steady, tap-tap-tapping. It turned out to be the leaves of a house plant, lightly tapping for no apparent reason. She explained that she had just moved it to the corner of her bedroom that day. Apprehensive and curious, she had investigated carefully. There were no drafts or vibrations that she could discern. She could find no reason for this plant to be tapping in this manner.

This plant had a story. She and her husband had bought it at the beginning of their marriage eleven years before. She was unhappy in this marriage, and just beginning to face this fact, which deeply threatened her sense of identity and security. Her marriage was romantic on the surface. From the outside, the couple appeared impressive. But in terms of her personal needs, the marriage seemed to offer her little in terms of emotional resonance, and their sexual relationship had never been satisfactory. She seemed to be unconscious of much of her emotional and sexual self.

This woman was fascinated by this plant tapping. She felt it was important. On the therapist side, I struggled with the strangeness of it, but wanted to understand all of the psychic energy it was generating. We explored its mystery, as if it were a dream. We collected associations. Symbolic interpretations were possible. In terms of its location and history, the tapping had occurred in connection with the bedroom and marriage, her primary issues. It also involved a newness of location, or we could say, growth in a new place. In associating it to her reactions, I heard its energy to be mysterious, undeniable, a new, gentle, seeking-in-the-night energy. It was expressing itself especially in the realm of intimacy and sexuality, in masculine/feminine relationship and marriage.

I articulated such themes and interpretations during that hour and the next. I did so carefully, aiming to create poetic resonance, hoping to hold the sense of mystery. But although I was in training to learn just such things, I felt that it was not quite right. Slowly, I began realizing that in articulating and interpreting, I was moving against a feeling in myself. Phenomena like this, involving plant or stone energy, occur at a very deep and slow vibratory level. Their very nature creates a resistance, in me at least, to trying to verbalize about them. From within the resonance of vegetable or stone, it feels strangely fast, hot-blooded and grasping. It is too far from the their nature, too animal in pace and style. It is *too much* in opposition to the nature of the phenomenon. Also, there was something so naked, so delicate, in this plant tapping. It seemed to require great patience and a slow and careful timing.

However, there seemed to be neither harm nor benefit from my articulations and interpretations. They seemed to have fallen on deaf ears. Despite my efforts to explain, to find a "place" for it, I, like my client, continued to feel the mystery and importance of this tapping. Boundaries recede when mystery arrives. This feeling was affirmed when this tapping began recurring in the consulting room. Twice, the ivy plant on the table between us began to vibrate (silently) in the sessions following. (Technically, this was auditory energy – tapping – moving into a kinesthetic energy – trembling.) We investigated carefully for natural law explanations. Was it the heat from the radiator? the traffic vibrations? surely not a minor earth tremor, recurring during her sessions!

Such moments are not reported very often in psychological circles in Western culture. Many would probably not even be noticed. Jung and Jungians, however, are part of the small group who respect and ponder such energies. On one level, searching for rational and scientific explanations for the plant trembling seemed off the point. For within the hour, within our vibratory vessel, some meaning had simply entered and resonated. We had noticed and re-experienced this trembling energy together. With the memory of her tapping plant as background, we were immersed in a sort of helplessness and wonder. The trembling and tapping had become a mysteriously accompanying energy. We said little. For some vague but palpable reason, its recurring nature seemed to function as a reminder of something.

Outside of the hour, I reflected on these moments, re-listening, re-resonating. I recalled an important moment in my auditory education, in a poetry class. It was this class in poetry which taught me the most about how *the way things sound* open out meaning. In my retro-hearing process with this plant tapping, I experienced again how a poetic moment can engage and amplify an event. What I remembered was learning to listen, in an ear-minded way, to a poetic phrase, Andrew Marvell's image of "vegetable love."

In the poem, "To His Coy Mistress," the speaker is elegantly, cleverly, passionately seducing his reluctant lady. He begins with spinning fantasies:

> Had we but world enough, and time,
> This coyness, lady, were no crime.
> We would sit down, and think which way
> To walk, and pass our long love's day.
> Thou by the Indian Gange's side
> Shouldst rubies find: I by the tide
> of Humber would complain. I would
> Love you ten years before the Flood:
> And you should if you please refuse
> Till the conversion of the Jews!
> **My vegetable love should grow**
> Vaster than empires, and more slow.

The meter established in this poem excerpt makes the reader, the listener, hear this starred line as moving slowly, deliberately. The word "vegetable" changes, becomes startling. Its three syllables now become four, and the word

seems vastly, grandly slowed. In auditory imagination, it
could almost – slowly, precisely – be growing outward.

After several more lines the poem then starts hurrying:

> But at my back I always hear
> Time's wing'ed chariot hurrying near.

Mortality looms. The speaker begins to scare his lady,
with images of ashes, dust and worms. After these lines, he
closes lightly, enticingly, reminding of his urging to "sport
us while we may."[93]

Differences in our native language and also educational
background made it impossible to share this poem with this
woman. She had other images, some of them from dreams,
which expressed the poignant and passion-bringing press of
the times and also, impending death. In retro-hearing, I
found myself wishing she had as enticingly gentle, erotic
and yet relentlessly truthful animus energy, inside of herself,
as the speaker in this poem.

The influence of this plant and poem quietly informed
me, evoking a certain style and content in the ways I was
working with her. Back on the mortal and everyday level, the
work began to change. She began admitting and working on
some of the conflicts in her marriage. The result was insta-
bility and drama. She had an impatient and demanding
side, full of harsh judgments and name-calling. She left her
husband and became deeply involved with a lover. Several
times, she ended up in stances she could not maintain,
deceptions and suffered violent splits as her husband and
her lover vied for her favor.

In these periods, I remembered with wonder this tapping
and trembling. In the turbulent times which followed, there
remained in my mind and ear the image of a slow and

[93] Andrew Marvell, "To His Coy Mistress" (1681). In *Introduction to Literature: Poems.* L. Altenbernd and L.L. Lewis, Eds., New York (Macmillan),
1963, p. 169.

delicate vegetative energy which was growing. It was steady. The subsequent vortex often felt like forced and violent actions and attitudes. It was helpful and centering for me to recall this image, its sense of natural necessities and passions. And it was true, a "garden" of positive feminine energy was slowly growing, as further months and years revealed.

Synchronicity, in all of its forms, functions to reveal or emphasize aspects of meaning which are relatively unconscious. It can broaden our consciousness. But it is the experiential, the vibratory aspect, that is often the most important. Auditory synchronicities bring that aspect home in a particularly effective way. Synchronicity rings a bell; it strikes its note, leaving us ringing and wondering in its resonance.

## C. Echo and Return

> *Echo is the soul of the voice exciting itself in hollow places.*
> Michael Ondaatje, *The English Patient*, p.250.

The world is full of echo. It is here, but not exactly here, and then it is there, but not quite there. Echo is everywhere, sounding in the most mysterious ways. It is found in the spaces between things. In modern times, echo may be trying to sound again, as we begin to listen again to the interrelatedness of things. Echo lives again when our ears are attuned to the way things vibrate back and forth between each other.

In communication, there are constant echoes. In responding, one person "tries on," in the moment, what she is hearing from the other. Some echoes simply turn over what is heard, in the mind, in the mouth. Or some may express reactions, incredulousness or sarcasm or outrage. In the therapeutic hour in particular, there are constant echoes. The art of echoing is one of the most common and effective tools that a therapist has. Nowhere more than in the process of self-discovery do people echo themselves and others, in such a variety of ways. They re-call and re-collect, learning to listen not only for the content of what they say, but for the quality of echo around their words and silences, for the ways things are being told. They quest and re-quest, singing out and listening in. People echo other people and beings and objects, imagined or "real" in the outside world. They echo the sounds of their past. They echo the present. And perhaps they could even be said to echo a future, existing in potential.

Echoes call up other times, places and people, sounding their subterranean energies to the auditory surface once again. It is most intriguing the way that people echo themselves. Returning to an idea or feeling, to a word or phrase, a laugh or exclamation, deepens contact with it. We "play it again." It vibrates onward. Its very sameness sometimes sounds different. It circles back, the same and yet new. Is it the sound that has changed, the space it is sounding in? Or is it the ear that has changed, in listening to it?

It is important to clarify from the start that "echoing" here refers to its specifically *acoustic* sense. "Echoing" means holding to the integrity of the *sound* of what has been expressed. In our non-auditory mind-frame, we do not always think of echoing as auditory. Psychologists, for example, use this term to refer to content, meaning that they rephrase a client's ideas or feelings back to him, with no particular attention to its original auditory form. However, in work attuned to auditory images, to change the sound of a communication is already a reworking of the image, the client's *acoustic* expression. It is not a *faithful echo*, for the original auditory image has been lost.

In a genuine echoing process, the therapist keeps to the exact sounds, the exact words, as originally expressed. She remains true to their melody, timbre, meter, pitch and rhythm, re-calling to the original moment in a resonant way. She is careful to facilitate the auditory image, letting it speak for itself, through her. She assists it in expressing its *telling* nature. The sense within the therapeutic hour is that the partners call and call back … call back … call back. …

Like the elements of auditory ritual and of rhythmic patterning, echo is primarily a phenomenon of re-petition. It is a re-seeking, an attempt to rediscover, sometimes again and again. And re-petition is an essential part of psychological work. While it might sound boring, repetition has many uses, and there are many ways to think about it. Granted, it has a meaningless side. We suggest senselessness, or even malignancy, in phrases like "neurotic patterns" or "reenactment in relationships" or being "caught in the same old complex." Likewise, we speak clinically of "obsessive thoughts," "compulsive actions," "perserveration" or even "echolalia."

But repetition can also be a primary indication of value. We suggest the meaningful nature of repetition in speaking of "role modeling" or "heroes" or even "influences." We notice when people are fulfilling "scripts," performed again and again; we mark the human need for "ritual." Jungians speak of "circumambulation," the spiral pathway of psychic development. The same issues and images come round, again and again, at deeper or higher levels. And there is the Jungian idea of "*voca*tion," the repetitious voice *calling*, demanding a person do or become something. This calling or necessity, when not listened to, may well result in a neurotic state, its real meaning lost in a "vicious circle."

Echoes make things alive in the moment. They single out certain elements, just as acoustic accent and synchronicity do. But what makes echoes so special is how they take on a life of their own. Echoes are tricksters. Sometimes, they seem to have plans of their own. Indeed, echoes in the consulting room do at least as many surprising things as they do in outdoor valleys and caves. Begun as simple repetition, suddenly some auditory fragment finds a totally new context. There is a startling new juxtaposition. A certain eerie, personal essence may suddenly be appear, as if echoes were revealing idiosyncratic drives or wishes.

No wonder in mythology, "Echo" is a nymph. She is a secondary divinity, charming, sylphlike, quicksilver, and not quite fully formed. Nymphs, who are not adverse to playing and pranks, mingle in affairs of all sorts. Out in nature, echoes show a lively, mischievous side, sounding as if they shift in volume, or even timbre. Trickiest of all, they move around in space. Suddenly, they ventriloquize our sounds back to us. We as sound-makers discover ourselves at a startling angle of experience in relationship to our own sounds. Subjectively, it is as if we are in some different space because of the way that echoes have re-sounded us!

We cannot really put a finger on an echo. We cannot grasp its essence at all. Many times, we do not even know what direction it is coming from. Yet echoes fascinate us, call to us. In an echoing tunnel or cave or valley, we find ourselves calling and calling again, as they call back, mingling our sounds with theirs. It is an ongoing interplay of auditory energy. We listen and linger, wondering at them, at their callings and at our own. Who is who? Where are things coming from? This fascination, this interplay, is in part, at some level, part of the pull of echo within the therapy hour too.

*Echo and Narcissus*

Many psychologists have shown interest in the Narcissus-Echo myth. It takes place in a world of resonance. With depth and profundity, it plays with boundaries and essences, with differences which are the same, and samenesses which are different. This myth speaks as movingly to the inherent dilemmas in soul work as to a poetic description of symptoms.

Much of the psychological work on Narcissus has been from a developmental standpoint. Like the echoing (and mirroring) which take place between caregivers and young children, this energy is clearly applicable to clients with young or little-developed egos. In Jungian terms, these are people who have not reached a level of ego development necessary to deal with the reality of the unconscious, that unsettling "otherness," much less integrate it into a wholeness of personality. However, a developmental viewpoint, taken alone, reduces Narcissus. He becomes too simple, just an undeveloped anybody who cannot get beyond himself. Reductiveness ruins the image, for it "explains" it. The reduced Narcissus is simply incomplete; he is held fixated in the past, rather than mysteriously evocative in the present.

Likewise with Echo, it is easy to type her as an insubstantial imitator, a hopeless repeater. She could be easily dispatched, a simple spirit stuck on rejection, married to impossibility. She thus becomes underdeveloped and reduced. Or is it we? As listeners, we too can feel the impossibility and rejection, next to this essence of Echo. In some ways, Echo and Narcissus are two figures who particularly invite reduction. Both are so insubstantial, so desperate for something or someone to "hold" them. We are easily taken in by this kind of energy. Who is who, and where? Echo, being nowhere, everywhere, somehow prevails.

In the psychotherapy process, in discovering and developing their own substantiality, such clients might well require reductive work, that is, a return to the roots of the situation. But that does not mean that psychotherapists have to be reduced to reduction! Helping a client become more substantial does not mean sacrificing an ear for image as the language of the psyche. Even if therapists cannot directly present this "as-if" approach, this inherently psychic reality to their "narcissistic," or "borderline" clients, they can still hold to the "as-if" as background for their own attitudes and style. Reduction is like a set repeat, an automatic playing out. But in following Echo, a resonant kind of repetition and return, image work can resonate, and resonate again.

There is a wealth of psychological material on Narcissus, who seems to capture a spirit of our times. He has impressive medical credentials as one of the few mythological characters to find a place in psychiatric diagnosis. His is the dubious honor of having a full-blown disorder, "Narcissistic Personality Disorder," named after him. In psychiatric literature, Echo is only, if poetically, recurrently, a symptom. She appears as "echo-lalia," "echo-phrasia," "echo-praxia," or "echo-pathy." In the medical model, Echo and Narcissus are linked with symptoms with pathology, with naming what is wrong. In the myth too, there is something wrong: they are doomed to isolation and wasting away.

Narcissus is well known for looking in the mirror. As illustrated in Kohut's term, "mirroring" and in phrases like "the gleam in the mother's eye," Narcissus's images are mostly visual. Narcissus gazes and gazes, falling in love with his own image. In the end, his curse is also visual. He is bound to his own surface shine. We might instead lend an ear to Echo, an auditory figure. The image and experience of "echoing" suggests a profundity of a different sort.

In the Greek myth, "Echo and Narcissus," Echo is a mountain nymph, longing for love. She is Narcissus's counterpart, as he is hers. She is desperately in love with this beautiful young mortal, who loves only his own image. Like Narcissus, Echo too is "disabled" or cursed. While *he* can only gaze at himself, Echo can only echo, only repeat the words of others.

These two mythic partners suggest some tantalizing parallels between seeing and hearing as partner modalities. As our two primary means of reception and expression, seeing and hearing, in our lives as in the myth, do not always make easy partners for each other. But their pairing is a given, a partnership of perception. The qualities that one partner lacks, the other has, sometimes to an extreme degree.

In the consulting room, in the acoustic vessel, therapist and client are also in a process of reverberating, back-and-forth contact, like Echo and Narcissus. Both "couples" are involved in a high energy exchange. And it is, resoundingly, one which centers around desire, as Freud proclaimed. Each partner, client and therapist, is a bit like Narcissus. Each is seeking images of self, seeking a deep and moving connectedness to that place of essential meaning. The work is entered on the client's images and "selfness"; but to keep the projections clear, the therapist's self must also be present as part of the background, and in moments, as foreground, at least to herself.

Each partner, client and therapist, is also a bit like Echo. Each is bound to Echo, bound to echo. The therapist echoes in her search for accuracy and genuineness of contact with the image, the energies, as given. By echoing, she can maintain a vibrant reactivity to the client, to both conscious and unconscious contents. She thus escapes too exclusive an enclosure in the mirror of her own psyche. By echoing, she can stay fresh and mischievous, avoiding illusions of so-called objectivity, of generalized or theoretical ideas which pre-organize hers or her client's perceptions.

A client's bondage to Echo is profound. Like all people, he is performing the natural psychic function of projecting his own unconscious material; but it is in a careful vessel, where things can be tracked and handled. In its auditory dimension, projection means the client is experiencing his own unconscious energy by hearing it as coming from outside of himself. In working with what he hears, as hap-pening in relationship to others, as well as within himself, he can experience aspects of his unconscious. They arrive back in his own ear, as he notes and explores his own reactions. Becoming engaged, indeed often enmeshed, in a constant play, interplay and replay of what is his, and what belongs to others, and what belongs to both, he undergoes processes of identification, overidentification, and disidentification. The discovery of his own essence and boundaries – a core of analytic work – is deeply rooted in a process of echoing vibration. The feeling tone is longing, pondering, demanding. The roots of the word "echo" have to do with "soughing" (Middle English) and "sighing."[94] Indeed, there is denial, frustration, perplexity … and ever more longing.

The nymph Echo seeks Narcissus especially in caves and grottoes, the most evocative acoustic vessels of all. Sometimes, the consulting room echoes like a cave, holding, reverberating with the longing, the dreams, the pain, the search. There is a beauty, a poignancy. Echo and Narcissus are somehow partners, searching for love and life. But they are always failing. It is a sad story, and a common one. Most essentially, they are seekers. Their real essence, as it emerges, lies in their state of being in potential. And like with psychic energy, this potential is rarely fulfilled. Each of them is searching, searching. This situation does not always describe tragedy. Longing is a given of human existence.

Having given this longing its due as an essential part of psychic life, we can ask what is it that takes the story further. What makes for its tragedy? What is it that holds Echo and Narcissus in a doomed position, as "receivers" for each other?

In Ovid's "The Story of Narcissus and Echo," questions of the inherent "togetherness" and "separateness" are handled with profundity and playfulness. A logical, linear standpoint only makes for confusion. When Narcissus, searching for his

---

[94] *Origins: A Short Etymological Dictionary of Modern English*, Eric Partridge, 3rd Ed., London (Routledge & Kegan Paul), 1958, "echo," pp. 175-76.

companion, cries, "Is there anybody nigh?" Echo responds, "I!" Her echo rings out, a response to Narcissus's words. Sounding similar, but becoming a different word, it has slid into an answer: "*I* am nigh!" In feeling terms too, it has slid into another kind of opposite too, an ironic one: Echo's certainty echoes Narcissus's uncertainty. In the myth, after several more exchanges, Narcissus proclaims: "I first will die ere thou shalt take of me thy pleasure!" And Echo's echo rings out, "Take of me thy pleasure!" Again his words have been taken up as hers, this time, exactly, word for word. Yet they have shifted in the air, into something "other." Something tantalizingly opposite to Narcissus's self-absorption has been constellated in this space of echo.

Hearing this echo as a surface communication problem, as if Echo had misunderstood or misused Narcissus's words, is inaccurate. Worse, it diminishes the complex integrity of the echoing space between the two. In this myth, just like in the therapeutic session, this echo has occurred within a world of Metamorphoses. Begun as mere repetition, Echo's echoes, like ours, are full of surprises, and often reveal opposites. Here, just like in the consulting room, echoes reverberate their transformative energies, back and forth, and back again, into the passionate search for inner and outer completeness, into the search for self.

This echoing process in the soul cannot be pinned down. It cannot really be understood rationally except to say that it is always shifting. But it is recognizable as a natural occurrence in the therapeutic process. It expresses the longing in our psyches, the call between our substantial and insubstantial selves. It has to do with the resonant words, ideas, thoughts, and feelings, and the way they are positioned in new and newly familiar ways. It is the call between concreteness and psychic essence; it is a call between inwardness and outerness. It is this quality of longing which holds us to the task, even when, wearied and confused, we cannot figure out a single thing.

The mythical Echo brings a sense of duet to the acoustic space where she and the "other" are heard together. But relationship fails. Echo has not had the chance for psychic definition, for that human crucifixion of being a specific something, yet not quite literally that specific thing. She has not received that curious and torturous gift that relationship with an opposite, or oppositely cursed figure, can offer. Surely it makes sense that Echo's opposite has to be a figure like Narcissus. He is thoroughly graced in self-enclosure. As potential partners, each offers the other something important. But they cannot receive each other. Echo and Narcissus rebound away from each other, like energies held between our own places of desperate emptiness and insubstantiality, like Echo's, and our own places of longing self-enclosure, like Narcissus's.

In the end of the story, like a bad joke, Echo has merely bounced between the polar opposites in her own soul. For in her sad and ironic fate, she does become "substantial" – in a concrete sense. Wasting away with longing for Narcissus, her bones turn to stone. In doing so, she returns to an essence of herself, to her origins as mountain nymph. This is poetic fate; it expresses a poetic logic or a poetic justice. By wasting away into nothing, Echo achieves substantiality, a literalized concreteness, held in stone.

With such a story as background, it is no surprise that receiving echo in therapy is difficult. It is by no means a given that Echo's energy, her longing, her passion and her highly tenacious demands, will be well received. Echoes can be disturbing and tricky. They often carry a confusing mix of chatter and profundity. Indeed, how can Echo be well received? Her essence demands staying in contact with her *as herself,* to be true to Echo as echo. Working with Echo involves helping her resonate to her own essence, her own truth.

It is tricky. Things in Echo's realm are catchy, permeable, back-and-forth. A therapist who is too wary of participatory energy, viewing it as "contamination," might attempt to protect the work from her own countertransference vibrations, rigorously trying to keep the "mirroring" polished and clean. But echoes cannot be relied upon as re-recordings. Highly reactive to varying types of enclosures and vibrations, they function in more complicated ways. The effects of echoes, including the attempts of the therapist to echo "cleanly" and "faithfully," are multiple, contradictory and – truth be told – quite beyond the control of the echo-er.

Echo's story speaks not only of exchange and re-sound-ingness, but also of the uses of verbal speech to speak the truth. In partaking in "the talking cure," we would do well to lend an ear to this aspect of the myth. According to Ovid, Echo, a member of Hera's retinue, has been deprived of normal speech as a punishment for misusing it. She has been chattering and singing in order to distract Hera from noticing Zeus's sexual forays. Echo's speech and song have been deceptive, disloyal to her leader and her group, a feminine one. Psychologically, the insubstantial Echo is at a stage of building of her basic sense of self. It is inauthentic, the wrong timing, and thus a "transgression" (developmentally) to form a liaison with the male "other," Zeus (as it will also be for Echo to connect with Narcissus, another "other").

Again, there is poetic justice in the resulting punishment. Hera's curse is that Echo can henceforth only echo. This limitation makes her, in one way, automatically loyal, in a purely auditory way. But of course, in a deeper way, it is true punishment, for it tortures and defeats Echo's process of becoming more of her true self. She cannot ring true. Since her expression of herself can only come via others' sounds, she is doomed to dependence, tricks, luck. Hera makes Echo unable to express her own truth, in either her own way or at her own initiative. As she repeats the words and sounds of others, the sounds from her own self ring hollow, lingering longingly in the air. How can Echo find herself? Echo poignantly portrays a being who is trying, and trying again, to become more of herself. Repetition reveals a form of loyalty, as Pat Berry points out, an attempt at continuity, at making things "take" or last.[95] Echo's story, psychologically understood, centers around a search for inner loyalty, loyalty to herself, to the truth of her own essence.

Echo's cursedness, her "stuckness" and useless persistence, suggest a pathological echoing. It is not only the parents of small children, but also psychiatric staff, who can be driven to distraction by the "echolalia" of their charges. But the mythic image of echo suggests, even demands, a possibility for resonance in a way that "mindless parroting" does not. A potential exists in echo, a possibility for deepening and perhaps, a shift or change. But as is clear from the myth, whose ears hear, and how, matters a great deal. Ovid's text shows Echo's echoing to be meaningful. In his story, in his language, in his very margins, he creates the kind of listening which discovers the significance in Echo's sounds and words. Therapists must, like Ovid, have "the ears to hear."

*Echo as an Entity*

Many of these illustrations of echo will ring familiar. Echoes, whether consciously recognized as such or not, are some of the most common and evocative interchanges in the consulting room, in the acoustic vessel.

---

[95] Patricia Berry, "Echo's Passion" in *Echo's Subtle Body: Contributions to an Archetypal Psychology*, Dallas TX (Spring Publications), 1982, p. 118.

One of the most familiar echoes is the echo of "possession." The client utters a sound or word or phrase as if it were his own, and suddenly, it sounds inauthentic to his "real self."

Often, it is only in the therapeutic space that this echo can be recognized as not his real substance. He speaks, the words resound in the air, and then, suddenly, he hears it as coming from someone or some place else: his mother, his brother, his childhood priest. Psychologically, the client is over-identified. He has been caught in a rebounding repetition. Until this vibrant moment of hearing his echo, he has been "possessed" by this energy, this sound. In that moment, however, he hears it as echo from someone else. Then, he can step back and realize that he is also different from it. He might even have a fighting chance of recognizing it as "that echo again," in later encounters.

This same type of echo can also occur in different kinds of transference reactions. The therapist may say something, which is then heard by the client as an echo. "That's just what my father always said" the client will accuse, or "You sound just like my mother – that's just her tone of voice!" When a therapist ends up sounding like a certain figure who "haunts" the client, it may or may not be a conscious move. Echo, remember, has a mind of her own. Her tricks remind him that he is "caught" again. Through the graces of Echo, he gets the chance to hear and react, in old and new ways, to these old, old strains.

People also find themselves sounding forth cultural, social and workplace sounds, which echo oddly in a space alien to them. It is as if the person has carried along his own acoustic world intact into the new space. In therapies which emphasize individual development, like Jungian analysis, slang and jargon may have the effect of focusing attention on the person's identification with collective values. They may signal a more "jive" style of understanding, rather than a more complicated and personally resonant standpoint.

Slang may signal a full-blown scenario in progress from the past, occurring in that particular moment in the hour. "Do your thing," "We were bummed out," "He was all fired up," such "period" phrases echo us back to former selves, from down the corridors of the past. They call to us, as we call to them, out of times gone by. Despite their being in the past, the energy in such phrases is vibrant: they are calling from times still ringing in our souls. Since slang is always changing, it is a particularly telling cue. People express a 1950s mindset with the word, "Neat!" And aging Hippie and Beat types sound forth with "groovy!" "bummer," and "Far out!" Voiced in present time, these expressions echo "out of time," from a past still encapsulated around him.

Phrases can echo out of time or place, out of a different culture, out of different geographical areas, as male or female, as old or young, as sacred or profane. Whether predictable or sudden, they echo from an auditory otherness of time and space, sounding forth a rootedness in that other place. Musically, as the client tells his story, session after session, such phrases may recur like an "*idée fixe*," a melody fragment which comes again and again. In extreme form, they can be very fixed indeed; if they sound recurrently, like clockwork, in a certain kind of situation, they approach "*fixation.*"

One important "out of time" period was childhood. Children are especially reactive to rhymes, songs and chants. Childish taunts and nicknames commonly become a leit-motif in the consulting room, echoing experiences from more freshly vulnerable times. For example, one client, a young woman, kept repeating the word "*doof*," meaning "stupid" in German. This recurrent, long-vowel ("oh") sound in "*do-o-of*," while having a certain comic edge, felt troublesome. So I asked her about her experience of this word. She vividly retold two memories of its occurrence. And indeed, its accusation, its power, was still resounding, now coming from her own mouth. Again, as she had before, she voiced and gestured her own impatient and arrogant rejection of her hurt, ashamed and insecure child feelings. This word, this world of "doof," had gone so intensely into her ears that it was still coming, insistently, out of her mouth. She had thoroughly introjected this accusation.

In our interchange, this woman could not seem to hear or react to how her own use of this word was an echo of what had entered her vulnerable ears long ago. She found no back-and-forth responsiveness to its insistent call. She rejected any mention of the insecure, hurt child, blaming only herself, and terminated the work after 15 sessions. She was young, in her early twenties, and had strong, heroic tasks immediately in front of her. Self-accusation, perhaps, helped keep her on her feet, since it seemed, as she stated, that depression, immobility, loomed. Did she have to remain harshly haunted by this word, echoing on, in her own head and also all around her? For the time being, it seemed intent on continuing, rebounding between the rigid walls of her denial, self-accusation and rejection.

The meaning discoverable in an echo might lie in the content of its words or in the sounds themselves: their rhythm, melody, pitch or timbre. Most likely, both sound and content carry the meaning. Meaning might also be tied to its memory field, the memories of significant events and feelings connected with the sound. Much of our auditory fantasy, at least that which is conscious, is based upon musical experience. So an echo commonly arrives in the form of a song, unrelentingly running on and on, in the ear.

Such an echo might be calling back to something reassuring, something which lifts the heart, supports, something necessary to pack up and take along in lightweight, acoustic form. Thus a harried, homesick American living abroad might find the well-known song from primary school, echoing in her mind, tickling her throat to get hummed, and pacing her through the hectic Christmas period:

> Over the river and through the woods
> To Grandmother's house we go.
> The horse knows the way
> To carry the sleigh
> Through the white and drifting sno - ow!

No matter how far the road home, geographically or imaginatively, and no matter what her plans for Christmas, this song suggested that like the horse, her psyche knew the way to keep on that path. It knew the way to a sense of reassurance and "home."

In their connection with unconscious energies, echoes are apt to carry a balancing or compensatory message. Lane Arye in his thesis on "Music the Messenger" describes how a song by Sting, "Sister Moon," popped into his head during a difficult period. He was disturbed at himself for being overcritical. The lines, "You watch every night./You don't care what I do" and "My mistress's eyes are nothing like the sun," helped him to feel the soft acceptance of moon energy, rather than the harsh, sharp energy of the sun. Arye's example also emphasizes the sense of echo as back-and-forth. He described his own singing back. It was an interchange, he said, with the spirit world; he was capturing the spirit of Sister Moon and returning her energy by singing her song back.[96]

An accompanying or visiting echo might as well feel unwelcome to consciousness. Then a sound or phrase becomes rankling. For example, a woman in the grip of a longstanding depression told me of the Walt Disney version

---

[96] Lane Arye, "Music the Messenger," Masters thesis for Antioch University, 1988, p. 22.

of "Zippedy-doo-dah," which pursued her mercilessly for weeks. In talking to her, I could hear and see its after-tones still, as she dramatically shuddered her rejection of "silly" lines like, "My-o-my, what a wonderful day!" and as she cynically rolled her eyes at "Plenty of sunshine coming my way." To her – still – it seemed ridiculous, a cartoon, a flattened, grotesque experience. Of course, Walt Disney renditions have their drawbacks, especially for students of fairy tales. But this much was clear: this light-hearted, zippy energy had been doing what it could to get into this woman's life. Its being "up" compensated her being "down." A less obvious dimension was also important. She seemed to have a strained overcomplexity in her life attitudes. It sounded as if the very simplicity of this song was compensatory. Cheering up, it sang, is easier than you think!

While the message in a song may sometimes be simple, it is not necessary so. We are so used to taking little care with sound, that we readily dismiss songs or melodies after only superficial contact. We may think we "have it" after connecting a song in our heads with the verbal meaning in the first line or with some remembered moment in our past. We are apt to neglect the kind of image work, slower and many-layered, that we would do in working with a visual image. Visually, we would examine the image carefully, discover its exact dimensions, color, texture, and surroundings. In auditory work, it is so easy to ignore the meaning in the sound itself, forgetting to ask what might be suggested in the melodic phrase itself, its pitch range, its intervals, its rhythms, timbres and vowel-sounds.

Indeed, just like the nymph Echo, some echoes are highly persistent, recurring in the session or in sessions, and even over months and years – or lifetimes. Through repetition, the meaning in the ear can suddenly "get through." Or it can shift. The following story illustrates how echo can occur within the confines of one session. A client dreamed that, amidst warnings, she was supposed to go back to a certain area to rejoin her mother and her mother's invalid mother, and bring them food. A burning issue in her life was her trouble saying "no" to her mother's requests for help, even when the request made unreasonable demands upon her.

As we worked with this dream, the word "invalid" began taking on a sense of echo, as if it had a life of its own. It rang oddly, persistently. "Invalid" at first meant "crippled," "unable," and elicited sympathy and care for these mother-figures. But as the word echoed on during the hour, it slipped into the new arena, a college course she was taking on psychological testing. Here, "validity" was a prime word. As "invalid" sounded again and again during the hour, its meaning shifted to her mother-figures being "invalid" in its testing denotation, that is, "not useful" or "not valid." It began meaning that their reliability was low, and they were no longer useful to her life.[97] In pulling her first into the all-too-familial, familiar position of a binding sympathy, this tricky echo suddenly made her hear, at least for a moment, the invalidity of these mother figures in her life.

Whether within the therapeutic hour or afterwards, a rhythm-based or melodic echoing often involves a cool, curious sort of "replay." It is as if the client and/or therapist were puzzling, turning the word or phrase or sound round in ear or mouth or mind, to perceive it more clearly, more deeply. It is an acoustic "rehandling." It invites thought, reflection and sometimes, a startling re-experience.

Echoes are sometimes used in a highly intentional way, the speaker auditorily driving home his or her meaning. Such situations, involving mimic or parody, may be uncom-

---

[97] In order to be auditorily accurate, I should mention that because we were speaking German, this word "invalid" did not change syllabic accent, as it does in English. In German, "invalid" is identically pronounced in both of its meanings.

fortable. A client once echoed my last phrase in a sharp and arrogant tone, adding, "says Dr. Kittelson"! This echo, this auditory caricature of myself, shocked me – in fact, it momentarily shattered me. She was throwing back what she had heard, something that had obviously violated her feelings. After asking her, it became clear to me that, in the midst of doing my inexperienced and over-eager best, I had indeed been explaining something in an ill-timed way. I had been performing my "expert" best, based on theory. Her echo was a highly effective way of communicating that I had been in a state of deafness to her feelings, and defending against their difficulty as well.

Sometimes echoes have a long personal development or history. One colleague who was interested in music told me the "musical history" of two verbal phrases. In her analytic work, she had been working on how incessant her conflicts were, how insoluble everything seemed. Her analyst repeatedly used the phrases, "on the one hand" and "on the other hand." At first, in great frustration, she had echoed them sarcastically back, like in the previous example. This was, as above, echoaic parody. As she continued trying to deal with her conflicts over the months, she described these phrases as taking on a mixture of styles, and even illustrated them. They sounded forth anger (loud, harsh-toned), questioning (halting, lilting), and depression (flat, dull, heavy sounds). Once they sounded in "a hysterical flurry," shrill and panting. She speculated on this being some sort of climax point, like the top of a crescendo. After this, she said she managed to relax more about the level and extent of her conflicts, rather like "musical resolution." Her use of these phrases began having a more singing, swinging sound, and she herself began using them as simply descriptive. She said the following about this acoustic and musical development: "The two-handedness, the two-armedness, had become a holding, and even in the end a comfort, like a lullaby. I felt

I could trust things more because I was not being too one-sided or naive."

A musical ear helps. As this woman noticed, an echoing phrase or sound often has a "musical history." A faster rhythm might be expressing new excitement or involvement; a slower meter and intonations in minor keys, in complex timbres, might express a more complicated or depressed attitude. A rising, piercing tone might express intolerance, flight or strong resistance; or it may express a climax point. It is the auditory qualities of phrases, and especially repeated phrases, that carry – or sing – their messages to us.

*Echo as a Quality*

Echo as a quality refers to the space around a person's words or energy. It is not that something specific is being echoed, but rather that a "sense of echo" is present, one which is its own experience. A client's talk during the session might sound as if he were alone. This basic quality of unrelatedness – to himself and others – might first take the image of too much acoustic space around him. The way that a sense of too much space, too lonely a space, occurs in a person belongs fits naturally and poignantly in the acoustic realm. Less artfully controlled, more "innocently" vibratory, the voice, the song, the silence around a person has a special place. It is resoundingly genuine. A quality of echo, like this lonely, space-filled unrelatedness, might appear as an over-all sense of a person's being and doing in the world. Or it might occur more strongly in relation to specific areas of a client's life, for example, when talking about childhood or a certain relationship. This is valuable information. Tuning to how it occurs, and well as when, is a natural evocation, like a call, to this lonely and unrelated place.

For some clients, there might be a sense of too little echo, too little space. It is as if the speaker were wrapped up in something. He is blocked up, smogged up, "encased" in something too solid or too concrete, too unalive. There are many possible images. In such a non-echo, the sound, the energy, cannot move, cannot move *through* to something or someone else. Earlier we discussed the necessity of some sound, but not too much, in everyday life. This statement is true of echo as well: there must be some, but not too much.

In her essay, "Echo's Passion," Pat Berry offers more images for echo as a quality: "Some things echo empty (like a Pinter play), some things echo overfull (like a heavily symbolic poem), some things echo flat and then big (like melodrama), and some things echo not at all – like jargon, say, or interpretation."[98] There is a rich array of ways that echoes present themselves as meaningful qualities. Focusing on such qualities of echo makes the experience clearer And it invites fantasies, which the therapist can then work with, alone or with the client.

Interpretation, says Berry, echoes not at all. The amount and manner of interpretation during a session vitally affects how much resonance, how much meaningful echo, can occur. What is often understood only as resistance to the therapist or to the content of an interpretation may instead be resistance to the therapist's departure from that space of resonance. The therapist has "abandoned" that acoustically-based experience of being and seeking together. The therapist is speaking or reacting from too separate or non-vibrant a distance, as clearly happened with my "Dr. Kittelson" client. However, interpretation need not always stop echo. If it is handled as if it were an answer that eliminates further seeking, if it stops the "call," then indeed, interpretation echoes not at all. And it must be admitted, interpretation is essentially an effort to "explain." However, its Latin roots simply describe the action of placing (*pretere*) between

[98] Berry, "Echo's Passion," p. 120.

(*inter*). An interpretation can be "placed between" the client and therapist in a less than conclusive, more poetic way that holds the sense of mystery. Then interpretation is basically a new image placed among the existing ones.

The most effective way to keep this sense of call and mystery in interpreting is to remain mindful of the acoustic expression of what is being worked on. The therapist remains auditorily accurate in her re-calling or re-petition, literally echoing, just like Echo. She thus remains loyal, faithful, to the original mystery (or "problem"). And it is, after all, constantly unfolding. Then each new event or interpretation functions like a stanza in a ballad. And the original sound is like a refrain, which is always returned to from an old, but new, angle, as the verses unfold.

Staying with echo takes energy. And it is a different kind from the effort used to formulate and articulate an interpretation. D.W. Winnicott stated that he felt one interpretation per session was satisfactory. Its expression, he said, should be simple and economical. He considered himself very tired and his work not good when he caught himself teaching or using the word "moreover."[99] In my understanding, this high level of energy in staying with echo involves the fact that sometimes it is more difficult *not to express* than *to express.* Speaking, expressing oneself, often involves a natural flow, a release of gathered energy. This echo level instead involves maintaining a state of "poised attention," poised listening. It means holding to a state of emotional and associative accessibility, so important to Freudian and Jungian styles of work, yet letting it shift (sometimes) into new spaces. Echo, says Pat Berry, is what psychological understanding is all about.[100]

[99] D.W. Winnicott, *The Maturational Processes and the Facilitating Environment*, Ed., John D. Sutherland, (The International Psycho-analytic Library, No. 64), London (Hogarth Press and the Institute for Psychoanalysis), 1978, p. 167.

For Jungians, it is not only interpretation which can shut off echo. It is also the Jungian process of amplification, which brings in collective associations. Amplification, when used well, is meant to echo more, or more largely, bringing in, as it does, layers of cultural and human context. Yet if done in a flat, closing-off way, its effect may be deadening. How to hold the echo, the back-and-forth, resonant energy, is a multi-faceted and highly individual matter.

It is a helpful image to think of the therapist as a musical instrument, with a resonant body and strings which are both relaxed and taut – tunable. By means of a balance between essential energies, she and her client work within the sensory and psychic experience of echo. Through music, through the music of echo and return, they stay alive to the calling, the shifting, and the longing so evocatively imaged in the Echo and Narcissus myth.

*Echo as a Symptom*

In her sixteenth month of analysis, a woman developed an echo in her right ear. At certain times, especially under psychological or social strain, her right ear would begin to echo what she herself was saying. Functionally, this was primarily a symptom of echo as a quality, since it was not what she was saying, so much as the experience of herself echoing which mattered. Experientially, it was a bit like an entity, in that she experienced it as arriving and departing, albeit uninvited. She talked to it. And as you might guess, it reliably talked back.

This echo was upsetting to her, and she tried in many ways to make it go away. Yet it recurred sporadically over the next 2 1/2 years. At first, she would become so nervous at its appearance that she could hardly bear to continue speaking, and would stop when circumstances permitted. She was

[100] Berry, "Echo's Passion," p. 12.

bothered by how strange this symptom was, and also by the way it interfered with her communications. But most troubling was the way it sounded in her ear. It sounded "not firm," "weak," and she expressed great upset to think that people would not want to listen to her because she sounded like that. Other people's responses were of vital importance to her. This echo functioned to turn this woman into her own audience: she *literally* became her own auditory witness. Her own ears, her own listening became filled with her own sounding self. For once, it was not primarily others' response which mattered.

In the hour following our first discussion of this echo, this woman reported that she had begun to talk to "it," her echo. "Active imagination," or dialog with an inner figure, was not a regular activity for her, and this conversation was her own idea. "What do you say?" I asked. There was a seemingly confused and embarrassed pause. "I tell it that we know it is shaky now, and insecure, and that that is okay now," she replied rather hesitantly. It was a new, shy relationship. The disturbing quality in this echo had evoked in her the wish to relate to it, to reach to it and care for it. She and her echo had become reassuringly involved with each other. Her reassurance to it was a reassurance to herself – even more so than usual in intrapsychic work! In the most literal sense, she heard it as coming back to her, back into her own ear.

In its revisitations, this echo symptom evoked various degrees of disturbance and curiosity in this woman. She was forced to hear the insubstantiality in herself, both intrapsychically and in relationship to others. This was a focal point in our work. Her right ear was making her hear and re-hear, insistently, an essential shakiness in herself. As a psychic partner, this echo suffered a blow when a medical doctor labeled it and explained it somatically (a result of too little fluid in the ear). It fled the analytic scene for several months. But then it returned. You can't keep a good symptom down!

This woman's consistent observation was that her echo seemed to occur when she was most engaged in "giving herself away." To her, this phrase meant losing the sense of her own reality in order to feel in contact with others or please them. The main function of this echo did indeed seem to be to fill her up with more of herself, with her own sound. It returned her to herself, to more of her own essence. This echo stopped in relation to no clear event around the end of her analysis. She had done considerable work on both her father and mother complexes, on transference issues, on work issues and on her relationship to her lover. Generally speaking, she had gained a more consolidated sense of herself.

### Retro-hearing

Finally, as a last appearance, Echo can present herself as "retro-hearing." Retro-hearing, like retro-spection, is an aspect of reflection, an essential part of the psychotherapeutic process. In therapy, it usually pertains to one important moment within the hour. This moment re-echoes, re-sounds in the ear or head. Imaginatively, it re-enters the very bones, organs and cavities of one's being. Perhaps the middle ear bones even move again, as they do in dreaming! Meanings may shift, becoming more distinct; or perhaps they become vaguer, or more mysterious. The moment may sound broader, narrower, or odder; or sometimes, it may suddenly sound familiar. Retro-hearing may be an experience of re-wonder, an attempt to deal with the impact of a moment. It may as well be a new hearing, a shift in how something is heard.

Retro-hearing makes a moment in a previous therapeutic hour find a new accent. Something may remain provocatively "sticking out." Or it may echo oddly in time. There in the privacy of one's own life, without the time and relational demands of the face-to-face hour, defenses are lower. In freely floating and relaxed moments like taking a walk, doing housework, feeding the birds, intentional thinking wanders away. Concentration is let down, and associative and emotional energies flow. Something new, or newly important, can slip into a new, or newly felt, place, and begin to wend its way into the inner ear.

Sometimes retro-hearing is an experience of what has been missed. "Oh, no," the therapist exclaims the next day to the vacuum cleaner. "I should have done this or that," she finds herself lamenting, staring at the odd-angle reflections in chrome facets of the faucet. Such moments can tempt the therapist into an attitude of rejecting the work she has done. To miss things is common, and indeed, it is sometimes lamentable. But such a self-rebuke might itself be missing something, occurring as it does outside the vibratory reality of the hour. It is a later awareness, a layer of the work occurring outside of direct relational field between the client and/or therapist.

The question is what it means, what sort of vibratory or musical reality accounts for the fact that this "connection" did not occur. Retro-hearing should not be assumed to correct a situation, but to add a layer to it. A self-rebuke which is too ready or too simple is an abandonment of the resonance of the space in which the moment took place. Would the client have been ready? Was the psychic material itself ready, formed enough, "safe" enough? Especially in a professional role, it is easy to identify with being the knower, to defend against the many difficulties of not knowing inherent in the job of psychotherapist, or anyone working with the soul. It is easy to get pushy and, in a way, *too clear*, outside of the resonance of the field in which the therapist and client were interacting. There is a truth to tell. But there is also the truth of the resonance. And that is the truth that is *telling* to the client's search for relationship to self.

There considerable interactional pressures in the face-to-face mode. There is as well an analytic or professional persona to maintain, at least in most moments. It is perhaps no coincidence that Jungians, and not Freudians, have given so much attention to a term like "persona." The word's roots have a direct bearing on audition, coming as they do from the Latin words, *sonare* and *per*, meaning "to sound" and "through." Originally used to describe a theater mask, this word suggests that the dramatic or experiential message – the speaking or telling energy in an event – is sounded through a set mask, covering the real human face. Persona allows the maintenance of an atmosphere in which the client can project unconscious qualities onto the therapist, so that they will eventually come to consciousness. And it also shields the client from the therapist's reactions, which might well be odd-appearing. After all, the depth psychologist's ear is usually tuned to a more unconscious level.

Hearing things later, in a protected and separate time and space, has a function similar to sounding through a persona or mask. Both provide as space to float in or be protected in, out of the more concentrated and hardline focus of visual contact and direct interpersonal exchange. Often it is only later, out of the hour itself, that something can clarify or deepen. Many previous examples which describe the process of realizing auditory-based meanings naturally involve retro-hearing.

Retro-hearing is, in one way, an acoustic "overtime" for the therapist, and must be reckoned with in assessing her workload. It is one reason why most therapists cannot work 40 client hours per week. Retro-hearing not only clarifies the past, but helps gather incentive and formulate new ideas for working with a client. It fantasizes the therapeutic process onward.

## D. Simultaneity And Flow

*The ear is the organ particularly capable of perceiving the dynamic quality of external events.*

Zuckerkandl, *Sound and Symbol,* p. 63

In the therapeutic hour, words, images, sounds, ideas, feelings flow along in a simultaneity of levels. It is impossible to understand such activity using rational modes of mental functioning, at least without distortion. Like psychic energy, auditory energy flows in a multi-leveled way. Linear rationality finds it overwhelming, and seeks to reduce it. In terms of conscious processes, it cannot be stopped, except artificially. How can we – how *do* we – deal with this simultaneity and flow in the therapeutic process?

Trying to understand something in the midst of an ongoing, many-leveled energy is a basic and common experience. The world we live in is in a state of constant flux. But following the flow is especially important in the therapy process. It is vital because accompaniment matters so much, to maintain a vessel, as well as to help in healing. Accompaniment during discovery or change, or even knowing that someone is along when things don't change, are often central, necessary experiences.

In the therapeutic process, it is of the essence to stop the flow at certain moments. There are many reasons. It may be to do a "re-take" in order to bring more clarity, or to re-experience something more deeply. It may be to say "no!" – or "yes!" – to something. Most generally, it is to focus, to shift perspective, to deepen understanding and reflection by making a little more space and time. However, most of the therapeutic hour is spent within the experience of the ongoing and shifting layers which characterize psychic life and human interaction. We are subject to this simultaneity and flow before any formal "analysis," before we can begin to separate anything out. "Undergoing" (motion) *precedes* "understanding" (stasis, standpoint).

Acoustic images form a natural way of working with the flow while staying within it, just as we do in listening to music. There is something static about using vision. It is so usual, and indeed, so central to culture and civilization, to take a visual moment out, to draw or paint it, photograph it, to freeze it, so to speak. A visual scene, when in motion, can usually be made into a still shot and still be meaningful – even if the focus might be different.

This sense of energy flow is, after all, an essential component to any sound. An acoustic image has a duration: it takes a set amount of time. It stays in time, even if re-created. Sound is not amenable to being prolonged or stopped. A change it its duration will usually alter its meaning radically. Prolonging the duration of a sneeze, say, to three minutes makes it a totally different auditory experience. Shifting a long high "C" to a duration of a quarter of a second shifts its meaning completely. Granted, a sound at a certain duration can move forward or backward to *another time frame* in imagination: it can be anticipated (forward in time) or remembered (backward in time). But it is still experienced as taking its own time. The sense of inherent flow in most sounds matches the ongoing quality of psychic life. Things flow along, but always shifting.

A many-leveled perception is intrinsic to depth work. Acoustic work means hearing a simultaneity of tones sounding on different levels, higher or lower. As already described, any single tone already has a sounding simultaneity of overtones, registered unconsciously as aspects of timbre. But even beyond overtones, a great deal is happening auditorily which is not registered consciously, but nonetheless subliminally, in the brain. What listeners select to hear from the myriad of possibilities, on both a conscious and unconscious level, are the sounds that we "have an ear for."

And that consists of two parts: what our auditory system is capable of hearing via the selective hearing process (ear to cortex), and our own psychic and physical state. Both sensory and psychic "organs" guide the process. As this kind of selective hearing is occurring, however, we also react – with little or no consciousness – to conductive hearing events, received by direct vibration through bones and skin.

This is already many-leveled enough! But things are still more complex in the realm of inner life, imagination. There is also imaginal sound, sound in dreams or fantasies or hallucinations. We now know that these inner sounds, for example, in dreams, produce somatic reactions, namely, Rapid Eye Movement during dreaming. A little known fact is that spontaneous middle ear activity also takes place during REM (Rapid Eye Movement) or dream sleep.[101] Eastern cultures have explored such matters much more thoroughly than Western cultures. Hearing is closely suited, by its very nature, to the moving and level-shifting nature of psychic experience. It offers meaning and image, not only in the ways that it can be shared between people, but also between a people and their outer and inner worlds.

The therapist can learn to sensitize herself to the client's voice as meaningful in its own layers and flow. A voice occurs from out of a quality of silence and within a field of resonance. As well, it moves through other sounds, rather like the brass or woodwind sections coming in and out during an orchestra piece. Hearing simultaneity and flow means hearing things, basically, as a "musical experience." A voice moves in linear fashion, horizontally metered, meshing and loosening within itself and among other sounds and silences. There are patterns, waves, forays out and about.

---

[101] Lawrence Kolb, M.D. and H. Keith H. Brodie, M.D., *Modern Clinical Psychiatry*, 10th Ed., Philadelphia PA (W.B. Saunders Company), 1982, p. 41.

There are echoes and returns, expressed by the client's various sounds and silences.

The client's voice is like a "main melody" among other acoustic events within the therapy hour. But the voice is only part of the auditory field. It is vital to maintain a sense of the "surrounds" of a voice, even as it is focused upon. Good listeners keep their ears open to the background, to the "underground" and to the overtones, as well as the main theme. The client's voice is part of the larger acoustic field. It wends its way through an auditory field made of various sounds only peripherally registered: the traffic outside, the rain pattering, the clock ticking, the heater coming on and off, the rustle of clothes and objects, etc.

The therapist's voice, her own vocal expressions and silences, also enter the acoustic field, in moments which are emerging from her own field of energy and her body. As already mentioned, it is very difficult to hear one's own voice with any accuracy. In the psychotherapeutic process, the therapist's voice is important. Like the client's, the therapist's voice creates images, as an energy coming around at the client. All of these acoustic elements around and within the vessel mingle with each other. Some become a background or animating environment. Others literally grab for attention as dramatic or synchronistic events. They may support, detract from, emphasize or comment on the client's voice and whatever is being "talked about" in the room. It is all of these acoustic aspects together which make up this flow, creating a layered simultaneity of energy and, potentially, of meaning.

Opening up awareness to the client's voice as a many-layered flow is full of potential for doing image work. As we have already heard, auditory fantasies in the area of the voice is rich – and often unexplored – territory. It is not uncommon for a voice to evoke different fantasies, at almost the same moment, some of which are fascinatingly incon-

gruent. In psychic terms, they may suggest ways that the
personality moves between its differences and opposites,
whether they rub up against each other, or swing between.
As images, they may present ideas for relationships between
the energies, and sometimes, for a balance of opposites.

Sometimes a client's voice carries the main energy as he
moves in and out of identifying with an inner figure. His
voice suddenly becomes that of an inner child, or an inner
tyrant, or his introjected mother. A voice can also be said to
carry a complex, that is, to occur when complex energy has
taken over. The victim voice pops in, suddenly having more
pauses and melody, the pitches swooping down. There is
often a certain progression, the child-lilt, the critic, the
growly bear, the public relations expert, the clown. Clients,
as well as therapists, can learn to hear this in their own
voices. One woman client used move reliably from her
normal adult voice at the beginning of a session, to a
childish lilting sad voice, and then right into an angry
outraged voice. As she herself began to offer, it sounded just
like her mother's voice. The child and mother were a pair,
a set pair, inside her as they had been without, to her ear. It
was when she began to hear the movement between this sad
child and rageful mother within herself, and not only a part
of her past, that serious work began. Her own attitudes and
structures, her own complexes, became real.

Using auditory images in concentrating on a client's
ongoing voice is an important way to receive the client. After
all, he is actually sending sounds, as well as silences, directly
into the vessel and "at" the therapist. It is a direct and
obvious pathway of energy. Sometimes, depth of auditory
imagination, going down into the layers of auditory fantasy,
is called for. Actually, it is unnatural, a stiffening and
flattening response, to hear someone's voice as only a thin
and isolated "melody." In normal speech, the voice sounds
forth in a flow of tension and relaxation. It moves in patterns

of climax-seeking, climax and resolution. Each aspect of a voice, its volume, pitch, fullness and timbre, evokes the listener's vibratory response. And as one listens in this acoustically imaginative way, more fantasies will probably emerge. But it is necessary to discover ways to give space – in time and within oneself – to this process.

This experience of simultaneity and flow is complicated to describe, in part because it can happen in so many ways. Auditory experiences, mulled over, are rather like what happens upon listening to one note, uniform and continuous, sounded on the harmonium for several minutes. Over time, all of the overtones of themselves successively emerge into full distinctness.[102] That is one image for a kind of auditory and psychic imagination process. But the ear must first be open to the possibility of auditory-based fantasy. It must be interested and trained to listen in an acoustically imaginative way.

In working with a client's voice as a many-layered flow of sound and silence, I recorded my perceptions and resulting fantasies and interpretations, most of which centered in sound. Many were "retro-heard," in response to the last twenty minutes of one session during the first month of work with this client. This woman was extremely intent upon telling her stories. Energy ran high. It was obviously important that I be responsive. She seemed to be asking mostly for nods, smiles, a kind of fixed affirmation which she was energetically and strategically orchestrating. Thus it was a good opportunity for this sort of "exercise." It left me a good deal of space within which to listen to her sounds and catch my own reactions.

[102] Ernest Mach, *The Analysis of Sensations and the Relations of the Physical to the Psychical*, C.M. Williams, Trans. for the 1st Ed. in German, Rev. and Supplemented for the 5th German Ed. by Sydney Waterlow, M.A., New York (Dover), 1959, p. 285.

I was listening to her childhood stories, which centered around the experience of being left alone in the evenings as a small child. Her words, I felt, were greatly minimizing the neglectfulness in her family. Although partly tuned into the content of the story, I began musing on how her voice sounded more important than the content of her words. Ringing high and clear, her voice cut a definite path. I heard her motivation as strong, and her directness precise, in terms of where she wanted to "take" me. The intonation patterns in her voice sounded melodic, with considerable movement and slide, expressing a stimulating amount of liveliness. Yet as I sought more focus, I realized that I was hearing her story as somehow practiced. No, "drilled." It was like a tight performance that had to be expressed in a certain way. Perhaps she had tried to hear and feel this story many times before. Perhaps this telling had occurred mostly within herself, or perhaps she had told it to others before. This sense of being "practiced" made me feel more clearly that her manner of telling stories was aimed more at holding my attention than it was at getting to what was truly inside of her.

In reflecting on moments like these, I realize that it was the auditory mode which kept me in close accompaniment with this woman. If a client is too practiced or too entertainment-oriented, the effect can be unreal, and attention wanders away from the unimportant. Or the effect can be irritating, since the therapist feels manipulated. This auditory mode kept me close to this woman's voice, held me to the phenomenon itself, occurring as it was, in the moment. This listening was my way of not becoming too separate ("viewing" her problems), but still perceiving it clearly, responsively. I was not the simple object of her voice, nor was her voice a simple object to me. I was held close to the necessity, the need, the drive in her voice.

As her voice continued, it sounded fairly steady in volume. There was an ongoing sense of its being carefully controlled. Its considerable energy sounded in the liveliness of her vocal pace, which was metered in a regular and ongoing way. Its timbre darkened slightly when she slowed and moved toward pauses. In such moments, and also in longer moments intermittently, she sounded less performance-oriented. Over all, her "song" felt natural, somehow humanly reactive, "conceivable," I thought, as I swung in and out of experience and reflection. But I could hear how pressured, how compelled she was, to tell her story in this way and no other.

As you can hear, I was moving in and out of auditory focus. Now, in moments, I began hearing something a bit eerie. It rang out only at certain moments. It was in the timbre, I slowly realized. Her voice had somehow a haunting quality at times, something hollow to it. I fantasized some sort of ephemeral being, like an "auditory ghost," wafting in and out of earshot. Next to this image, I had another strong sense: her voice sounded hauntingly lonely. It was as if it were seeking roundedness, fullness. I then felt how strongly she was filling my ears with her sound. And this was indeed what she was doing, non-stop, and with considerable energy.

In listening on, in and out of auditory focus, I found that I was not yet finished with the timbre of this woman's voice. To my ear, it was its most striking, and also most complicated aspect. It was especially curious next to the incongruence of its images. In general, her presentation was "happy," with bouncy gestures and cheerful facial expression. But as I focused further on the exact quality of this timbre, its edges, its *edginess* began to sound more and more. It became difficult to listen to. This thin, sharp quality seemed to be taking up a great deal of her energy. It was as if her energy were centering in on and sharpening, honing, this thin and cutting edge. I had the fantasy that it was draining her solidity, keeping her from sounding like a powerful person with a full shape.

This was disturbing. And so was my sense of boundariless-ness. For this sharpening was indeed just what I was doing at this moment, as I honed in on its edge. Who was who? But in asking, I became clearer to myself. I had stepped back, and now noticed how curious this reaction of mine made me about this edge. Then the discomfort returned, full force. I will return to this feeling shortly.

But here I pause to reflect upon the considerable poten-tial in this acoustic work. Listening carefully, imaginatively, seeking for the layers, and going in and out of the flow, I was poised in the space vibrating between us. Here, I could gather many ideas. Once I had caught them, I still had the task of checking if and how they might be accurate. And of course, I had the task of following them in their further directions. But this listening was to me as rich as any dream. It was full of ambiance, rhythms, and images.

What I felt in particular was that I had made contact with a deep level of this woman's loneliness, an essential quality of her personality which manifested especially in the haunt-ing tones and cutting edge. It seemed that this was percepti-ble in large part only through her voice. As is often the case, it was *not* present in her facial expression or gestures. However, her stories, which sounded disconnected from emotion, did include some mention of loneliness, at least in her childhood. But without these vocal characteristics, it was by no means *palpable* in the experience of listening to her story. This client's haunting quality and cutting edge were far from consciousness. Clarity for me was only slowly emerging. Indeed, as it turned out, a good deal of time in therapy was required before any real work on these areas was possible. Yet hearing, reacting to such auditory and psychic manifestations, means that the therapist can tune into and perhaps maintain contact with important energies in a way that invites their emergence. It is an inviting perceptivity.

In my approach, I was, in Theodor Reik's language, "listening with the third ear." That is, I was utilizing the analyst's emerging unconscious processes as having something to do with the client's unconscious processes. However, I was using an important Jungian idea, the discipline of returning to the image. I did not allow my fantasy to wander far from the original sound, which was the image. The actual auditory image was held in my mind's ear, as I explored in the depths and breadth of where it took me.

Making such perceptions conscious is especially important for clients who are seriously out of touch with their personal world and their emotions. For this woman, it seemed to be the aloneness of her remembered childhood and also her unresponsiveness to her real feelings, which was like her leaving herself all alone. At this early stage of the work, it was unclear how much was my fantasy only and how much was syntonic, or similar to her psychic experience. As I have been stressing, auditory work, by its very vibratory nature, involves the partners in boundary issues. Later in the work, it became clear that this woman's loneliness and the neglected child inside of her were indeed at the center of our work, as was her desperate need for response from others. In terms of content, she addressed these issues rarely, and in a way which was cut off from her emotions. However, she continued expressing them freely and unconsciously in her auditory presentation.

Only toward the end of our 50 months of work together did this "cutting edge" come clearly into the foreground. It involved her aggressions and separating energies. These themes were present in varying ways, and at various levels, repeated, reinforced and extended in dream work, relationship issues, drawings, sculptures, fantasies, and transference/countertransference work. The need to be edgy, to yell at her father, to say "no" to friends and lovers, to be alone despite its being sometimes miserable and uncomfortable, the urge to cut a career path in the world, all these issues were where this edge, this edginess, began to become real to her. This edge was indeed an important image.

This particular piece of work involved the sound of a client's voice as "solo," as an acoustic, vocal flow. I have emphasized sensitive reception by the therapist. Often, all a client is really seeking is an attentive listening to this solo-level. This simple, yet intense desire can present frustrations to a therapist who wants to begin exploring the depths *immediately*! Good listening, including to oneself, takes humility and a tolerance of confusion and ambiguity. And it takes time. Often, a client is attempting what amounts to a "virgin" hearing of himself. If he has been able to hear himself in a new way, or a deeper way, if he has heard something better, this experience might be what has been sought, in and of itself. It can be interference, static – or even violation – to do anything more than help contain the experience and listen. It might even be destructive to change or modulate any of the sounds, and even to echo. Sometimes, this simple state of uninterrupted receptivity of flow is what is needed.

It should be realized that many people are sensitive about their voices. The voice is closely connected with unconscious contents. The therapist might sense the possibility of doing some further work with a vocal auditory image. In respecting the client's defenses, especially about his voice, it is important to approach things carefully. The therapist might reason that the client's immediate "solo" voice, with its more obvious qualities, would be a safe place to start. However, people are surprisingly unconscious of the major qualities of their voices – even of such basic characteristics as volume level or pitch. And after all, we are not apt to hear our voices very accurately. Not only do we have poor listening habits and little training. The reason is also acoustic. We hear our own voices from inside of our bodies, so to our own ears, they sound louder and lower in pitch. Over all, working with a person's voice as an auditory image is very different from visual work. It is experienced as coming so immediately from the body, so vibrantly in the moment. And in its close links to the unconscious, it can sound so surprising, and so strange.

Deciding which elements or levels of a person's voice to work with usually takes care of itself. It is often the odd and surprising vocal happenings which fascinate. When speaking during the therapy session, the client is apt to be concentrating on his "solo" level, and thus be deaf to deeper and more distanced layers. But he might lend an ear to them, if only briefly, as an engaging "musical" offering from the therapist. In the listening process, the therapist hears some auditory element as "intriguing" – perhaps a certain rhythm, or an over-full quality to the voice, or some quality in the timbre. In trying deepen and clarify the acoustic experience, it is useful to try going in and out of auditory focus, as I described doing in the previous example. The emerging element might be a rhythm of throat-clearing or breathing, a segment of an intonation pattern, or a distinct accent in a word or phrase. It might involve some non-vocal element, something occurring next to body movements, or even objects in the room.

Whatever intriguing aspect has been "constellated," or called to notice, could be maximized to increase experiential intensity and increase consciousness. A soft tone could be made softer, a raspy tone raspier, a breath still breathier, a high tone still higher, etc. It can also be "amplified" to its opposite, that is a soft sound made loud, a low-pitched growl made high-pitched.[103] It is a strange process at first, for we are not used to working with sound, unless perhaps musically. To invite this kind or work/play and to loosen things up, the therapist might well have to lead in the repetition and amplification of sounds, like an "acoustic modeller." However, it seems to be important for the client to make his sounds again himself. This returns the auditory energy directly to him so that he can feel himself as its source and/or instrument.

Often a childlike playfulness will occur in doing auditory work. This is a liberating energy which helps the partners move into a sense of more freedom and self-expression, while at the same time, opening up the associative process. However, such a process could slip into a distancing mimic or even taunt, as it often does in childhood. It should be remembered that much of the work is apt to involve the darker, more unconscious shadow aspects of the personality.

What about the previous case example of this woman's voice and its most interesting auditory element, its "cutting edge"? We could have worked with making this client's voice more cutting – sharper, thinner. We could have tried having her make her voice softer and fuller, to provide a defining contrast. This would have been closer to her ego-based presentation of herself and more acceptable to her, offering more ego support. Perhaps encouraging auxiliary qualities, like making her sound louder or clearer, or higher or lower, might have been interesting. Asking for and exploring accompanying memories and images (auditory, visual and kinesthetic) might have helped round things out.[104] However, working with this cutting quality would not have been indicated. Our vessel was too new. This cutting edge, the most intriguing element for me, was too far from, and probably in too much conflict with, her conscious state. An approach which is too quick will "orchestrate" superficial or

[103] Arye, Seminar, "Working with Music and Sound," Nov. 19, 1988; also, Dee Bass, Seminar, "The Body in Psychology," July 20-23, 1987, Zurich.
[104] Ibid.

numbed reactions in the places which are actually in the most need of attention. Authentic contact, even when it is at a more superficial or more accessible level, gives the client the chance to discover where his own authenticity lies. Then the client can himself learn to trust the step-by-step, layered richness of the psyche and its images.

Auditory fantasy can range wide, lured by its expanding and many-layered nature. In my listening process with this woman, I also recorded some broader fantasies. In one, I was fantasizing a cavity, an empty psychic space, surrounding her sound. It was a vibratory void. I especially heard a void of tenor and bass level, like an absence of "grounding." In its deepest tones, lower than any bass tone and heard only as the loosest of vibration, rumbled a darkly solemn throbbing, a sound of basic mistrust. These auditory images seem much more generalized than the others. Indeed, they range a good distance from the first layer of images I heard. Perhaps in Jungian terms, such auditory fantasy material could have to do with the collective and archetypal levels.

Psychic energy, like a rich, musical piece, strikes and enters the ear in a moving simultaneity of levels. Phrases and statements, like returning musical motifs, vibrate out more clearly with each hearing. It is just like in music, when a listener begins to "understand" a piece of music as she re-listens and retro-hears it in her head. It takes patience and time, as well as willingness and training, to hear the psyche well. And this is especially so in hearing the enriching subtle and furtive tones. Many emerge and become distinct only upon re-hearing.

# 3. Around Sound

## A. Hearing What is Not Said

> *Since my phone still ain't ringin'*
> *I assume it still ain't you.*
>
> Dwight Yokum, "Is It Over (still)?"
> (*Buenas Noches* album)

Depth communication is as much about what is *not* said, as about what is said. The contents of the unconscious take shape in images, with their layers and reverberations. They communicate in the margins, the spaces, the resonances, the silence. As Theodor Reik says, "In psychoanalysis … what is spoken is not the most important thing. It appears to us more important to recognize what speech conceals and what silence reveals. It is that feeling that 'there was more in that remark than met the ear.' "[105]

This hearing is sometimes experienced as magical. The client is, naturally, unconscious of what his own unconscious is expressing. It is exactly the depth psychotherapist's job to help in this task. However, picking up unconscious messages is also simply part of the human communication process. We are social animals, hardwired and socialized to pick up

[105] Theodor Reik, *Listening with the Third Ear*, New York (Farrar, Strauss and Giroux), 1948 and 1975, p. 126.

cues of all kinds. Understanding unconscious meanings involves listening for indirect information of all kinds. It means including incongruities in what is understood. And it involves associative links. To the trained person, this type of listening is far less magical than it can seem.

This more indirect approach to communication has been explored from many angles, for example, as intuition, as empathy, as the unconscious level of language, as connections to the realms of myth, symbol, archetype and image. This section explores how material which is almost or approximately expressed, or verbally unexpressed ties up with auditory experience.

It is of vital importance to state outright, from the start, that when one person hears something which has not been said, it does not always describe unconscious messages from the speaker. Rather, it might describe what is present in the ear of the listener, that is, what the listener has "inserted" from her own world. In therapy, the partners are then said to have a "*dystonic*" or "discordant" experience. The client's standpoint is not being shared. The psychotherapist has not heard the material, and each person remains in a separate world. Good listening involves *syntonic* perception. The therapist picks up indirect cues as well as direct ones, asking, checking, and weaving back, in order to clarify and include the unconscious energy the client is in. However, these terms are relative. A case can be made for "dystonic" experience never being purely dystonic, and as well, for "syntonic" experience never being purely syntonic. The partners are operating in a shared field, rather like shared air. They are never purely separate; rather, they are relatively separate. Further, they share the collective and archetypal levels, which are always present. "Syntonic" really means "syntonic enough to be useful."

There are many ways to pick up this subterranean level of hearing. Sometimes we hear it because it is defined by its being missing. Its very lack has created what seems like a void-shaped "entity"[106] in the acoustic vessel. This void, the not-talking-about-X, has itself become an area, defined by its absence. If, for example, a client acts as if his brother simply did not exist, and never did, a "brother-shaped" void comes into being. An unexpressed awareness is present because of its not being expressed. It is "telling" because it is not telling anything.

A topic might also become defined or important through picking up a field of sensed resistance around it. There might be a pulsing-against, a resisting resonance, in the sound and feel of the words and pauses which have to do with a particular subject or area. Perhaps it is nameable to the client. It may even have been spoken aloud at some point: "my father," "jealousy" or "being gay." It is as if the words or sounds were treading nervously, furtively, around this topic. Painstaking avoidance defines it, draws attention to it. A peculiarly distinct silence makes audible the weight of the client's resistance. Such moments are a strong experience, for client and therapist alike. It is as if the thought that was pushed aside demands attention and expression or it will impose silence or interfere with every other train of thought. Reik told of one woman analysand who, after one such disturbing silence, finally declared, "Let's be silent about something else!"[107]

---

[106] A somewhat similar visual image is the "white" or "blank shadow" described by M. Gallard; it, however, describes an area that cannot be defined since it is not definite enough to be repressed. While its influence is significant, it can only be discovered by working on the parents' unconscious or collective cultural experience. White or blank shadow in this sense concerns massive trauma, as in war or political persecution (Martine Drahon Gallard, "Black Shadow – White Shadow," transl. by Paula Kondrick, in *The Archetype of Shadow in a Split World,* Proceedings of the Tenth International Congress for Analytical Psychology, Berlin, 1986, Mary Ann Mattoon, Ed., Zurich  Daimon Verlag, 1987, pp. 199-213.).

[107] Reik, *Third Ear*, p. 124.

At times what is not said is *almost* said. To the careful listener, by a process of associative and/or logical extension, words are heard to stretch farther, to become more intense than their usual meanings. The listener registers their resonance, beyond their literal meaning. "I like her," said stiffly, surrounded by a panicky resonance, slides forward to a heard "Oh, I am desperately in love with her!" A field of anxious excitement reverberates out from the emotional core of such a statement. Or sometimes sentences or phrases, especially emphatic ones, are heard to slide into their opposite. "Methinks the lady doth protest too much," is much quoted from the master listener and psychologist, William Shakespeare. What sounds in the ear is this unstated opposite, yet this shared ground – the poison (and the healing), the love (and the power struggle), the great gains (and the great losses). A statement or word or sound bounces off and returns, transformed, into its partner-opposite.

It is striking how, and how often, people, in and out of the therapeutic hour, seem to state the opposite of what they meant to express. As Jung described, the flow between opposites is a basic activity of the psyche. An avowal of "I am finally cured now" can ring more like, "I am in more and more trouble." "I need to 'introvert'" can throb out a message more like, "How I long for a friend, a lover!" The depth therapist is in the role of hearing the opposite. In Jungian thought, this is so by the very fact of working with the unconscious, whose role is to compensate or balance.

Transference and countertransference work also provides an opportunity to notice energy which is not directly expressed. For the therapist, this means not only noting keeping an open ear for the client's assumptions, but sorting through her own responses as countertransference. "The analytic response," said Reik, "is … the emotional and intellectual reply to the speech, behavior, and appearance of the patient, and includes awareness of the inner voices of the analyst."[108] The subjective aspect is always present; therapists are working every moment with a combination, an interweaving, of their clients' and their own responses. The therapist considers how much her own reactions have possibly been "transferred over," at least in part, from the client, because of the shared field. This process can go on whether transference issues are addressed directly or not.

Reik's book, *Listening with the Third Ear,* essentially focuses on the psychoanalyst's process of listening to what is happening inside of himself as related to the client's unconscious material. Reik explores his own responses to his own inner and mostly auditory events as they relate to the analysand's psychic life. What he hears inside and how he associates to it might illustrate aspects of the client's life. Reik mostly reports hearing theater scenes, speeches and musical pieces. These inner auditory events, he says, involve a deep level of reverberation, one that non-focused and participatory listening evoke. Reik illustrates with case and life examples how, from such initial vibratory diffuseness between two people, a specific auditory image can be coaxed into consciousness and increase understanding. Many of his examples are musical, like operatic passages, which played in his head, lead him to emphasize a certain theme or mood. Indeed, Reik's ear is highly musical; another book of his is entitled *The Haunting Melody: Psychoanalytic Experiences in Life and Music.*

So in mostly musical terms, Reik too is suggesting that the therapist use herself as a sounding board, registering within herself first, through listening to her own reactions and images. She will go on to check the accuracy of this information-from-the-inside, sometimes indirectly and sometimes with direct questions. It is necessary not only to gauge its

[108] Ibid., p. 269.

correctness, but also to understand more about the client's readiness to receive and process it. If it is timely, in "Takt," if she can discover a fitting key, a matching rhythm, she can "play back" what she has heard, sound him out, and then listen to what happens next. She might decide to communicate directly something she heard, or mention it in somewhat modified form. She might try to "translate" her auditory image, or it might translate itself naturally, into a visual or kinesthetic image. Or, she might put all or part of what she has heard "on hold," in order to work with it at a later time.

One of my first conscious experiences of this "third ear" phenomenon was so dramatic that, frankly, I had little choice about listening or reacting. In the first session with a Swiss woman, she related an initial dream which included a scene in which an old man was being forced to move too fast. As she spoke, her voice sounded light, sharp, fast-paced, even a bit jolly. In the dream, however, the vocal sounds were dramatically different: as the old man was arduously, painfully, forced into his descent, both he and she as observing dream-ego began screaming. As she continued talking, her voice suddenly became unbearable to me. Somehow, from within the experience of this woman's voice, the dream-scream energy had entered my own ears. The dream had enter me. Or had I entered it?

This was a strong and shocking experience. In my considerable distress, in this first hour with an unknown client, I left my seat and actually broke the "seal" of our vessel, ostensibly going to the door to check if the "Do Not Disturb" sign was outside on the door. It was. But it was only of temporary help for the disturbance inside of me. However, after this brief pause, I was able to go back to working. I sat down and verbalized, with considerable feeling, that going slowly was extremely important. Then to my relief, I could hear her voice more "normally" and listen further. Strange

as it was, my peculiar experience turned out to have beneficial effects in several ways. This event, in its drama and
immediacy, forced upon me a strong level of disturbance
centering around "moving too fast." I knew of nothing in my
own life which would cause me to have such a reaction. Was
it that major – and torturous – a defense in this woman's life
to move too fast over painful events?

As we discussed the dream in this first session, she stated
that going too fast was not a serious problem. However, she
had been affected by my distress in this initial hour. Over
the next few months, it was impressive how she disciplined
herself to go slowly. She seemed to be doing this for me,
stopping at times to see if I was ready for her to go on. In a
practical way, my strong reaction had become our brake,
our *ritardo*. For the time being, it was I who had to carry the
suffering of this going-too-fast.

As this woman began telling the events of her childhood
and adolescence, she was distrustful of, yet fascinated by, my
subsequent reactions, which were also strong. It soon
became clear, especially from dream figures, that levels in
her psyche were suffering. They were sometimes very much
on the "scream level," as this first dream and my countertransference response had shown. During our 56 months of
work, there were many more dream-screams and unbearable images. She gradually slowed down, in a natural way. It
was no longer a self-conscious discipline, nor done ostensibly for my sake. She came into more contact with herself and
also with me. She also entered a few depressive periods
which, although brief, were very slow-moving indeed.

This dramatic acoustic "prelude" to our work – a forceful
one – revealed aspects of my psychic reactions and defenses
in working with this woman, as well as hers. It was an
acoustic warning of my own vulnerability to her psychic
state, and its intensity. In this initial incident, I actually acted
out one image for my instinctive defense: to run, break the

seal, leave the scene. Since it was early in my training, I did
not take this initial acoustic event seriously, except as per-
taining to that session. Thus at first I bypassed a clear image
of what I was, on one level, to encounter long-term in the
work. Over the months and years of our work, I did indeed
have to meet difficult demands in relation to this woman's
energies and issues. This is not uncommon, especially at
deep levels of work. At times I suffered a contagion of her
pain and despair, which necessitated working on my own
psychic spaces which had some similarity. Such a strong
reaction on my part showed the threat; but also my ability to
respond, to be shaken up, by this client. But I had to learn
to be willing and able to use my permeability in a differentiated way. Through my vulnerability, I had considerable
ground from which to receive and work closely with her.
Potentially, I had many levels of access to her.

There is no problem in "catching" an auditory image as
intense as this scream. In fact, it is more accurate to say that
it caught me. With so strong an experience, the problem lies
more in responding to the images and emotions in an
adequate way. It is challenging, and we may feel inadequate.
We may long for a replay, a chance to do it better. However,
the phenomenon of resonance is on our side. If, in the
impact and confusion of the immediate moment, an adequate reception was not possible, it is perhaps possible later
or over time. Reflecting, re-calling to such a moment, after
it happens, offers possibilities for adding to and sometimes
shifting responses.

Dramatic acoustic events, however, are not necessarily
the rule. Many, perhaps most auditory experiences are low
key. The flowing, reverberating aspects of the listening
process guarantee that the experience will be vibratory and
many-layered, and thus difficult to "catch." How we are
listening and hearing in any one moment is not a result of
conscious choice as much as it is our total, and also uncon-

scious, state. What we hear is, in part, based on unconscious aspects of a situation and of our own state of receptivity. The very fact of this bond with the unconscious is what makes acoustic work so necessary, and so richly informative.

Body movement and sound go together. Of all the channels of expression that we move in and out of, these two are perhaps closest. As we dream and think and feel, our eyes and ears react, our hearts and throats and brains make sounds and words. Whether active or still, noisy or silent, in a simple and ongoing way, we are in spontaneous motion. In communicative gestures and in conscious and semi-conscious movements, our bodies are naturally expressing our energies. We are constantly creating what is really a continuum of exchange between auditory and kinesthetic energy. This connecting-up of movement and vocal sound is a major theme in the work of many artists and therapists like Noah Pikes and Paul Newham, to name only two.

The familiar gesture of cocking the head, or turning the head in a new direction, could indicate that a particularly attentive listening or a new kind is occurring, inside or out. Such movements can also take place in potential, as only a slight leaning or checked urge. If the listening therapist finds herself or her client *almost* making certain movements – or half-making them, or only wanting to – she can be alerted to new energy. If the therapist is listening predominantly through one ear, she might want to try out, in momentary or periodic shifts, intentionally listening with the other ear and see what happens. Most people are used to listening with a certain slant. Perhaps therapists and clients use different ear emphases and different patterns of ear positions with different partners or in response to different types of situations. Do people in a depth psychotherapy session use the right ear more, turning their heads to the left, so their right ear receives the dreaming side of the psyche? Perhaps in depth work, partners move their heads more often, as they move between different listening modes and between different psychic levels.

How the chairs are placed within the listening space also affects the listening style. Of concern are not only issues of practicality and aesthetics, but also, essentially, acoustics: the placement of sound-producers and listeners within a resounding space. Some angles might encourage listening to occur more predominantly in one mode or one style over another. What is the angle of encounter? It is interesting to explore the many different images that chair, body and head positions suggest, to think and dream about what they could mean. Shoulder movements, shaking the head, covering part of the body, crossing the arms, or just the feeling of wanting to, even starting to, clap the hands over the ears, or curl up and hide the head are full of meaning. A wide and sensitive awareness means attention to both auditory and body signals [see next chapter].

Oliver Sacks narrated an event to ponder, which has to do with the importance of body signals and nonverbal auditory messages. It involved a situation in which all possibility for verbally-based messages was eliminated: the aphasiac ward in a hospital. He was visiting a group of severely aphasic patients, during which time a U.S. President was giving a television speech. Due to their medical condition, these people had no capacity to understand verbal content. Nonetheless, their reactions were plentiful and intense: roars of laughter and also outrage, bewilderment and apprehension. Their reactions were based solely on extraverbal cues like tone of voice, intonation, suggestive emphasis or inflection, gestures, facial expression, and posture.[109] Words themselves easily lie. But the "truth" comes through all of the cues surrounding communication and speech, of which auditory and body signals are such an important part.

---

[109] Oliver Sacks, *The Man Who Mistook His Wife for a Hat*, London (Pan Books, Ltd.), 1986, pp. 76-77.

## B. Hearing Silence

> *Silence is a condition of sound as sleep is a condition of life.*
> V. Zuckerkandl, *Sound and Symbol*, p. 3

Silence is not the same as soundlessness. It is not just the absence of sound. Silence is a meaningful experience around sound. While we may have given silence little thought, we find in the dictionary that we do have many ideas about it: stillness, quiet, hush, lull, aphony, tacitness, peace, deadness, dullness, inaudibility, and soundlessness. There is suggested here a wide range of feelings and reasons for silence. Silence is so essentially a part of therapeutic work that it scarcely needs saying. Silence is an experience of meaning. It is full of resonance.

Within a surrounding atmosphere of silence and its containing resonance, hearing oneself speak is resoundingly different from just thinking within one's own head. Indeed the Catholic Church takes into account the same principle when it recognizes as valid only a spoken confession. Jungian analyst Harry Wilmer[110] muses: "I am interested in silence because I work in silence, I listen into the silence of my patients. Sometimes I meditate. Sometimes I contemplate." He asks: "Could it be that true dialogue occurs not when we are listening to dreams, or to stories patients tell us, or the histories we hear, but only when we listen into silence?"[111] Silence lets things sink in. Contact is clearer, more concentrated. Commonly, a client remembers or connects deeply for the first time to a dream or experi-

---

[110] For another Jungian analyst's remarks, see the summary of Yvonne Federer's work in the accompanying excerpt; and for those who read Italian, note the thesis by Caterina Wolf, C.G. Jung Institute, Zurich, 1983.
[111] Harry Wilmer, from the text of a lecture given at C.G. Jung Institute, Küsnacht, Jan. 19, 1994, p. 5-6.

*In her diploma thesis for the Jung Institute in Zurich, entitled "Silence: Non-verbal Aspects of Analytic Psychology," Yvonne Federer concentrates on the many kinds of silences which occur. As archetypal background, she presents three divine figures:*

*- Choosing to remain silent: The Greek god Harpokrates, who sat on a lotus flower with finger at his lips.*

*- The pain of suppressed and anguished silence: The Roman goddess Angerona, her mouth bound and sealed.*

*- Silence in connection with punishment: Another Roman goddess, Lara, who talked so much that Jupiter cut out her tongue, whereupon she was called Muta or Tacita.*

*Federer mentions further images from myths and fairy tales, describing healing silence, silent families, numinous silence, punishing silence, pathological silence and the silenced child. Her work includes case examples and discussion of countertransference reactions within silence.*

*Silence, says Federer, is to be considered within the framework of Winnicott's "transitional space." It is "a dynamic no-man's land which is shared equally by analyst and client, belonging to neither and yet to both." She warns against being stuck at the cerebral and verbal levels, encouraging a "receptive condition in which our whole being is open to the unspoken messages from the other."*

ence only within the therapy hour, as he himself will often comment.

However, experiencing more reactivity, within and without, can also be threatening. Silence, which is encouraging of a deeper reaction, is by no means always felt to be beneficent. Wilmer lists four tentative classifications of silence, the last three of them involving danger: Sanctuary, loss of identity, daemonic danger, and portent of death.[112] Indeed, many clients consistently avoid silence, and perhaps most do during certain phases of the work. Silence is sometimes feared as too heavy an experience. It can have a weight, a pressure, that pushes emotions and contents into "deep water." When a client is resisting, and a therapist too, they may attempt to keep discussing, to keep amplifying and interpreting and moving along, rather than entering into the vibratory realities of what is present. They avoid silence, holding off what is happening at a deeper level. The speaking runs on, the explaining, elaborating, the talking *about*. They are not sounding or being sounded into that deeper space, both psychic and physical, which silence can help create.

Some silences, just like sounds, are distinctive moments with distinctive meanings. Rather than being background or surroundings, they appear like visitants, during the hour or during a phase of the work. They arrive and go, a definite felt sense in the room. Some are unwelcome, at least from the conscious or ego standpoint. There is, for example, the sullen, hostile silence which literally pulsates with the dare, "Break me! Force me!" The air is full of a passive demand for struggle. A particularly unwelcome silence is the silence of embarrassment or shame. One kind has a hot, sprinting energy, with images of prodding sprites and sneering devils. Another kind is heavier, much heavier, with long, heavy

112 Ibid., p. 20.

flushes of heat, and hot prickles of flesh. Time stands nightmarishly still. It impales nonspeaker and listener alike upon its endless red-hot moment.

Other silences are warm, enveloping. They are nurturing moments for the soul. For many clients, they may be more important, and also more memorable, than things that were verbalized. Sometimes they steal into the space without particular notice of arrival. They bring a comfortable attunement in which partners simply do not need words. Especially in working with the unconscious, silence goes a long way in creating a place of gentle relationship and wonder. It is a companionship of being. Silence is also a teacher of dreaming. It invites a field of dreams. Images and feelings interweave, slipping in and out of each other like ribbons waving in the air. Sometimes, there comes a silent dreaming-together space. Each person is wandering in a vague, yet foxfire place, in associative mode. As they move along their pathways, they may brush into contact, in response to a feeling, a sound, a momentary startle, a few words. The one person's parallel dreaming space encourages the other person to dream on, silent, together and apart. Such a silence is not only a dream time, but a dream time in concert.

However, for some people, silence is an uneasy place. Their silence is "way out there," spacy. This silence vibrates out as diffuse, dispersed. It is a difficult place to be in for the listener. It seems to be increasingly prevalent in our space age of both fantasies and realities and may be related to the purported increase in narcissistic disorders. The client's world as a personal space seems lost, spread out in the vast expanse of unknown infinity. This experience of silence might come from a world that has never come together at all. The therapist will shoot through this expanse like a missile in space, and miss the mark completely, unless she drops all notions of bringing light or clarity. She must simply attend. Specificities are not so important. Establishing a vessel at all is the main point, discovering a basic sense of resonance and holding it. But that may be light-years away. For now, only resonant companionship can befriend the vagueness of this kind of silence. Only it can call to and coax the fragments in space to come into some human relationship – with the therapist, within the client himself, and with "the world" as a solid planet around the client. Auditory sensitivity, that sense of containing resonance, is of the essence with such a case. The "Rhythmic Patterning" chapter has an example of working with this kind of silence.

Without ever considering it, many people, especially in extraverted American culture, feel it is wrong to be silent. This idea suggests that silence is lonely. Silence can bespeak an isolated, deadened experience. People sometimes need help to escape their silences, to find something in themselves, to find something in the interaction which an empty silence prevents. But silence does not have to be lonely. It can be full of a feeling of companionship, even within oneself. Between two people it can be a place where a person can simply be, can simply live along, without making any effort to communicate or focus. There is a mutual sense of the space, a natural place of being. Developmentally, its roots lie in what Winnicott describes as playing in the company of another. It is being separate, yet with the sense of the other person being reliably there, and eventually remembered after being forgotten.[113] There is a feeling of safety, a sense that you can follow your own dreams and feelings and thoughts, without attack, without being cast into outer space. Neither are you tracked too closely. You do not have to worry about the other's reaction. It is a profound experience of just being, just playing, together. With all of

---

[113] D.W. Winnicott, *Playing and Reality*, London (Penguin Books), 1971, pp. 54-56.

the emphasis, the frenetic demand always to be "doing" in Western culture, no wonder we are hunger for silence, for the quiet. It answers some of the deepest of our longings.

Sometimes, a silence portends an especially strong coming together. When I was first grappling with Jungian psychology, I was in a class where the analyst instructor was explaining the relationship of the ego to the Jungian Self. He was explaining that the ego was a prototype of the Self, that the ego could, in a potentiality that could never be achieved, be like the Self. I could not grasp this at all. In the grip of my analytic work, involving new levels of confusion and shadow, my limited personal ego seemed light years away from the all-inclusive Jungian Self, the center and circumference of all of psychic life. Despite my usual shyness, I began waving my arm. I protested, asking how that could be true, how the limited, narrow ego could be trying to become the other, which includes all. My vocal vehemence still rings loud in my ear. So does the next memory. After my words, there was a strong, vibrant silence. It seemed to last a long time. Within it, I felt the teacher to be very close, very alive, to my energy. Then, in what was actually a rather godlike gesture, he moved his hand in a wide arc, and at the top, suddenly stretched his fingers up and out. There was another brief pause. "*Lodestar,*" he said. A remarkable feeling of energy and union followed. I felt accompanied, helped, stimulated beyond measure. My energy had been witnessed and duly, indeed beautifully, met with this silence, this gesture, and this word.

In the therapeutic process, the archetype of the Self is constellated. Holy persons, gurus, and shamans are one kind of image for Self energy. In their holy places and in the places they bring holiness to, silence falls upon entering. It is a resonant experience of peace and wholeness. "Nothing in the universe is so like God as silence," Meister Eckhart said. He spoke of the unspoken and of silence in the core, the essence of the soul, from which the God or Word comes, unspoken.[114] Such a silence can, in and of itself, be deeply moving. It is complete.

There is some of this energy in the background of therapeutic work, in a largely impersonal way. Perhaps it is in relating to just this sense of silence that we often reach to deeper levels in working at a soft volume, with a sense of stillness. A quiet sort of hearing into something, with silence around it, often rings truer than a louder and more ray-like insights. Much of psychic phenomena is subtle. It is elusive, vibrating its energy only indirectly. It is often the fringes of experience, the aftertones, that open out deeper understanding.

And last, there is the silence around a span of therapeutic work. The silence before the therapy can often be sensed. As a client struggles to remember and understand his stories, it can be heard that his words have grown out of a silence. This is the silence before the speaking of these words, the realization and enduring of this inner and outer world. And this is so, even if the client was "talking about his problems" before starting therapy. It is before the talking became "telling." And there is also the silence after the work. In the long run, in the larger sense of personality development, what matters most is how a person's life is lived onward, during and after the work. It is often the case that therapists do not hear about their clients' lives following the work. In a mystery of silence, they may never hear what occurs, after the sounds and silences of the therapeutic process are only echoes and memories.

Beaulieu states that the deepest level of listening is silence, that the center of all sound is silence. "All sounds rise from and lead back to silence," he says. "Listening is the

---

[114] Joachim-Ernst Berendt, *The Third Ear*, Long Mead, England (Element Books), 1988, p. 72, and *The Best of Meister Eckhart*, Halcyon Backhouse, Ed., New York (Crossroad), 1992, p. 62-63.

art of discovering silence. Silence is the key to the many adventures the world of sound has to offer. Through silence we are truly safe and free. We know the beginning and we know the end." [115]

---

[115] John Beaulieu, *Music and Sound in the Healing Arts*, Tarrytown NY (Station Hill Press), 1987, p. 17.

# 4. Therapy Considerations

All clients will have auditory-centered experiences at some point. People naturally move in and out of different types of images, visual, auditory, body movements and proprioceptive (feelings in the body). They give them expression in their language, gestures, facial and vocal expression. However, at times it may be especially important to stay with the auditory channel. Working with sound or resonance or silence might be necessary in order to receive a particular image in its deepest and most natural sense, to accord it its full resonance. Within the repertoire of the session, the possibility of doing acoustic work should exist.

Acoustic work is especially important for some people and for some types of work. At times, it is probably irreplaceable. Firstly, some people are "ear-minded." They are responsive, perhaps uniquely responsive, to images when they are in an auditory form. They respond most naturally, with the most differentiation, to the sound of a voice or a hum in the air. Their best communication is via the ear. It is "speaking a foreign language," to communicate with them primarily in another mode, through a picture or written language or the meaning in a gesture.

Secondly, auditory processes have special resonance with early work, with contacting the young developmental levels of the psyche. Infants and children are highly receptive, acoustically. Without even thinking, we interact with them using songs, animal noises and sing-song, rhyming, playful, vocal sound and speech. Acoustic sensitivity is important with adult clients who are working at an early developmental level, as they contact their musings, memories, emotions and inner figures. It is not only that infants and young children are pre-verbal. The fact is, auditory experience is primary in early life. The sounds and resonances and silences which have surrounded infants and children are the primary way they have received meaning. This fact affects what we theorize to be a child's sensory-based reality, as well as the ways that adults in therapy fantasize and remember about their childhoods.

And finally, some people have had acoustic experiences which have been psychically unmanageable, resulting in a feeling of imprisonment or fixation within a kind of sound or silence or resonance. Although often unconscious or vague, a complex has taken "acoustic form." It requires auditory sensitivity to the client's images, as well as to the handling of the interaction in the session, to do this kind of work.

## A. Sensory Channels

> *Now I heard there was a secret chord*
> *That David played, and it pleased the Lord.*
> *But you don't really care for music, do you?*
>
> L. Cohen, "Hallelujah"
> (*Various Positions* album, 1984)

In describing the development of children, T. Bower states that the perceptual system is originally prepared to use any information present, regardless of its sensory modality. But this flexibility does not last long. In the first year or so of life, the perceptual system of a child gets accustomed to certain modalities of input, becoming more and more specialized and precise.[116]

Such a statement suggests that people narrow their perceptions to operate in certain typical sensory modes. Neuro-linguistic Programmers work with the visual, auditory and kinesthetic channels of information. Process-oriented psychology workers use these three, but include other channels, namely, proprioception (feelings inside of the body), relationship (to figures perceived as "other"), and the world (relationship to events in the world). They define "primary process" and "secondary process," that is, a more conscious and a less conscious channel. Besides its being typically primary or secondary, an individual's channel is also typically extraverted or introverted, that is, directed outside or inside of oneself.

Perhaps preferred channels are a result of inborn traits. Or perhaps they are defined during certain stages in the developmental process. Familial or societal factors may be significant. Choice of sensory mode is influenced by the environmental field in the given moment and also within the larger context of history. But whatever their causes, it is clear that some people are strongly auditory in the way they function. When an image comes up in auditory form, a switch to another sensory channel may be counterproductive. A communication mismatch between the partners will easily occur, masking the image and throwing obstacles into the communication. And aspects which are unique or primary to auditory energy may be lost in the "translation" to the other mode.

The auditory channel is especially important to depth workers because it tends to be relatively unconscious. As stated earlier, for most people in Western culture, the

[116] Tom Bower, *The Perceptual World of the Child*, London (Fontana Press), 1977, p. 84.

auditory channel is relatively unconscious; the phenomenon of sound is close to unconscious energies in its layered quality, in its vibratory associativeness, and in its position in creation mythology before the light. In Process-oriented work, clients are helped to discover their unconscious and conscious processes by following the flow of energy accessible in their sensory channels, keeping close tabs on body signals and word choice, and monitoring the client's conscious and unconscious feedback to the moves that they as therapists make. These signals naturally express the channel the person is in. Using what they have learned to be the client's process of receiving information, workers might then suggest "amplifying" an emerging image, that is, intensifying its expression in some way. They lend an ear, an eye, and an intuitive nose, to the client's "edges" or places of strong resistance. Sometimes too they themselves switch channels or suggest the client switch channels to make the information more accessible or conscious.[117]

The perspectives and skills of Process-oriented psychologists and Neurolinguistic Programmers are of value. They help therapists become conscious of the auditory channel and learn to do auditory work (as well as to work in the other channels). But even without specific training, most good listeners in any situation will find themselves naturally responding to a person's being, say, highly visual. Just as we pick up a person's gestures or vocabulary or speech rhythms, we may also adapt, without thinking, to the channel a person is in. We unconsciously adjust our natural modes of communication, in our words and image choices and movements, reacting to the sensory style of those we are in contact with.

[117] Lane Arye, Seminar, "Working with Music and Sound," Nov. 19, 1988, Zurich, Switzerland, and Joseph H. Goodbread, *The Dreambody Toolkit*, New York (Routledge & Kegan Paul), 1987; see the script of casework for detailed, practical suggestions.

However, if a person meets with images or information in a sensory channel that is secondary, or awkward for him or her, a blockage of communication can occur. In such cases, it requires some consciousness to notice what is happening, and some skill to deal with it. In psychotherapy, where communication and understanding are often difficult, we especially need this kind of training. The therapist might be stuck in one sensory mode, or denying or evasive of another, just when the need to be otherwise is strongest. The right attitudes and actions are not always enough; we need a workable channel for communication, as well.

Previous experience with the client helps. Memory of what channel a client has used in the past is part of remembering his images and stories. Therapists return to a channel ("that picture you drew," "that tone of voice") to re-evoke an image, to recall it to heart and mind. Perhaps such an awareness comes up during discussion of an elusive dream or fantasy figure. If the therapist remembers a channel's having been especially moving, she may make what are really channel decisions. In "bringing home" an image, she may ask the client to use the gestures of a dream figure or to make the roar of a fantasy lion. The first is a move from the visual channel, in which the client is simply seeing the figure making gestures, to an enacted, moving portrayal (a switch to the kinesthetic channel). The second example is a move from seeing or drawing a lion in fantasy, to a gut-filled, reverberating vocal experience (a switch to the auditory channel).

The partners might decide to continue working with an image. Following the auditory channel further with such an image (in Process-oriented terms, "amplifying the image"), might mean making the lion's roar softer or louder, or asking the client to roar out a word. The partners could explore what it is like making that roar, or being inside of the roar, or in the resonance or silence after the roar.

Channels can shift quickly, with or without forethought. Maybe the client begins to make movements that go with a sound, or perhaps the client begins to imitate the voice of a speaker in a dream. Such moves, especially using the auditory and kinesthetic channels, tend to make access to that image less verbal, less visual – and more vibratory. In Jungian terms, such work has the potential to sharpen the image, to release its impact. And sometimes, it augments or expands the image. Therapists help such image work along by suggesting and facilitating such moves in the actual session. They may also encourage clients to work and play in these ways outside of the hour.

However, despite the natural propensity that therapists have to be sensitive about images, some case reports sound like a battle of sensory channels. Some therapists show little or no regard for the communication problems constellated by a rigidity of channel usage. Perhaps a therapist reports the client as flooding her with painting (visual communication), and she responds with what the client complains of as "a lot of useless words" (ideational or auditory-verbal communication). It is off the mark to treat such events simply as resistance to the material or to the content of what the therapist said. Sensory channel problems in therapy sound like two partners speaking different languages, with no one translating or mediating. That necessary sense of resonance, of being on the same wavelength, is harmed, and the work may not proceed.

However, while a therapeutic alliance requires "speaking the same language," it is also true that too common a language, too many assumptions shared, is a problem. Jerome Kagan states, "The mind grows at the edge where the expected does not occur or is moderately transformed."[118]

---

[118] Jerome Kagan, *The Nature of the Child*, New York (Basic Books, Inc., 1984), p. 39.

At times, a "misfit" of communication modalities is beneficial. It can lead into an awareness of hitherto unconscious
material or communication modes. When somebody says,
"Nobody understands what I am saying," there is a great deal
to explore! Communication difficulties can lead deeper
into issues, and in a way that speaks to the everyday processes of people's lives. The way that clients use their voices,
their silences, their words, their bodies – all of the ways that
they respond or do not – becomes interesting, something to
work with. A client can be challenged by having to communicate, especially to the stimulating realities of someone
different. So a good therapeutic alliance requires partners
who can speak only *enough of* the same language.

In transference/countertransference work too, it can be
the misfits, rather than the good fits, which bring meaning.
These problematic moments bring up images and memories, bringing the awareness of projections and counter-
projections: "You're blathering, just like my mother," or
"You're cold and silent, like my stony father." The client's
and therapist's communication processes become clearer
with important figures, inside and out.

Work with channel awareness can become technically
engaging, and then especially, it can move too fast. It is not
lack of accessibility to psychic material which presents problems. The fantasies and images of less conscious layers lie
everywhere, in gesture and posture, in all of the aspects of
language usage, clothing choice, vocal presentation, body
sensations, in night and day-dreams, social interactions –
and even in synchronistic events. Unconscious meaning lies
in the evocation of mythological themes, even in the sim-
plest telling of the incident on the road on the way to the
hour. Switching between channels, like TV channel "surf-
ing," only skims the surface. The vital realm of resonance
may be lacking. Significant elements regarding timing, containment and a grounding background for difficult material

are bypassed. All of those things make deeper awareness possible. Finally, in following the mercuriality of the images and channels, boundary issues between workers may receive little attention. Information is gained, but individual relationship to it remains unclear.

The real challenge lies in allowing the material to be deeply, and at times murkily, felt and understood. It is finding a right relationship to the images that is the real difficulty. Essentially, this process requires slowing down, so that images can radiate their essence into the space around them. Between consciousness and the unconscious, between the separate and unified realities of the partners, space and resonance are necessary. In general, it is a slow, step-by-step process which creates responsiveness and respect.

A person for whom auditory energy is primary – whether during certain moments or as a typical mode – needs response on her or his own wavelength, at least some of the time. The therapist needs to be able to notice the sensory channel an image is occurring in. If it is in auditory form, she needs the flexibility to move into the auditory mode of reception, adjusting her acoustic antennae so that the reception is good, or good enough. Auditory work also means that she herself sometimes communicates auditorily, in reaching to the deepest level of contact. Sensitivity to channel usage is valuable, and often necessary. It can prevent unconscious barriers to communication, in the hour and outside of it. And this is particularly important in working with sensory modes like audition, which are so little attended to.

# B. The Preverbal Level

> *children guessed (but only a few*
> *and down they forgot as up they grew*
> *autumn winter spring summer)*
> *that noone loved him more by more*

e.e. cummings, "anyone lived in a pretty how town" (1940)
3rd stanza

Acoustic emphasis is indicated, and perhaps necessary, in working with infant and early childhood states. In Jungian terms, such work is resoundingly in "the first half of life." It is to be differentiated from work in "the second half of life," where the ego has established itself adequately. At this later stage, it has developed enough continuity, stability, and flexibility to manage things in the world, as well as in its own inner world. So it now turns to the task of meeting the reality of the unconscious, bearing the crucifying tension of opposites and the necessities of a more spiritual life. In contrast, work in the "first half of life" is regressive work, concerning the earliest developmental levels of the psyche.

For Jungians, this early work is also to be differentiated from archetypal work on "the Divine Child," with its emphases on creativity, renewal and redemption as qualities within the wholeness of the psyche.[119] Regressive work concerns the basic grounding of an individual psyche, the building of a stable ego. It is clear that a solid ego identity must first be in place, before a client can find a bridge to the inner, imaginal and archetypal world. While this Divine Child archetype might seem to be at the center of this work, the archetype of the Self, of wholeness, is its real center. It is the ego, or the ego complex, that is being built up, and thus it is the archetype of wholeness which resonates at its center.

---

[119] Eleanor Mattern-Ames, "Notes on Early Damage and Regression," Diploma Thesis, C.G. Jung Institute, Zurich, Switzerland, 1987, pp. 6-7.

Jungian depth work is of great value in reference to psychic situations involving early wounding. For many clients, their basic sense of identity and security is at the core. We have heard how auditory experience is primary to a basic sense of being contained, of being in vibratory contact with the world, with other people and beings, and ultimately, with oneself. What a person experiences sensorily (that is, what is experienced directly in the moment, and not imagined afterwards) feeds and forms psychic experience. Children born deaf, for example, do not have auditory images in their dreams. Apparently, patterns of cerebral organization fail to evolve without actual perceptual experience in the early years.

Infancy was a time before vision mattered much. Sound, movement and skin contact were the most important. It was a time when the auditory meaning of words was primary, as sounds, vibration, as an acoustic holding which both soothed and stimulated. Infancy was a time of vulnerability and malleability. The absolute dependence of early infancy gradually lessens over the months and years. According to A. Balint, when the basic ego is still forming, life is "a harmonious, interpenetrating mix-up" – like a fish swimming in water.[120] Adequate containment and reactivity from caretakers is essential at this point. In everyday life, we tend to be overextended, but at this early level of work, a high level of attentiveness is vital. In fact, for the client it is a survival issue, psychologically speaking. Attention and reactivity are *necessary* to the basic establishment of one's sense of being – and being oneself – in the world.

People who have received inadequate responsiveness as children are apt to be acutely sensitive regarding the issue of reactivity to themselves. If they feel improperly responded

[120] Michael Balint, *The Basic Fault: Therapeutic Aspects of Regression* (The Brunner/Mazel Classics in Psychoanalysis, No. 5), New York (Brunner/Mazel), 1968, pp. 65-66.

to, they experience it as a repeat of previous suffering, one which actually threatens them psychologically in maintaining their very sense of themselves. They will be experiencing, once again, the crying need for some definition, for some grounded sense of who they are. In the therapeutic vessel, all of this energy comes directly at the therapist as care-giver. For such clients, this deep need to come into "being" is mostly unconscious, and often profoundly so. But their behavior makes clear their need for basic affirmation. The therapist is called upon to listen and react in the right way.

This careful kind of listening, echoing, and replaying is like reparenting in one way. However, psychological work with early wounding is by no means reducible to an acoustically improved "re-run" in any concrete way. It is unlikely that a client could be "healed" simply by the literal or technological "reparenting," with the therapist being highly reactive and acting out early parental activities. There may be certain "acted-out" moments, like giving the client a drink, or saying a playful verse, which may become important moments in healing. However, at least in the Jungian framework, the work is much more complicated. It involves the activation and freeing of psychic experience, finding the images and fantasies which call to necessary energies, inside of and around the client. They might be talking about a dream or remembering another moment, in terms of verbal content. But acoustically, it could be as if the therapist were singing a song. In early work, the client's experience of the therapist's voice is highly influential. Sometimes, it will be the most basic mode of attunement.

The following information evokes both thought and imagination on the topic of the care of children and child-energies within adults. Besides describing the assumed experience of "real" fetuses, infants and children, it suggests ways of imagining and feeling for this early psychic field around therapist and client. This material is best heard as both fact and image.

There is a growing body of research and literature on the topic of preverbal experience. This increase is in recognition of the fact that, according to clinical and laboratory research, the cerebral processes associated with learning in early life seem to be fundamentally different from those that take place after maturation of the nervous system. Many researchers believe that psychic life begins before birth. Nerves connecting limbs, trunk, ears and eyes with the brain are present starting from the seventh or eighth week after conception. They are already feeding back environmental stimuli such as sound and light. The rudimentary connections between the primitive parts of the brain are also recognizable as early as the eighth week. "Brain life" is said to begin as early as the seventh month of gestation. Ultrasound pictures show fetuses sucking their thumbs, grabbing their umbilical cords, hiccoughing and smiling. Especially interesting to depth psychology is the fact that all phases of sleep have been recorded in an unborn baby.[121] This includes REM sleep, with Rapid Eye Movement, which indicates dreaming.

So it is possible that fetuses dream. Some clients tell of dreams and fantasies involving fetal life, and a few people even report memories. Dream material and fantasies, of course, are not necessarily a sign of something having happened literally, in "reality." What they do indicate is what is happening in the psyche. Certainly fetal life is "real" in terms of the psychic realm.

It is significant that the auditory system is one of the first systems to develop. The second and third trimesters of gestation are when the fetus is accomplishing some of its

---

[121] Mortimer G. Rosen, "The Secret Brain: Learning before Birth," *Harpers*, April 1978 (pp. 46-47), p. 46; Michal Baggish, "Fetal Life," *Science Digest*, Dec., 1982 (pp. 47-53), p. 53.

most basic stages of growth and brain development. The fetus reacts to auditory stimuli very early, as compared with other sensory systems. At only 4 1/2 to 5 months, fetuses have been recorded as jumping, making limb movements and averting their heads in response to sounds.[122] Thus hearing is one of the first experiences in an increasingly differentiating set of perceptual processes. Audition is a first base in establishing how individuals receive and process the world around them.

Another important fact concerns the surprising amount of sound in fetal life. Researchers have established that the womb is actually a rather noisy place. Its volume is estimated at about 75 dB, the level of a fairly loud conversation. And what sounds does a fetus hear? There is controversy on this question. But it is generally agreed that it is mostly the sounds of the mother eating, drinking and chewing, as well as her digestive and muscular movements.[123] Noises in the womb are thus intermittent and linked with the mother's activity. Periods of quiet are not unusual.[124]

The fetus is also in muffled contact with sound in the outer world. Early studies found that sounds from the outside were reduced by between 19-90 dB. A later one, the first done from microphones inside the wombs of sheep, speculated that the spectrum of difference is less than believed and the sounds less reduced as well. This study concluded that the auditory experience of the fetal mammal may be considerably more extensive, varied, and, as in

---

[122] J.C. Birnholz and B.R. Benacerraf, "The Development of Human Fetal Hearing," *Science* 222:516-18 (Nov. 4, 1983), p. 517.
[123] To get a sense of how loud muscular movements are from the inside, close your ears tightly with the palms of your hands. The steady humming you hear is actually your hand and arm muscles continually contracting.
[124] *Ibid*. And S.E. Armitage, B.A. Baldwin and M. Vince, "The Fetal Sound Environment of Sheep," *Science* 208:1173-74 (June 6, 1980), p. 1173.

birds, possibly of greater postnatal significance than has been believed.[125]

Although it runs contrary to common fantasy, some studies found that the mother's heartbeat was not a significant auditory experience for the fetus. Mentioning this finding to friends and colleagues has invariably produced upset, protest and even statements of outright disbelief. Such emotional reactions suggest that we have a strong psychic investment in the fantasy of the mother's heartbeat, comforting the fetus. This heartbeat is an image for the fetal "paradise" of love, warmth and safety. It auditorily expresses an archetypal experience of the paradisal womb.

According to many sources, what a baby seeks, once outside the womb, is the mother's voice. That a baby is differentiated and highly reactive to its own mother's voice is common knowledge among parents and researchers alike. It is the higher frequency sounds, and especially the higher-pitched female voice, which a baby most responds to. Body or visceral sounds are low frequency, low in pitch. If our ears were too receptive to these lower sounds, we would be hearing mostly our own body sounds, and especially our bodies in movement. A.A. Tomatis states that in the womb, the fetus's hearing is geared toward higher frequency sounds precisely in order to mask these relatively loud visceral sounds from the mother's and fetus's own body. The fetus, infant and young child, he says, are biologically primed to tune into the mother's voice and to human vocal input.[126]

Actually, there is evidence to suggest that it is not only infant, but also fetal, experience which determines this high sensitivity to the mother's voice. In one study in a hospital in

[125] Arthur S. Freese, M.D., *You and Your Hearing*, New York (Charles Scribners Sons), 1979, p. 32; and Armitage, above, pp. 1173-74.
[126] Patricia Joudry, *Sound Therapy and the Walk Man*, St. Denis, Sask. (Steele and Steele), 1984, pp. 49-51.

North Carolina, where infants experienced a mixture of female caretakers and little time with their own mothers, newborn babies consistently distinguished and preferred their own mothers' voices. The experiment was described as follows:

> *Newborn infants less than three days old learned to suck on a nonnutritive nipple in such a way as to elicit their mother's voice in preference to that of another female. In this ingenious experiment the mothers recorded part of a Dr. Seuss children's story shortly before delivery. Babies got their own mother's recording by sucking in one way and another voice if they sucked differently.[127]*

Babies may well become accustomed to their mothers' voices while still in the womb. Although their mother's voices were previously filtered through flesh and fluid, and now sounded different filtered through air, they were recognized and preferred by these babies.

The founder of Audio-Psycho-Phonology (APP), A.A. Tomatis, believes that if an infant has experienced too little care, or too non-adaptive a response to its basic needs, it will hear the world differently. Mainly, it will not learn to suppress its own inner, visceral sounds. Instead, it will remain attached to its own inner world. Either the eardrum will be too rigid and nonresponsive, or else improperly tense to external stimuli. APP therapists work to change hearing and listening habits. In the APP process called "sonic birth," a mother's voice is first recorded and filtered to approximate how it could have sounded to the fetal ear in water, in the womb. A typical reaction to such a tape, in the case of a 14-year-old autistic child, is to curl up in fetal position in his mother's lap and suck his thumb. The recording is then gradually reduced until the voice sounds like the mother's normal, air-conducted sound, outside of the womb. Tomatis believes that only then can selective

[127] Baggish, p. 51.

hearing, the cochlear-to-cortex reception of the outer world, begin to function properly. Only then can listening become differentiated.[128]

This sonic birth process is in essence a carefully timed, step-by-step emergence from safety, from the paradisal and acoustic womb, where all activity is centered, by its very functioning, around the fetus. This auditory procedure is gradual, so that adaptation can be achieved slowly, so that it does not traumatize. The sonic birth process sounds like a literal enactment, in auditory terms, of one of D.W. Winnicott's ideas. He says that it is the task of the mother to accustom her child slowly enough to the loss of "paradise" or life centered around the child's needs. This necessary loss should occur only in increments, by means of slowly increasing levels of frustration and disappointment.[129] The child must not be "ripped untimely" from its womb, from its necessary experience of trust and dependence. This step-by-step process in separating is like the move from union in water, with its interpenetrating energies, to separation in the thin air.

Tomatis' language suggests profundity, a primordial experience: "By means of filtered sounds through the medium of memorized ancient audition, we arouse the awakening of the most archaic relationship desired: the relationship with the mother."[130] These are the overtones of the archetypes in the sonic birth process. In its archaic connections, it sounds like an opening up to the positive side of the archetypal Great Mother. As Tomatis makes clear, differentiation is the goal: a selective, cochlea-to-

---

[128] Joudry, pp. 54 and 50-51.
[129] D.W. Winnicott, *The Maturational Processes and the Facilitating Environment*, John D. Sutherland, Ed., The International Psycho-analytic Library, No. 64, London (Hogarth Press and the Institute of Psychoanalysis), 1987, pp. 87-88.
[130] Joudry, p. 50.

cortex hearing. It is a step-by-step journey into consciousness, where an individual has the ability to differentiate. It is
a move from unified vibration, from hearing the mother
and world through bone and flesh and fluid, to hearing her,
and the newly sonorous outer world, through the separating
air.

Once out of the womb, the infant and young child
continue to be highly dependent upon hearing. The very
youngest of babies exhibit impressive auditory capacities.
They depend mainly upon sound through the first six
months of life. Babies can localize sounds just moments
after birth, an ability involving a high level of differentiation
regarding timing and volume. With its first babblings, as
early as eight weeks of age, babies start dealing with the
complicated task of understanding and producing speech.
Learning to speak, much taken for granted, is in fact
astoundingly complex. Just in terms of bodily mechanics,
the word "church" requires twenty different adjustments of
the lips, tongue, larynx and jaws in correct sequence and in
less than one quarter of a second![131] Accurate production of
speech is inextricably tied to hearing. To speak properly, a
person must first hear in a highly differentiated manner.
Only when a person can *hear* the differences in pronunciation and intonation, can they produce the sounds.

For most people, the mechanical production of the
sounds in a language occurs quite naturally, once careful
listening is established. Babies naturally play with almost all
of the sounds found in different human languages, and
babies in different language groups produce highly similar
babbling sounds. Only gradually, as they become more
aware of the sounds around them, do their babblings begin
to approximate the specific sounds in their own language.

[131] "Learning to Talk: Speech, Hearing and Language Problems in the
Pre-school Child," Office of Scientific and Health Reports (NIH No. 77-
43), Rev., 1977, Bethseda MD, pp. 16 and 11-12.

Babies experiment with and echo a wide range of sounds, which become the groundwork for producing the verbal sounds in their own language. Deaf infants, by the way, also babble from this large pool of human language sounds; but they stop babbling at about 4-6 months.[132]

An infant's real precision lies in his perceptions of people. There is a high degree of reactivity in the spontaneous echoing and "goo-goo-ing's" of infants and their caretakers. Diverse and startlingly complex duets take place, long before real speech occurs. It is on the way to differentiated speech. A certain amount of this kind of communication occurs in the psychotherapeutic process too. In one sense, it is a layer of the work with all clients. Therapists who are personally attached to subtle language and careful verbal differentiation may minimize this "babbling." However, it is both a "natural" and musical level, even if often unconscious, and it is both fine-tuned and subtle in its musical manifestations. It is a back-and-forth, ear-based contact, where speech is, first of all, a carrier of sound. A babble level of speech, for some clients, is by no means always defensive; nor is it, in one way, a superficial level. It is sometimes a necessary place, especially if the work is to contact the young child within.

There is a pleasure in oral expression and oral speech. We are so taken up with verbal meaning that we rarely think about the sound of words. Conscious awareness of speech as satisfying sound is relegated to the realms of poetry, the rhetorical speech of sermons and politics, and a few kinds of music, like rap music. But there is something satisfying about the sound of words. Apparently, this love of speech begins early on. According to one study, infants prefer the sound of recorded speech or vocal music to the sound of

---

[132] Peter A. and Jill G. deVilliers, *Early Language* (The Developing Child Series), Cambridge MA (Harvard University Press), 1979, pp. 21-24. and 17.

instrumental music or other rhythmic sound.[133] This appreciation seems to be rooted in fetal and infant experience.

The way we verbally interact is complex, and much more sound-based than most people are aware. On one level, our interacting speech is less based on verbal responses than on a musical duet or a musical dance. Physical movement is a vital aspect of the interaction, along with sound. According to the field of interactional synchrony, both speaker and listener are making movements which are extremely slight and very difficult to detect. They begin and end on "phoneme breaks," the places which determine the accent and rhythm of an utterance.[134] They are based on the *sound* of words, rather than their verbal content.

Surprisingly enough, newborn babies only hours old are equipped and ready to engage in interactional synchrony. No wonder babies are so engaging! Their movements, like adults', begin and end on phoneme breaks, seemingly in any language. They have an astonishing ability to analyze the flow of sound in any language into its component parts. This ability to respond to the flow of language is an area where the newborn might well do better than the adult.[135] This is a humbling thought for therapists invested in their interactional acuity!

Actually, the meaning in words is slow to come. It is only gradually that words take on the assigned meaning that they will have in adult usage. This preverbal experience of vocal sounds and words fades slowly into the background, and this fact is an important one to remember in keeping attuned to some clients. The use of language and the way it is under-

---

[133] deVilliers, p. 16, quoting E.C. Butterfield and G.N. Siperstein, "Influence of Contingent Auditory Stimulation upon Non-nutritional Suckle," in *Proceedings of the Third Symposium on Oral Sensation and Perception: The Mouth of the Infant*, Springfield IL (Charles C. Thomas), 1974.
[134] Bower, pp. 32-33.
[135] Ibid.

stood in early childhood is a fascinating field for researchers and parents alike. Some writers present striking and evocative contrasts between children's and adults' use of words. While an adult client who is doing work on early childhood does not become a literal child, there is a child energy within him who is listening and expressing things. It is that "as-if" place, *as if* he were a child. This is a place which needs to become *psychically real.* Considerable confusion can result for a therapist who assumes that a client is using and understanding words in an "adult" way.

In a child's world, words' meanings are not yet clearly defined. They are clustered in ways that may be highly associative. The meanings of a child's words may be mostly idiosyncratic. What the child understands as defining an object may be radically different from how the adult has learned to categorize or describe it. One striking example involved a 13-month-old, Nicholas, and his favorite pet, a shaggy sheepdog he called "Nunu." In a restaurant, Nicholas was served a salad on a round plate, consisting of shredded lettuce with two shiny black olives placed in the middle. He pointed to his salad and said, "Nunu"![136]

Listening carefully to the way that a client uses language and associates to things is already the task of a depth psychologist. This child level of talk rings profound, close to the unconscious and associative roots of awareness. The world of association and idiosyncratic linkage, which Jung worked with in his Word Association Experiment, is the language of young children. For them too, Klang, the sound of words remains important. Balint reports that children's words do not yet possess the overriding symbolic function that they will have in adult language. They are mainly pictures, images, and sounds, which may sometimes change their meaning or merge into each other, as they do, in fact,

[136] deVilliers, pp. 31-39.

in dreams. Only in adulthood are they suitable for use in a concise, clearly defined way. Balint also comments on how the analyst must enter into this space of verbal interpenetration. It is an experience of close involvement, he says, and requires careful work with the analyst's subjective, emotional state.[137]

So the fetal and infant world is primarily, profoundly centered in audition. Early developmental stages exert a formative influence on an individual's life, laying a groundwork and building its foundation, layer by layer. The understanding and use of words only slowly emerges out of a field which is auditory, associative and idiosyncratic, as it slowly moves into "adult" language usage. Often, more than one level will be sounding through. As they emerge more clearly over the course of time, it is helpful to stay aware of how much nodding or smiling or auditory echoing a therapist feels like doing. It may, in sorting things, be different from how much she is actually doing.

Interactional cues from clients are usually clear, if the therapist will stop to notice them. They are also insistent. However, they are often conflicting. It may be difficult, but it is vital to sort through these different communication levels, both emotionally and intellectually. It is common that adult clients are staunchly defended against the great difficulties caused by the childish, dependent part of themselves. Some people who have suffered early wounding have achieved considerable outer success. They might well have an impressive persona in place, in their work and social roles, as well as in the session. Yet they may be engaging in early interactional demands.

One example of differentiating levels happened in the early stages with a client of mine, (also mentioned in the next chapter), who presented a friendly demeanor and an

[137] Balint, pp. 97 and 20.

intellectual style of speaking. In terms of content, he voiced a stream of philosophical and political ideas, well thought out, and exhibiting independence of mind. As he spoke, he had frequent, brief and intense moments in which seemed to be seeking affirmation. He would nod and beam at me, as if to say, "Now you do this back." Feeling confused by this incongruent combination of words, ideas and manner of interacting, I was at first experimenting with how to respond. He seemed to want intellectual exchange, yet he felt very eager, even desperate, for an emotionally affirming response. In trying to differentiate from within the flow of interaction, I tried out ideational response, emotional response, and imaginal response. He appeared to get satisfaction from all of these.

As I tracked my own reactions, I began noticing how strongly I felt that I had to respond. And the clearest message came when I tried moving against that urge. With little or no response, he would become visibly upset, talking louder and faster. At times, he seemed to want to start a "fight," a disagreement, rather than simply be listened to in an interested, but not actively affirming, way. It was as if he was trying to get relief from any non-nodding, non-smiling facial expressions, even if it meant disagreement. When I would return to nodding and smiling, he would beam and his energy would sail forth again.

In the ensuing work, the air between us was full of energy, which I basically "read" as unconscious anxiety and demand. It was becoming clearer what was being asked, indeed, unconsciously demanded, of me. Conflicting as it was, this was a strong experience, present from the first hour, of this man's difficulty in bearing a lack of affirming response from me. This was despite his intellectuality, strong masculine presence and outer success. If I had functioned primarily in response to his words and ideas, I would have been lost. A psychologically unthinking, but "thinking," response would have had me trying to make psychological sense of his ideas, and riding roughshod over his emotional self. I would have been caught up in his thinking self, with which he was over-identified. His messages, involving this early developmental level, were communicated almost completely from within the "music" of the interchange.

This experience, based mainly on auditory experimentation, illustrates the fact that something responds naturally, acoustically, and at its roots, quite unconsciously, to the psychological level of a client. A therapist's instinctual interactional responses to a client are usually an accurate gauge of his developmental level(s). Granted that in a less auditory or interactional mode, this client might have "taught" a therapist what was needed, using the longer route of the therapist's constant "failure" – if both partners had been able to persist. But the acoustic and participatory field offers the clearest and most immediate learning situation. The ear picks up what is often deeply unconscious in the layers of a client's psyche. Indeed, in the subsequent analytic work, the strong negation and domination from his mother, from infancy on, was a major theme. Meeting his need, rather than confronting it, was the first step.

In doing therapeutic work with early psychic levels, developmental research, especially on perception and speech, is stimulating to both fantasy and fact. While the difference between fantasy and fact is not always easy to distinguish, it is clear that the emphasis needs to lie with the experience of the client, with his world. The need for responsivity is a central part of therapy for all clients, and it can occur at many levels. It is important to be in touch with the possibility that for some clients, words may sometimes be a primarily auditory experience. In such moments and phases, language is being heard and spoken as an associative mixing-in, rather than as content-based speech. Interactivity is primary.

If a resonant mainline to words has not yet developed, or if it has got "lost," perhaps in the transference field, then content-based verbal work is not really possible. At least, it is not possible without leaving these deeper layers untouched. The real work has to based on this elementary – yet highly refined – level of acoustic interactivity.

## C. Sound and Silence as Fixation

> *I call to you,*
> *I call to you,*
> *But I don't call soft enough.*
>
> L. Cohen, "There Ain't No Cure for Love"
> *I'm Your Man* album)

Some people have had formative, and even traumatic or fixating acoustic experiences or images. When some difficulty with audition has been too great, a fixation may occur. A person remains arrested in a certain psychological space, unable to process and "work through" the feelings, thoughts and events associated with it. Perhaps a parent's voice has been habitually overpowering, or a certain timbre in a father's voice has threatened a scalding scorn, or physical punishment. Or a mother's silences may have been like impalement in guilt or shame. The person will live his life expecting recurrences, and trying to defend against their reality, or even possibility. But his unconscious structures will invite these situations to recur. The world will seem wrong, overwhelming and cruel in the old familiar, familial ways.

In auditory terms, his psychic ear has not "recovered." He remains imprisoned or fixated in an acoustic experience. In Jungian terms, his complex, like a shell of emotion-laden assumptions easily set into motion, has taken "acoustic shape." Discovering a relationship to such experiences might well entail work in the auditory mode. A careful ear and well-tuned resonance from the therapist is vital. Without a reactive and imaginative ear and an evocative response, the client's images and memories could be lost. Indeed, the therapy might never even get established.

It is possible that more people have had acoustic "trauma" than might be thought. Noisy and ugly acoustic experiences are rampant in modern society, sometimes in long-term situations. It is not uncommon to live in an unhandleable acoustic environment and not perceive it as such. Vocal harshness is quite common. Many people's voices are high in volume and pitch, and unpleasant in timbre. They often sound tight, pressured and demanding. In the stress of modern life, people have few outlets for their tensions and aggressions. And perhaps more for women than men, voices are a socially condoned medium for such expression. In speaking over background sounds, and in our hurried and competitive messages, our voices rise and sharpen. It is not only a bland sort of societal unconsciousness, but also a necessary denial or repression which make up many people's responses to sound.

Trouble with listening and hearing may occur many situations. Therapy necessitates dealing with it within the acoustic vessel. The therapist's voice is important. A client may be hearing, at least in moments, a harsh, rasping mother-voice, a soothing, enfolding mother-voice, a sharp, arrogant animus voice, a deep, stabilizing father-voice, a throaty seductive anima voice, or a musically inspiring Orpheus voice. Or sometimes vocal images suggest more what is missing: a "cold" voice, a monotone or a "dry" tone. In the client's hearing of the therapist, where projection is involved, there are as many transference voices as there are transferences.

Whatever the constellation or typical pattern of energy, it might have little to do with the therapist's voice as it is more commonly heard. On the other hand, it might have a great deal to do with it. Therapists would do well to listen with openness to what a client says or shows about how their voices are being received. After all, therapists, as well as clients, tend to be unconscious regarding how their voices sound. The therapist's own ear, her own listening skills applied to her own sounds, are important to the process. In working with the countertransference, in the sorting through of her own reactions, the therapist might hear how she has one kind of voice with one client and another voice with another, within the different vessels. She might hear how her voice changes in a particular moment or constellation. Audition allows new perceptions to emerge.

No matter how hard a therapist tries to speak clearly and simply, the effort is sometimes of little avail. There are some clients, and more than might be thought, who have trouble listening to the sound of their therapist's voice. To make matters worse, many will be unable to verbalize their auditory experience. They, like most of us, will not have noticed their auditory reactions. So their responses, their images, must be coaxed into consciousness, whether they regard events in the present, their own past experiences, in regard to the therapist's voice or silence. Even without verbal explanations, clients will be offering many cues.

If a client is not receiving the therapist's voice, the problem might not at first seem to be voice-centered. Indeed, anything, everything, might be going wrong. If the means of communication sounds "wrong," then the words, the meaning, the interactional field, will be infused with negativity. In such a case, it is not the words or the accuracy of interpretation which matter; the meaning, the image, lies in the *experience* of the communication. If the therapist has too little consciousness of the way that the sound of her voice can be full of meaning, she will miss the forest for the trees. She will not realize that talking at all, or her specific vocal expression, or the way she is being silent, is itself being experienced as a complex.

When a therapist's voice, verbal meaning aside, is sounding like haranguing father or cold mother, then that is the strongest part of its message. Great frustration and confusion can ensue between the partners. Essentially false questions will be futilely addressed and re-addressed *ad nauseam*. The partners will be waylaid, and waylaid again, by vaguely hurt and angry feelings, misunderstandings, and questions about verbal content. The interchange will get mired in impossibility. Meanwhile, the therapist will have little sense of what the client is resisting. Nonetheless, the message of rejection will be present, and often strong. The client may communicate by means of silences, irritating smalltalk, indirect or direct attacks. Trouble may manifest in facial expression, tone of voice, gestures, dream or fantasy or verbal images – and even smells. Resistances will follow no clear path in terms of content. It is "crazy-making," if the partners remain on the track of verbal content or interpreting psychic material.

In tracking this auditory field through her own countertransference, the therapist may be experiencing her own uselessness or powerlessness, feeling rejected and even punished for her presence and her efforts alike. Neither being nor doing suffices. She will experience herself rarely, if ever, getting heard, resounded to. Her rhythms, her timbres, her accents will be met with a dull thud. Or else they will evoke a negating or even annihilating counter-response. Obviously, it is vital that the therapist not identify personally with this experience. She must catch what is happening and explore it as an unconscious field, a communication from the client about *his* experience.

Psychoanalytically, this kind of interaction may reveal a transference/countertransference situation which is "syntonic." Unconsciously, via acoustic exchange, the client may be playing out a need to make the therapist experience his own feelings of emotional and acoustic rebuff, torture, or void. Intrapsychically, within his own self, he may also be dramatizing his own relationship with himself, that is, the way he cannot communicate and respond to himself. Obviously, this information is important. Even though a therapist may be skilled in discovering regressive patterns of behavior or in doing dreamwork or discussing the transference, such "insights" will be of little therapeutic use if they cannot be experienced, resonated to, by the client. The experiential element – that which can be immediately listened to and felt – reverberates in the moment, in the hour, waiting to be made real.

While fixation in the auditory realm can manifest in many ways, the two case examples which follow offer some illustration of auditory fixation. A colleague responded to a request of mine for stories about auditory dreams and psychological work. In the ensuing interview, it was clear that she was especially interested in audition. She stated that the auditory dimension of her analysis had been primary. During these six years, she felt that she had reached the deepest experience of her disturbed relationship to her mother through recontacting her mother's voice. As she slowly discovered, she had felt her mother's anxious neediness primarily through her mother's strained and compulsive talking. The elusiveness of this kind of work was clear in her case, for it had taken four years of time and effort to "catch" this basic reality.

The first part of her story involved a brief period when she had just started with a new analyst. She was disturbed to notice that this analyst talked a great deal, and seemed to be talking more, and more loudly, with each session. After the sessions, she had almost no memory of what this woman said, or of the sessions in general; she only remembered their auditory reality. She felt confused and overwhelmed. In this state, it was not until the third session that she complained to the analyst. She said she used a quiet and rational manner, and the analyst responded the same way, saying that she too had noticed her own talking, and felt she just had to go on – she did not know why. In their fourth session, the issue crescendoed to a climax. The medium was the analyst's dog, who lay beside the client on the couch. It would howl for the first few sentences, whenever its mistress began speaking.

Animals and even plants and objects appear to express the reality of human energies at certain moments, especially at intense ones. This dog seemed to be sounding forth, in an animal and excruciating way, the client's energy. It sounded like her own pain and rage at this overwhelming, unrelenting, analyst/mother voice. Despite the howling, the analyst continued talking, during this fourth session and the next. A couple of times, the analyst mentioned the howling. After the fifth session, the woman said she gave up, and terminated the work.

What might have been going on here? From the description, it seemed that in this brief period, the devouring mother versus the victim daughter had constellated. In the first three sessions, it expressed itself in a torrent of talk versus a numbed silence. In the fourth, the talk was accompanied by an animal howling. The "right" energies – a strong, conflictual suffering that needed attention – had entered the vessel. At this intensity, could this energy have been met and worked with? Not, perhaps, without a fight. The analyst, who verbally expressed consciousness of her talking, did not relent in her behavior. According to the woman, to stay in this vessel, she would have had to stop the analyst/mother-voice, perhaps outtalking, outshouting, or confronting it more forcefully. The daughter as powerful, as fighting the mother, would have had to occur. Had this happened, it might have sounded like torrent to torrent, howl to howl.

However, the vessel did not hold. To the client who withdrew, the dog's howling seemed more like a helpless expression of torture than a rallying call to stop the voice. It moved like a dream-event, that the protest to this voice came from the dog, and not the client. It came from the vulnerable animal, a carrier of nonverbal energy who could not, did not, inhibit or transpose the experience. Apparently, this client did not depend on the instinctual reactivity of animal energy, the dog's or hers. Her five sessions of upset, numbed silence was humanly, inhumanly, maintained, trapping her in the inability to deal with this voice.

This woman's energy must have been intense, in transferring to the dog. And its mode of expression, howling, also indicated intensity. Intrapsychically, we could surmise that she could not deal with her own inner pain and protest, her own inner howling. The strength of emotion and sense of helplessness could indicate that this woman's level of wounding was early, like the vulnerable desperation, yet the powerful howling, of a small child. She could not meet this voice, this perceived vocal overpowerment, like an adult or a hero. It seems that the analyst had acoustically overwhelmed her, or we could say, re-traumatized her.

The analyst's response was to go with this auditory energy, to play it out. She verbally expressed that she was aware of her own flood of talking and the dog's howling. Might this dog have howled like this frequently, so that the analyst was used to it? Did it sound like upset howling to her? In this client's perception, at any rate, the analyst was not experientially responsive to the pain and desperation that her talk was causing. The analyst might have been caught at a content level, receiving verbal information but emotionally unresponsive to what was happening in the moment. She might have been talking about it or around it, instead of experiencing it.

Perhaps this woman made the analyst feel aggressive or needy herself. She was probably presenting a numbed rejection of the analyst's considerable mental and verbal efforts. Perhaps the analyst was in unconscious need of validation. A trained therapist knows that it is an ongoing difficulty to disentangle what is actually helpful to a client from what can sometimes be the therapist's push to help, a need which stems in part from the therapist's own difficulties or ego concerns. Perhaps the experience was touching on the analyst's own unworked places, ones she had to avoid. With too little sensitivity to the field of energy present in the vessel, this process of unconscious communication by the interactive field is easily misperceived or lost.

Another possibility is that, consciously or unconsciously, the analyst was trying to constellate the client's pain or anger, allowing it to happen and even inciting it. She was then sounding the call to rouse the client to protect herself and stop her mother. The client had unsuccessfully tried to stop the analyst by being calm and rational. She would have had to shout and insist, in her perception, to "overreact" to accomplish this task. Stopping this mother voice would have immersed her in difficult shadow issues. She would have had to move beyond a polite, rational, please-be-nice-to-me stance, becoming more forceful. The situation called for more breadth of personality.

The phenomena of this interchange suggests that this woman needed to experience and react to this recurring mother-voice energy, and somehow deal with it. In Jungian terms, it was the task of the therapist to discern the client's needs from within the vibratory field of the negative mother complex vibrating in the vessel, where the needy and verbally aggressive energy was so strongly felt. In the client's perception, a sense of basic emotional response did not occur. For her, a tolerable acoustic and emotional exchange was lacking, and the vessel broke.

While this attempt could, in and of itself, be called a resounding non-success, it proved useful. This woman's story has a sequel. These five sessions alerted her to what had been unheard, vague, involving the trouble she had always had with her mother, as well as with hearing other people talk. It offered direction, helping attune her and her next analyst. It became the opening image, guiding their work, holding them to working carefully with the sound of talk and with silence. When she told this story to her next analyst, she listened carefully, and remembered it. As they began working, this analyst spoke little, and at first allowed the client to stop her from talking with only the slightest gesture or the softest vocal sound. Over a two-year period, as trust grew, the analyst challenged her more and more. The client had to learn to be more assertive in stopping the talk when she could not listen. And she found out she could. This experience was also central in her learning to speak with more connection to herself, as well as with more strength and conviction. This development, reflecting the intrapsychic aspect of her negative mother complex, helped her connect and feel more secure within herself, as well as in her self-expression.

Slowly, in listening and speaking, this woman learned to attend to her own state when she could not listen. It had become possible in increments. She stated that she gradually used more and more emphasis in responding, until she could use even dramatic gestures and sounds. She was naturally illustrating some of them as she told her story, and I could well understand how they rounded out her basic soft-spoken presentation. She had been able to escape entrapment in this intolerable mother-voice only from a base of feeling acoustically "held." This second acoustic vessel had been individually tailored to her auditory needs. She said that she had learned more than simply to endure listening; she had learned to want to listen. This woman's description calls to mind APP theories regarding how a child learns to be interested in verbal and vocal meaning. Slowly, she had started believing that her analyst's sounds and words and silences could signify both an emotional caring and an expression of meaningful ideas in relationship to her. She had learned that she wanted to get into the acoustic exchange, here and in her wide life. Now, she said, she could hear the positive side of things, like comfort, invitation, and stimulation.

A second example centers around the dream of an analysand whom I worked with in Zurich. It portrays a scene of auditory torture:

> *(Shortly before falling asleep.) It is day and I find myself in the bedroom. At first I think I am alone, but later I diffusely sense that my wife and the children are also present in the room.*
>
> *A boxer (fighter) of* UNHEARD OF *strength tries to force his way into the bedroom. Since the door is locked, he hits his fist through the door. We barricade the door further with the bed so that it is impossible, even with the greatest use of violence, to get into the room.*
>
> *I provoke him with* SCORNFUL WORDS AND LAUGHS *and thus incite him to new attack in the hope of finally wearing him down. He seems to have* UNHEARD OF *power at his disposal and soon we reach safety by climbing out of the window.*
>
> *We are somewhere in complete safety. The black man has managed to force his way into the bedroom. It has become night. Somehow I had had the possibility to shut off the electric current to the house. The criminal finds himself in complete darkness.*
>
> *By means of an infra-red camera, we can still observe him further and by means of* BUILT-IN LOUD-SPEAKERS *in the ceiling, we can also* PROVOKE HIM ACOUSTICALLY *more and more and break him down until at the end, he finally almost loses his mind.*
>
> [translation and acoustic emphases mine]

This man was clearly much attuned to auditory wave-lengths. In our work, he often described sounds and voices, and spoke about music. Much of our 2 1/2 years of analytic work centered around his experience of his mother. She had been strongly, even forcefully, nurturing, insisting on his obedience, help, and profuse gratitude. At the age of eleven, he had begun to stutter. It had been a torture to him and was, in fact, clearly a torture even to remember. This dream came within several days of the analytic session in which he had realized, with considerable upset, that it was his mother who had been a prime reason for his stuttering. She had constantly interrupted and contradicted him. She had forced him to obey, under threat of emotional and physical punishment, without any discussion or protest.

The images in this dream suggested a strong conflict between the dream ego (the "I" in the dream) and the black man figure. To echo the story, the black man has an "unheard of" amount of power, an "unheard of" amount of strength. His power has not been heard or recognized. As strongly as his power is affirmed in auditory terms, it is even more strongly rejected by the dream ego. In a dire struggle, the dream ego literally tries to break the black man down and drive him crazy. What exactly was this black man energy doing in entering the bedroom, and then remaining impris-oned and tortured there? The client said he did not know. He had no idea what the black man wanted and no sense of any conflict he himself might have been feeling. His responses, as well as the dream images themselves, made it loud and clear that his resistance, his fight against this dark energy, was intense.

Indeed, this black man is imaged as a complete outsider to the house and family, a criminal, with no right to break in. Later, he is kept imprisoned in the disconnected dark-ness. Since he is a boxer, this figure has to do with a fighter, an aggressive aspect. It is caught and tortured in a bedroom space, associatively a place of intimacy with both mother and wife. This image could suggest family or marital intimacy, and perhaps sexuality. Was his anger or aggressiveness being trapped and tortured in these areas of his life? Intra-psychically, within himself, the home and especially the bedroom could suggest this man's most intimate and private inner places. These two masculine dream figures or sides of himself are locked in battle, in a torturing provocation. Might the auditory images suggest that this interaction especially involves auditory energy?

In our work together, I understood such themes to relate to this man's strong conscious and unconscious rejection of aggression, especially his own. He stated that aggression was inferior, that he could not justify such feelings. Apparently when angered, he either denied it, repressed or suppressed it. It did seem to manifest auditorily, in his voice and words. When his wife opposed him, he would, as he described, explain the rightness of his position, and patiently, at length, if she would not agree. Then she would usually withdraw, stating that his voice was "aggressive" and that she felt "bullied." The *sound* of their talk seemed to be revealing the energy underlying it. Realizing that he did not always sound like a cultured, controlled man was a difficult admission for this man. He had invested a great amount of energy in his ideals and worked hard on his self-image. I admired the honesty and courage he showed in facing his shadow qualities.

The image of the intrusive, aggressive black fighter was linked to this man's experience of his powerful mother. In her imposing nurturing, she had not listened, except to him as an idealized musical son. Her voice, he said, had been loud, sharp, and unrelenting. Like his mother, he had also tried to "take care of things" with words which, as he was learning, sometimes sounded harsh and intrusive to others. Previously, dream figures had appeared, sometimes masculine, which he had spontaneously linked with his mother, especially in her aggressively active, overcontrolling aspect. The masculinity of the black figure functions to draw the dreamer closer in their shared male roles. However, the conflict was strong: the black man looked dangerous, criminal, deserving of total defeat and mental annihilation – at least to the dream-ego.

The way that this man used his voice was important in the hour. He spoke steadily, his tone insistent. At certain moments, without knowing it, he fairly pounded his message into my ears. Particularly then, it sounded tense, filled with amorphous, upset emotionality. The part of him which had ideas, his thinking self, represented his identity, his main sense of himself. His presentation, including his voice, seemed to be seeking, and simultaneously fighting against, affirmation. With such a conflict, I could understand the image of acoustic torture, as an image applying to him, as well as me. Intense energy was present.

Despite its difficult and conflicting energies, I felt like staying alive to this man and his voice. I played both a supporting and challenging part in helping him discover and then mediate these fighting, needy energies in himself. His rejection of them was formidable. Early in the work, as I slowly heard more about his experience of his mother, I found that my ear was mostly trained on the fear and need that his voice was expressing. I reacted in a soft-voiced, calming manner, when I could. Unconsciously, in trying to provoke me with his energy and ideas, his voice seemed unrelenting, like his mother's. I felt that I had to resist becoming like his mother, loud, rejecting, and insistent. In the first few months, he did not appear to "hear" my voice or reactions as soft and containing. It was out of his psychic frequency range. He seemed anxious, resisted any input and kept talking.

As time passed, trust became stronger – trust that I was really responding to him. Slowly, he began to be able to hear my softened voice. It was moving to hear how his sound screen, so auditorily defensive in its intensity, was slowly mellowing. Increasingly over the months, his own voice softened. His posture relaxed a bit. His presentation of his opinions, and perhaps even his opinions themselves, became more humorful, looser. His wife and colleagues commented on his being more relaxed and flexible. And in his work evaluation, he was praised for increased confidence and improved relationships with co-workers.

The power that feminine energy held for this intellectual and artistic man was not only found in negative mother energy. On the inner feminine or anima level, there was an en-chanted, enchanting anima, running concurrently. He seemed in moments to be "swept away," apparently with powerful, positive emotion and inspiration, in reacting to interchanges with women. A few times, his dreams portrayed such powerful experiences. This intense anima energy was coming into more contact with human feminine energy. At least, he seemed more able to let women in his life come a bit closer. He engaged with them and with me in a less unconsciously overpowering (and overpowered) manner. It was a beginning for a more real relatedness to anima energy, inside and out.

For me, this work involved a strongly acoustic experience. It was oddly intangible, essentially inarticulate, as it was happening. This is often the case with auditory work. Slowly, an auditory constellation formed between us, of working with tone, resonance, rhythmic interchange, echo, and duet. In the imagery of the acoustic torture dream, it was a place where imprisonment could transform – into containment. Fighting could become intense responsiveness. This man's need for affirmative feminine response continued strong. But he became able, sometimes consciously, to mediate his behavior and attitudes.

This man had several intensely powerful dreams, with religious overtones. Several other individuals who shared acoustic dreams and experiences with me described strongly numinous auditory images, often in connection with anima/animus figures. Obviously, numinous dreams were the ones which stayed in memory. But other reasons are also possible. Auditory images can also be a powerful experience because we are not used to them: the surprise of the medium adds to the message. Sometimes too, auditory experiences tie in with that spirit or godlike level, which is one aspect of auditory energy. In terms of developmental work, this numinosity could be also echoing early auditory-based experience which partakes in an archetypal paradise.

Numinosity, with its overwhelming energy, has a redemptive/healing aspect, as well as a potentially wounding one. Auditory images, like any images, are unlikely to be directly damaging, or experiences which are only negative. However, working with them does present threats as well as challenges. For people with weak or rigid egos, they can tend in the direction of psychotic auditory hallucinations, just as religious, "visionary" experiences can. Strongly numinous auditory images may possibly require long term work, or a long time, before they can be integrated into everyday, ego-related energy.

Sound is a reverberating bridge upon which we find ourselves, as we reach to the unconscious and our larger selves. We can work on developing and refining our accessibility to auditory energy and sharpening our skills in working with it. Then, in situations where auditory energy calls, we can resound and respond in helpful ways.

# Conclusion

Violinist Yehudi Menuhin is eloquent in pointing out our neglect of the auditory world, as well as in praising the paths of audition. "We seem to think that the ear is dispensable," he says.

> *We concentrate overwhelmingly on what is visual. Everything that we cultivate or build impresses through the eyes, by size and colour and shape. We ignore the miracle of the ear, which conveys images that are far deeper, more subtle and more penetrating than the eye. Light bounces off surfaces and conveys its message through a greater abstraction than sound. Sound goes directly into our bodies. What the aural can do to the inside of our brain, to the "within" of our lives, nothing else can do.[138]*

What has struck me, again and again, is how close auditory energy is to psychic energy. In exploring what experiences and images are like by means of the ear, I have often had to examine whether I was really describing something auditory, or something more like "psychic vibration." Since sound is mostly experienced as a flow of energy, as a force, it is always elusive, just like psychic energy. The meaning in auditory images can be difficult to "catch," and even more difficult to hold. Auditory images easily elude clear perception and are easily forgotten.

---

[138] Yehudi Menuhin, quoted in P. Joudry, *Sound Therapy for the Walk Man*, St. Denis, Sask. (Steele and Steele), 1984, p. viii.

Auditory energy is fraught with a rich and resonant confusion. Especially when worked with from within the containment of a vessel, it can sound the depths of the soul. But it takes patience and a tolerance of (k)not knowing. Another of its many vexing profundities is the way that sound manifests as a surrounding resonance, while at the same time carrying precise and distinct images. It has been difficult to describe the work with this in-and-out energy, this process of defining the participatory base, while at the same time seeking for auditory specifics. Just how auditory experiences take on meaning, inside and outside of us, is complex. In keeping with its vibratory essence and relative boundarilessness, it is often easier to suggest than to pinpoint.

If images are the language of the psyche, and images come via the sensory channels, we find ourselves circling back to the questions of early psychologists about perception. Bower explains that we are mostly dependent upon our perceptual processes before we have a bank of experience to rely on (just like small children or foreigners). As we gain experience, we depend less upon sensory impressions, and more upon the judgments we have already formed, many of which actually contradict our immediate sensory perceptions.[139] Overall, this is a gain in efficiency, as we simply recognize things: "Oh, it's chocolate-flavored." "Ah yes, Beethoven." As individuals and as members of different groups, we depend upon well-practiced response. We do not have to explore each impression or image as new. Yet, although each of these moments of recognition has its own assigned and refined world, with its own kind of impact, we have nonetheless lost out on a certain vividness of experience. We have retreated into an already formed world of

[139] Tom Bower, *The Perceptual World of the Child*, London (Fontana Press), 1977, p. 84-85.

preconceptions and judgments. It is to the detriment of the keen, and often raw, edge of the fresh and new.

Bower also comments, "The more we grow away from the perceptual world, the more we are compelled to return to primitive certainties of perception."[140] The therapeutic process shares with poetry, music, theater and all of the arts the essential goal of trying to reach again to an original moment. This originality has essentially to do with being vibrant, "young," creative, with not being stuck in rigid assumptions. At its core, it has to do with psychic health. We need, we hunger for fresh encounters through inner and outer sensory processes. The dreams, images and fantasies of our lived lives widen and shift awareness. This imagination in our lives, of our lives, is understandably, centrally, the stuff of psychotherapy, the care of the soul.

Auditory energy is both powerful and subtle. Uniquely expressive, it vibrates us to our core. Sound is ever-present, yet little attended to. Difficult as it can sometimes be, it is a vital and vitalizing process to explore the auditory perceptual process, to hold to the unique and poignant qualities of auditory experience. We can learn to let them work on us, as we learn to work with them.

---

[140] Ibid., p. 85.

### All Lives, All Dances, & All is Loud

*The fish does ... HIP*
*The bird does ... VISS*
*The marmot does ... GNAN*

*I throw myself to the left,*
*I turn myself to the right,*
*I act the fish,*
*Which darts in the water, which darts*
*Which twists about, which leaps –*
*All lives, all dances, and all is loud.*

*The fish does ... HIP*
*The bird does ... VISS*
*The marmot does ... GNAN*

*The bird flies away,*
*It flies, flies, flies,*
*Goes, returns, passes,*
*Climbs, soars & drops.*
*I act the bird –*
*All lives, all dances, and all is loud.*

*The fish does ... HIP*
*The bird does ... VISS*
*The marmot does ... GNAN*

*The monkey from branch to branch,*
*Runs, bounds and leaps,*
*With his wife, with his brat,*
*His mouth full, his tail in the air,*
*There goes the monkey! There goes the Monkey!*
*All lives, all dances, & all is loud.*

(Africa: Gabon Pygmy) *Technicians of the Sacred*, p. 36

# Bibliography

Adams, John. "The Chairman Dances/Two Fanfares/Other Works," Elektra/Asylum/Nonesuch Records, New York, 1987. San Francisco Symphony, Edo de Waart, conductor.

Appelbaum, David. *Voice*. Albany NY: State University of New York Press, 1990.

Armitage, S.E., B.A. Baldwin and M. Vince. "The Fetal Sound Environment of Sheep," *Science 208*:1173-74 (June 6, 1980).

Arye, Lane. "Music the Messenger," Masters thesis for Antioch University, 1988.

— Seminar: "Working with Music and Sound," Nov. 19, 1988, Zurich, Switzerland.

"The Aural Root of Paranoia," *Science Digest*, Jan., 1983, (no author listed), p. 90.

Bachelard, Gaston. *The Poetics of Reverie: Childhood, Language, and the Cosmos*. Trans., Daniel Russell. Boston: Beacon Press, 1969.

Baggish, Dr. Michael. "Fetal Life," *Science Digest*, Dec. 1982, pp. 47-53.

Balint, Michael. *The Basic Fault: Therapetic Aspects of Regression*. The Brunner/Mazel Classics in Psychoanalysis, No. 5. New York: Brunner/Mazel, 1968.

Bandler, Richard and John Grinder. *Frogs into Princes: Neurolinguistic Programming*. Ed., John O. Stevens. Moab, Utah: Real People Press. 1979.

Barnwell, Ysaye M., "The Power of a Vocal Community," Tape Cassette of a Workshop, "Nourishing the Soul, Discovering the Sacred in Everyday Life." Nov. 12-14, 1993, Crystal City, VA. From Sounds True Recordings, Boulder CO.

Barthes, Roland. *The Pleasure of the Text.* Trans., Richard Millner. New York: Hill and Wang, 1975.

Bass, Dee. Seminar: "The Body in Psychology," Intensive Week, July 20-23, 1987, Küsnacht, Switzerland.

Beaulieu, John. *Music and Sound in the Healing Arts.* Barrytown, NY: Station Hill Press, 1987.

Berendt, Joachim-Ernst. *The Third Ear: On Listening to the World.* Trans., Tim Nevill. New York: Owl Book, Henry Holt and Company, 1988. Orig. publ as *Das Dritte Ohr,* Rowohlt Verlag BmbH, Reinbeck bei Hamburg.

Berry, Patricia. "Echo's Passion" and "Hamlet's Poisoned Ear" in *Echo's Subtle Body: Contributions to an Archetypal Psychology.* Dallas, TX: Spring Publications, 1982, pp. 113-26 and 127-146.

Birnholz, J.C. and B.R. Benacerraf. "The Development of Human Fetal Hearing," *Science* 222:516-18 (Nov. 4, 1893).

Bliss, Barbara. "The Singer and the Voice," Diploma Thesis for the C.G. Jung Institute, Küsnacht, Switzerland, 1983.

Borg, Erick and S. Allen Counter. "The Middle-ear Muscles," *Scientific American,* Aug. 1989, pp. 62-68.

Borg, Susan Gallagher. "Sound: Bodywork for the Soul," Casette Tape of a Workshop, "Nourishing the Soul: Discovering the Sacred in Everyday Life, Nov. 12-14, 1993, Crystal City, VA. From Sounds True Recordings, Boulder CO.

Bower, Tom. *The Perceptual World of the Child.* London: Fontana Press, 1977.

Campbell, Don G. *The Roar of Silence: Healing Powers of Breath, Tone & Music.* Wheaton IL: The Theosophical Publishing House, 1989.

Chatwin, *The Songlines.* London: Pan Books Ltd., 1988.

Chessick, Richard D., M.D., Ph.D., *The Technique and Practice of Listening in Intensive Psychotherapy.* Northvale, NJ: Jason Aronson Inc., 1989.

Cooper, J.C., *An Illustrated Encyclopaedia of Traditional Symbols.* London: Thames and Hudson, 1982.

*Cymatics: Bringing Matter to Life with Sound.* Videotape, Pt. III of a 3-part Composite Tape from a film by Dr. Hans Jenny. MACROmedia, P.O. Box 1223, Brookline MA 02146.

Deutsch, V. Seminar: "Der siebenstufige Tonzyklus" ("The Seven Tones of the Scale"), May 9, 10, 11, 1990, C.G. Jung Institute, Küsnacht, Switzerland.

deVilliers, Peter A. and Jill G. *Early Langugage.* (The Developing Child Series). Cambridge, Mass.: The Harvard University Press, 1979.

Eliade, Mircea. *The Sacred and the Profane.* New York: Harcourt Brace Janovich, 1959.

Federer, Yvonne. "Silence: Non-verbal Aspects of Analytic Psychology," Diploma thesis for the C.G. Jung Institute, Küsnacht, 1989.

Ferenczi, Sandor. "Confusion of Tongues between the Adult and Child," *International Journal of Psycho-analysis XXX*(1949), iv, pp. 225-30.

Fischer, Emil A, "On Creative Achievement" in *C.G. Jung Speaking: Interviews and Encounters.* Eds., W. McGuire and R.F.C. Hull. (Bollingen Series XCVII). Princeton NJ: Princeton University Press, 1977, pp. 164-67.

Fort, Julius and Barbara. *Talking between the Lines.* New York: Viking Press, 1979.

Freese, Arthur S., M.D., *You and Your Hearing.* New York: Charles Scribner's Sons, 1979.

Gallard, Martine Drahon. "Black Shadow – White Shadow." Trans. by Paula Kondrick. In *The Archetype of Shadow in a Split World.* (Proceedings of the Tenth International Congress for Analytical Psychology, Berlin, 1986). Ed., Mary Ann Mattoon. Zurich: Daimon Verlag, 1987, pp. 199-213.

Galouye, Daniel F. *Dark Universe.* Middlesex, England: Hamlyn Paperbacks, l961.

Gardner, Kay, *Sounding the Inner Landscape: Music as Medicine,* Stonington, Maine: Caduceus Publications, 1990.

— One-day workshop, "Sounding the Inner Landscape," Sept. 9, 1991, Minneapolis, Minnesota.

Garfield, Laeh M. *Sound Medicine: Healing with Music, Voice and Song.* Berkeley CA: Celestial Arts, 1987.

Goodbread, Joseph H. *The Dreambody Toolkit.* New York: Routledge & Kegan Paul, 1987.

Greenberg, Joanne. *In This Sign.* New York: Harper & Row, 1980.

Hall, Nor. *The Moon and the Virgin.* New York: Harper & Row, 1980.

"Hearing Loss," Office of Scientific and Health Reports, NIH Publication No. 81-1613. U.S. Department of Health and Human Services, Bethseda MD, 1981.

Hillman, James. *Insearch: Psychology and Religion.* Irving TX: Spring Publications, 1979.

The Holy Bible. King James Version. Cleveland OH: World Publishing, Company, (no date).

Isakower, Otto. "On the Exceptional Position of the Auditory Sphere," *International Journal of Psycho-analysis* 20:340-48 (1939).

Jaynes, Julian. *The Origin of Consciousness in the Breakdown of the Bicameral Mind.* Boston: Houghton Mifflin, 1976.

Joudry, Patricia. *Sound Therapy and the Walk Man.* St. Denis, Sask.: Steele and Steele, 1984.

Jung, C.G. *The Collected Works of C.G. Jung.* Eds., H. Read, M. Fordham, G. Adler and W. McGuire. (Bollingen Series 20, 2nd Ed.) Trans., R.F.C. Hull. Princeton NJ: Princeton University Press, 1953-1979.
Vol. I: *Psychiatric Studies*
Vol. II: *Experimental Researches*
Vol. III: *The Psychogenesis of Mental Disease*
Vol. V: *Symbols of Transformation*
Vol. VIII: *The Structure and Dynamics of the Psyche*
Vol. X: *Civilization in Transition*
Vol. XI: *Psychology and Religion: West and East*
Vol. XII: *Psychology and Alchemy*
Vol. XVII: *The Development of Personality*

— *C.G. Letters.* Eds., G. Adler and Aniela Jaffé. (Bollingen Series CV). Trans., R.F.D. Hull. Vol. I (1906-1950) and Vol. II (1951-61). Princeton NJ: Princeton University Press, 1953 and 1973.

— *Memories, Dreams, Reflections of C.G. Jung.* Recorded and ed. by Aniela Jaffé. Trans., Richard and Clara Winston. Rev. Ed. New York: Vintage Books (Random House), 1965.

— *Selected Letters of C.G. Jung,* 1909-1961, Sel. and ed. by G. Adler and Aniela Jaffé. Trans., R.F.C. Hull. Bolligen Series. Princeton, N.J.: Princeton University Press, 1984.

Kagan, Jerome. *The Nature of the Child.* New York: Basic Books, Inc., 1984.

Keats, John. Letter to George and Thomas Keats, dated Dec. 21 (or 27), 1817. In *The Norton Anthology of English Literature, Vol. II.* Ed., M.H. Abrams, Ben. New York: W.W. Norton and Company, Inc., 1962.

Kittelson, Mary Lynn. "The Acoustic Vessel" in *The Interactive Field in Analysis: Volume One.* Murray Stein, Ed. Wilmitte IL: Chiron Publications, 1995.

Kolb, Lawrence, M.D. and H. Keith H. Brodie, M.D. *Modern Clinical Psychiatry.* 10th Ed. Philadelphia PA: W.B. Saunders Company, 1982.

Kugler, Paul. *The Alchemy of Discourse: An Archetypal Approach to Language.* Toronto: Associated University Presses, 1982.

*The New Larousse Encyclopedia of Mythology.* Ed., Felix Guirand. Trans., R. Aldingon and D. Ames. New Ed. Hamlyn NY: The Hamlyn Publishing Group, 1968.

"Learning to Talk: Speech, Hearing and Language Problems in the Pre-school Child." Office of Scientific and Health Reports. (NIH No. 77-43). Bethseda MD: 1977.

Levin, David Michael. *The Listening Self: Personal Growth, Social Change and the Closure of Metaphysics.* New York: Routledge, 1989.

Mach, Dr. Ernest. *The Analysis of Sensation and the Relation of the Physical to the Psychical.* Trans. for the 1st German Ed., C.M. Williams. Rev. and Supplemented from the 5th German Ed. by Sydney Waterlow, M.A. New York: Dover Publications, Inc., 1959.

March, Robert H. *Physics for Poets.* Chicago IL: Contemporary Books, Inc., 1978.

Marguilies, Alfred. "On Listening to a Dream: The Sensory Dimensions." In *Psychiatry 48*:371-81 (Nov., 1985).

Marvell, Andrew. "To His Coy Mistress" (1681). In *Introduction to Literature: Poems.* Eds., L. Altenbernd and L.L. Lewis. New York: Macmillan, 1963, p. 169.

Mattern-Ames, Eleanor. "Notes on Early Damage and Regression," Diploma Thesis for the C.G. Jung Institute, Küsnacht, Switzerland, 1987.

Matthiessen, F.O., *The Achievement of T.S. Eliot: An Essay on the Nature of Poetry.* Boston and New York: Houghton Mifflin Company, 1935. "The Auditory Imagination," pp. 81-96.

*The Best of Meister Eckhart.* Ed., Halcyon Backhouse. New York: Crossroad, 1992.

*Meister Eckhart: A Modern Translation.* Ed., Raymond B. Blakney. NY: Harper & Row, 1969.

Mindell, Arnold. *Dreambody: The Body's Role in Revealing the Self.* Eds., Sisa Sternback-Scott and Becky Goodman. Santa Monica CA: Sigo Press, 1982.

Munn, Norman L. *Psychology: The Fundamentals of Human Adjustment.* 4th Ed. Boston: Houghton Mifflin, 1961.

Newham, Paul. *The Singing Cure: An Introduction to Voice Movement Therapy.* Boston: Shambhala, 1993.

*Ovid: Selected Works.* J.C. and M.J. Thornton, Eds. (Everyman's Library, No. 955). London: J.M. Dent & Sons Ltd., 1939, pp. 180-89.

*Origins: A Short Etymological Dictionary of Modern English.* Ed., Eric Partridge. 3rd Ed. London: Routledge & Kegan Paul, 1958.

Pardo, Enrique and Liza Mayer. Special Conference and Master Class, "Hermes: Mercurial Creativity," (The Voice of the Body), July 23-29, 1991. Mythos Institute, Minneapolis MN.

Pikes, Noah. "Giving Voice to Hell," *Spring 55: The Issue from Hell.* Putnam, Conn.: Spring Journal, 1994, pp. 51-66.

— Seminar: "Exploring the Body Voice," March 3, 10 and 23, 1990, Zurich, Switzerland.

— Seminar: "Introductory Course: The Body Voice," Weekend Course, March 24-25, 1990, Zurich, Switzerland.

— Tape: "Vocations: Travels with the Whole Voice: Demonstrations, Compositions, Improvisations." Privately Produced Tape by Noah Pikes, C.A.I.R.H., Maleragues, Thoiras, F-30140 *Anduze.* Explanatory booklet is included.

Purce, Jill. "Sound in Mind and Body." Interview by S.K., *Ham & High*, April 6, 1984. Reprint in *Resurgence*, No. 115, March/April 1986, p. 1.

Reik, Theodor. *The Haunting Melody: Psychoanalytic Experiences in Life and Music.* New York: Grove Press, 1953.

— *Listening with the Third Ear: The Inner Experience of a Psychoanalyst.* New York: Farrar, Strauss and Giroux, 1948 and 1975.

Rosen, Mortimer G. "The Secret Brain: Learning before Birth.: In *Harper's*, April 1978, pp. 46-47.

Rudhyar, Dane. *The Magic of Tone and the Art of Music.* London and Boulder CO: Shambhala Press, 1982.

Sacks, Oliver. *The Man Who Mistook his Wife for a Hat.* London: Pan Books Ltd., 1986.

— *Seeing Voices: A Journey into the World of the Deaf.* New York: HarperPerennial, 1990.

Schwaber, Evelyne, M.D. "A Particular Perspective on Analytic Listening." In *The Journal of the American Psychoanalytic Association*, 1983, pp. 519-46. See especially pp. 521-22.

Sheff, David. "George Lucas." Interview in *Rolling Stone: The Twelfth Anniversary Edition*, No. 512 (Nov. 5 - Dec. 10, 1987), pp. 241-45.

Shepard, Paul. *Thinking Animals.* New York: The Viking Press, 1978.

Stanford, W.F. *The Sound of Greek.* Berkeley CA: University of California Press, 1976.

Stevens, Stanley Smith, Ph.D. and Hallowell Davis, M.D. *Hearing: Its Psychology and Physiology.* New York: American Institute of Physics, Inc. and the Acoustical Society of America, 1983.

Storr, Anthony. *Music and the Mind.* New York: Random House (Ballantine Books), 1992.

*Technicians of the Sacred.* Ed., Jerome Rothenberg. 2nd Ed. Berkeley CA: University of California Press, 1968 and 1985.

Tiberghien, Monique, "Connecting Sound with Dreams," Cassette Tape of a Workshop, "Nourishing the Soul, Discovering the

Sacred in Everyday Life," Nov. 12-14, 1993, Crystal City, VA. From Sounds True Recordings, Boulder CO.

Tilly, Margaret. "The Therapy of Music." In *C.G. Jung Speaking: Interviews and Encounters.* Eds., W. McGuire and R.F.C. Hull. (Bollingen Series XCVII). Princeton NJ: Princeton University Press, 1977, pp. 273-75.

Tomatis, Alfred A. *The Conscious Ear: My Life of Transformation through Listening.* Ed and Trans., Billie M. Thompson. First Draft Trans., Stephen Lushington. Barrytown NY: Station Hill Press, Inc., 1991.

Tusler, Robert L. "If a Music Therapist Had Been at Waco..." *Fellowship,* Sept./Oct. 1993, p. 31.

Vetter, August. "Hauptgesichtspunkte für die Beurteilung der Sprechweise" ("Major Points in Judging the Way a Person Speaks"). From "Merkmalsschema aus den Seminar-Übungen an der Universität München," Winter Sem., 1960/61, in Rudolf Fährman's *Die Deutung des Sprechausdrucks.* Bonn: Bouvier and Co., 1960.

Whitfield, Dr. Philip and Dr. D.M. Stoddart. *Hearing, Taste and Smell: Pathways of Perception.* Tarrytown NY: Torstar Books, 1984, pp. 7-65.

Wilmer, Harry, M.D., Ph.D. Written text of a lecture given at C.G. Jung Institute, Küsnacht, Switzerland, Jan. 19, 1994.

Winnicott, D.W. *The Maturational Processes and the Facilitating Environment.* Ed., John D. Sutherland. (The International Psycho-analytic Library, No. 64). London: Hogarth Press and the Institute of Psychoanalysis, 1987.

— *The Piggle: An Account of the Psychoanalytic Treatment of a Little Girl.* Ed., Ishak Ramzy. London: Hogarth Press and the Institute of Psychoanalysis, 1978.

— *Playing and Reality.* London: Penguin Books, 1971.

Wolf, Caterina. "La Funzione del silenzio nel processo individuatio," a thesis for the C.G. Jung Institute, Küsnacht, Switzerland, 1983.

Zuckerkandl, Viktor. *Sound and Symbol: Music and the External World.* Trans., Willard R. Trask. (Bollingen Series XLIV). New York: Pantheon Books, 1956.

*References for opening quotations not otherwise listed*

Opening poem from *The Selected Poetry of Rainer Maria Rilke*, ed. and trans. by Stephen Mitchell, New York; Vintage International, 1989, p. 229.

Alexander, Lynne. *Resonating Bodies*. New York: Atheneum, 1989, pp. 216-17.

Andrews, Donald Patch. Quoted in D. Rudhyar, pp. 154-55 from Andrew's *Symphony of Life*, Lee's Summit MO: Unity Books, 1966.

Cohen, Leonard. "Ain't no Cure for Love," *I'm Your Man* Album. CBS Records, 1988.

— "Hallelujah." *Various Positions* Album. CBS Record, 1984.

cummings, e.e. "anyone lived in a pretty how town." In *Introduction to Literature: Poems*. Eds., L. Altenbernd and L.L. Lewis. New York: Macmillan, 1963, pp. 469-70.

Kundera, Milan. *The Unbearable Lightness of Being*. Trans., Michael H. Heim. New York: Harper & Row, 1984.

Nyro, Laura, with LaBelle. "The Bells," *Gonna Take a Miracle* Album. CBS Records, Re-issue, no date listed.

Ondaatje, Michael. *The English Patient*. New York: Vintage International (Random House), 1993.

Travis, Randy. "Is It Over (Still?)" *Old 8 x 10* Album. Warner Bros. Records, 1987.

Closing poem from *Technicians of the Sacred*, 2nd edition, ed. by Jerome Rothenberg, Berkeley CA: University of California Press, 1968 and 1985, p. 38.

# Index

Alan McGlashan
**Gravity and Levity**
The Philosophy of Paradox
162 pages

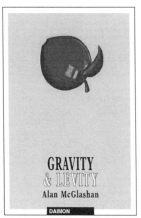

This book heralds a breakthrough in human imagination, not a breakthrough that may take place in the future, far or near, but one that has already occurred – only we may not have noticed it. Life, as the author shows, is open-ended and full of paradoxes. Its principles cannot be understood by logic and causal reasoning. We can only come to terms with life if we accept that there is no final answer to it and that adjusting to life's natural rhythm is the key to finding release from the horrors and problems around us.

**TALKING WITH ANGELS** Budaliget 1943
A document transcribed by Gitta Mallasz
474 pages, revised second edition

*Budaliget 1943:* A small village on the edge of Budapest. Three young women and a man, artists and close friends are gathered together in the uneasy days before Hitler's armies would destroy the world as they knew it. Seeking spiritual knowledge, and anticipating the horrors of Nazi-occupied Hungary, they met regularly to discuss how to find their own inner paths to enlightenment.

For 17 months, with the world locked in a deadly struggle for survival, the four friends meet every week with the spiritual beings they come to call their "angels"; Gitta Mallasz takes notes, the protocols which form this book, along with her commentary. The angels' message of personal responsibility is as meaningful and as urgent today as it was for its initial recipients half a century ago.

*I am deeply touched by the dialogues with the angels.*
Yehudi Menuhin

*I could read it over and over again and never get tired of it.*
*Thank you, thank you, thank you for sharing this book with me.*
Elisabeth Kübler-Ross

## Hayao Kawai
### Dreams, Myths and Fairy Tales in Japan

The well-known Japanese author, university professor and Zürich-trained Jungian analyst, Hayao Kawai, presents here the long-awaited second of his works in English. Originally presented as lectures at the historic Eranos Conferences in Ascona, this book describes five Japanese fairy tales, insightfully examined from Eastern and Western vantage points by an author intimately familiar with both.
(158 pages, illustrated)

## Rainer Maria Rilke
### Duino Elegies
Translated by David Oswald

The *Duino Elegies* are one of the twentieth century's great works of art. In the space of ten elegies, presented here in a bilingual edition, an impassioned voice struggles to find an answer to what it means to be human in a world torn by modern consciousness. (128 pages)

## C.A. Meier
### Personality
*The Individuation Process in the Light of C.G. Jung's Typology*

Carl Gustav Jung never produced a systematic treatment of his own work – he was always moving forward. His assistant-of-many-decades, Carl Alfred Meier, made it his life-task to gather and present in detail the various aspects of Jung's far-reaching discoveries. This final volume of Meier's work addresses the human personality in its encounters between consciousness and the unconscious, a process referred to as *individuation*. In describing such encounters, the author extensively explains the notion of Jung's *psychological types*. (192 pages)

## Susan Bach
## LIFE PAINTS ITS OWN SPAN

On the Significance of Spontaneous Paintings by Severely Ill Children with over 200 color illustrations

Part I (Text): 208 pp., part II (Pictures): 56 pp.

*Life Paints its own Span* with over 200 color reproductions is a comprehensive exposition of Susan Bach's original approach to the physical and psychospiritual evaluation of spontaneous paintings and drawings by severely ill patients. At the same time, this work is a moving record of Susan Bach's own journey of discovery.

## Susan Tiberghien
**Looking for Gold** – *A Year in Jungian Analysis*

The author relates an experience that belongs to everyone – the experience of soul, of tapping the depths of the unconscious. Here is the search for wholeness, for bringing together the visible and the invisible. The author calls it "seeing with her eyes closed."

Susan Tiberghien shares one year of dreams, analysis, daily life. A writer, mother, woman in love, she enters her inner world, experiencing vertigo and breathlessness until she lets the light and darkness fuse within her.

Each of the sixteen chapters marks a turn, with a dream and an epiphany. Thus they build upon one another, as the reader comes into cyclical time, discovering that dreams, too, have their seasons. (192 pages)

*Forthcoming: A Festschrift for Laurens van der Post*

## The Rock Rabbit and the Rainbow

edited by Robert Hinshaw

Authors from around the world have combined their talents in a tribute honoring this one-of-a-kind writer, soldier and statesman, a man of his time. Contributions include: Joseph Henderson: "The Splendor of the Sun"; Alan McGlashan: "How to be Haveable"; Ian Player: "My Friend Nkunzimlanga"; Jean-Marc Pottiez: "Rainbow Rhapsody"; T.C. Robertson: "A Triad of Landscapes – a Day in the Veld with Laurens"; and numerous other essays and works by Aniela Jaffé, Jonathan Stedall, Harry Wilmer, Jo Wheelright, C.A. Meier and many others.
(ca. 240 pages, illustrated)

# ENGLISH PUBLICATIONS BY *DAIMON*

Susan Bach  – *Life Paints its Own Span*
E.A. Bennet  – *Meetings with Jung*
George Czuczka  – *Imprints of the Future*
Heinrich Karl Fierz  – *Jungian Psychiatry*
von Franz / Frey-Rohn / Jaffé  – *What is Death?*
Liliane Frey-Rohn  – *Friedrich Nietzsche*
Yael Haft  – *Hands: Archetypal Chirology*
Siegmund Hurwitz  – *Lilith, the first Eve*
Aniela Jaffé          – *The Myth of Meaning*
                      – *Was C.G. Jung a Mystic?*
                      – *From the Life und Work of C.G. Jung*
                      – *Death Dreams and Ghosts*
Verena Kast      – *A Time to Mourn*
                 – *Sisyphus*
Hayao Kawai  – *Dreams, Myths and Fairy Tales in Japan*
James Kirsch  – *The Reluctant Prophet*
Rivkah Schärf Kluger  – *The Gilgamesh Epic*
Paul Kugler      – *Jungian Perspectives on Clinical Supervision*
Rafael López-Pedraza      – *Hermes and his Children*
                          – *Cultural Anxiety*
Alan McGlashan  – *The Savage and Beautiful Country*
                     – *Gravity and Levity*
Gitta Mallasz  (Transcription)  – *Talking with Angels*
C.A. Meier      – *Healing Dream and Ritual*
                – *A Testament to the Wilderness*
Laurens van der Post  – *A «Festschrift»*
R.M. Rilke  – *Duino Elegies*
Susan Tiberghien  – *Looking for Gold*
Ann Ulanov – *The Wizards' Gate*

Jungian Congress Papers:
Jerusalem 1983  – *Symbolic and Clinical Approaches*
Berlin 1986  – *Archetype of Shadow in a Split World*
Paris 1989  – *Dynamics in Relationship*
Chicago 1992  – *The Transcendent Function*

*Available from your bookstore or from our distributors:*

*In the United States:*                                    *In Great Britain:*

Atrium Publishers Group      Chiron Publications      Airlift Book Company
3356 Coffey Lane             400 Linden Avenue        26-28 Eden Grove
Santa Rosa, CA 95403         Wilmette, IL 60091       London N7 8EF, England
Tel. (707) 542 5400          Tel. (708) 256 7551      Tel. (607) 5792 and 5798
Fax: (707) 542 5444          Fax: (708) 256 2202      Fax (607) 6714

*Worldwide:*      Daimon Verlag
                  Hauptstrasse 85
                  CH-8840 Einsiedeln Switzerland
                  Tel. (41)(55) 532266
                  Fax (41)(55) 532231      *Write for our complete catalog!*